C000303425

PEMBROKESHIRE

Past and Present

Brian John

with a Foreword by Lord Parry of Neyland

Greencroft Books

1995

Enjoy the things that glisten bright
In crystal rays of noonday sun;
But then delve deep in shifting shade
And find the treasures left
By kith and kin long gone to earth.

The hidden phantoms of their land
Will whisper revelations.

Conspiring in your soul, they say
All this is yours, just for today.

Copyright © Brian S. John 1995

Typesetting: Sally Rudman and Brian John

Printing: Lewis Printers, Carmarthen

Design: Brian John using Claris Works software on Apple Mac LC475 computer

Illustrations: Sketches, Brian John. Photographs, see individual credits.

Greencroft Books, Trefelin, Cilgwyn, Newport, Pembs SA42 OQN. Tel: 01239 - 820470

ISBN 0 905559 60 6

Contents

Foreword

As much as anyone, and very much more than most, Brian John has written Pembrokeshire into the hearts and minds of people who might, otherwise, have had only a passing acquaintance with our county. One of Pembrokeshire's favoured sons, academically distinguished and successful professionally, he was drawn back to Preseli from university research and lecturing by that mystic *hiraeth* for home that expresses itself so attractively in his writing. It is Brian's love for his homeland, particularly the Pembrokeshire peninsula, that brings his work to life.

A geographer, he is able to build, on his understanding of the physical forces that shaped the rocks, the hills, the valleys and river estuaries, a relief map in the mind of anyone taking up this book. An historian, he counts and recounts the events that peopled the land north and south of the Haven with two very distinct groups of Welsh men and women. A researcher, by nature and by training, he revises and brings up to date the detail of the past and the present of Pembrokeshire's idiosyncratic communities.

It is, though, as one Pembrokeshire born out of "Honey Harfat" (Haverfordwest) that he breathes life into his prose, humour into his understanding, and dedication and affection into his portrait of Pembrokeshire as it was and is.

Lord Parry of Neyland

*Pen-y-holt Stack, near
Linney Head (Studio Jon)*

Preface

This book has been written because I love Pembrokeshire. Since my school-days in Haverfordwest I have been fascinated by the complicated history and the scenic richness of my native county. I have been particularly intrigued by Pembrokeshire's two halves and by the invisible dividing line between them. To my (entirely biased) way of thinking, Pembrokeshire is more beautiful than Ireland, more interesting than Cornwall, and more varied than Brittany. It has the densest cultural weave and the richest landscape texture of any of the regions of Wales.

After twenty-one years as a part of the overblown county of Dyfed, Pembrokeshire is coming back into existence as an administrative unit in its own right. The old county is entering a period of rapid change, during which it will rediscover its own identity. This book looks at the main features of the landscape and the way of life in this little corner of Wales at the end of the twentieth century. The viewpoint is very much a geographical or topographical one, concentrating on what can be observed rather than on what can be read or remembered. In fact, the book has grown out of a volume first commissioned more than 20 years ago, revised and reprinted in various formats since then, and out of print for the last ten years. This new volume represents a very substantial revision, with the addition of several new chapters and many new illustrations..

In the re-writing of the text I have tried to make it easy to read, but also authoritative enough to satisfy those with an academic turn of mind. The chapters are organized so that they can be read out of order, or so that the specialist reader can simply pick out relevant chapters. But at the same time I appreciate that there are many who will buy the book simply because they love Pembrokeshire and because they want "a good read." I have therefore introduced legends, anecdotes, and snippets of folk-lore here and there, since such irreverent material helps, in my mind at least, to portray the **character** of Pembrokeshire. By the time that you reach the end of the book, I hope that you will know Pembrokeshire as you might know an old and special friend.

This is a book about places and the people who have made these places what they are. Some of them will be difficult for the visitor to find, but hopefully the maps in the text will provide some help. So many places are mentioned in the text that I have decided to omit grid references; however, the standard holiday guides often give grid references to important sites, together with information concerning access. For those who wish to use the book during the course of intrepid expeditions into the Pembrokeshire outback, the OS 1:50,000 Landranger maps (Sheets 157, 145 and 158) are essential items of equipment. For more detailed studies the 1:25,000 Pathfinder maps are widely available through local bookshops, newsagents, and TICs.

While hunting for fascinating localities, please remember that most of them belong to somebody or other. Pembrokeshire has a National Park and its residents are used to visitors; nevertheless, you are asked at all times to respect the private property and the proper privacy of those who have the good fortune to live somewhere interesting.

Brian John
October 1995

Chapter One

The Region and its Character

"A hamlet -- three cottages and an inn crouched under low cliffs. A man is burning brushwood cut from a tree, bleached and washed by the sea. The flame looks incandescent in the evening light .... Herons gather. They fly majestically towards the sea. I wish I could give you some idea of the exultant strangeness of this place ....." (**Graham Sutherland, 1942**).

Pembrokeshire is something of an enigma, and visitors are never quite sure what to make of it. They should not worry too much about this; Pembrokeshire people themselves are not quite sure what to make of their mysterious and turbulent history or of their complicated landscape.

The county is mostly lowland, but earth scientists have always referred to it as a part of Highland Britain since the gentle mountain of Mynydd Presely and its rolling foothills are geologically a small part of a once-extensive mountain range that covered most of Scotland, Ireland and Wales. For geographers and historians, the old county occupies one of the "Atlantic ends" of Europe, looking to the west and sharing at least a part of its heritage with Brittany, the South West Peninsula of England, and Southern Ireland. It also shares many landscape characteristics with these other lands which jut out into the Celtic Sea and the "south-west approaches" of the British Isles. And yet, since 1536 it has been a part of the United Kingdom and its political destiny has been determined far to the east by a London-based parliament.

Land and Sea

Another of Pembrokeshire's "identity crises" arises out of its relationship with the sea. It is often said that the Pembrokeshire economy depends ultimately upon the success of farming and the multitude of local businesses that spring from the soil. But as many writers have pointed out, the county's long coastline, its instant access to the St George's Channel sea routes, and its multitude of little harbours and creeks, have combined to give local people salt in their veins. Even in the centre of the county the magnificent sheltered waterway of Milford Haven and the Daugleddau estuary carries sea water as far inland as Haverfordwest and Canaston Bridge; every community in the county has had more than a fair share of mariners, shipowners, fishermen and merchants listed in parish registers and remembered in graveyards.

It would not be too much to claim that Pembrokeshire's destiny and landscape have been shaped by the sea. For a start, the mild, wet, windy climate is influenced above all else by the proximity of the Atlantic Ocean. In every month of the year Atlantic depressions sweep in from the west. The landscape has been carved out, over many millions of years, by waves and rain rather than by frost and snow. From the summit of Mynydd Presely, on Foelcwmcerwyn, on a clear day, you can see the sea in a great sweep from south-east through west all the way to north-east. No point in Pembrokeshire is more than 15 km from salt water.

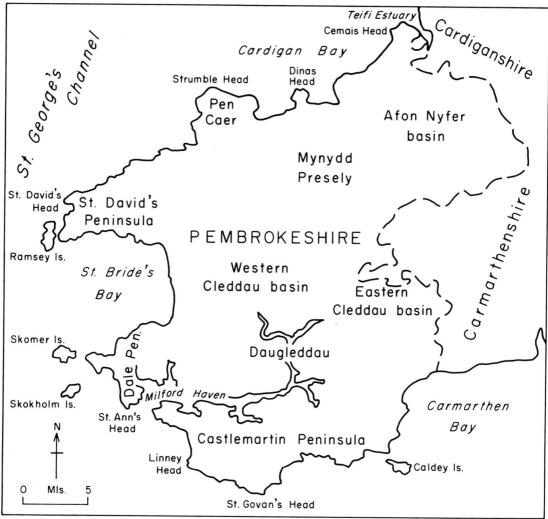

Pembrokeshire location map, showing the configuration of the coastline and the main landscape regions.

Pembrokeshire has grown up with its feet in the sea. In its early days the Stone Age settlers, the Celts and the Viking sea-rovers all dragged their sea-going vessels up onto Pembrokeshire beaches. During the Dark Ages, Pembrokeshire looked westwards across St George's Channel towards Ireland for much of its cultural inspiration, and the land and people blessed by David and his fellow saints played a key role in the flowering of Celtic Christian culture on the western fringes of the British Isles. Even those architypal landlubbers, the Normans, built their castles on the coast where they could and depended upon the sea for the maintenance of their supply lines whenever their new colony in "Little England" was at risk from the fury of the Welsh princes. Following the advent of more peaceful times, the sea asserted its influence yet again, when the little ports of the Pembrokeshire coast (and the inland port of Haverfordwest) became the focal points of the local economy. Shipbuilding, fishing and maritime trading maintained the fortunes not only of coastal communities but also of squires, farmers and businessmen who lived far from the sound of the sea. Later still, Pembrokeshire's little "industrial revolution" was only possible because the coastline provided easy access to mineral wealth and export points for shipping out coal, limestone, roadstone, bricks, woollen cloth, pig iron and a host of other goods. The major industries of the nineteenth century (for example, shipbuilding at the Royal Naval Dockyard in Pembroke Dock) and the twentieth century (for example, the Milford fishing industry) again fed on Pembrokeshire's maritime traditions.

After the Second World War the Pembrokeshire Coast National Park was created because the government ministers of the day felt (and who can disagree with them?) that the Pembrokeshire coastline was the most beautiful and unspoilt in Britain, and was therefore worthy of protection as a national and even international asset. The Coast Path, running all the way from Amroth in the south to St Dogmael's in the north, was created to allow public access to the whole coast, and has become an economic asset in its own right. And in our own time the Milford Haven oil industry and the tourist industry have grown as they have, as major contributors to the modern economy, simply because the sea washes into the heart and soul of this place.

Welsh and English

Then we come to the matter of the people and their culture. Pembrokeshire people can be classified as either Welsh-speaking Welsh or English-speaking Welsh; both groups feel that they are the real guardians of Pembrokeshire culture. As mentioned above, Pembrokeshire is a part of the Celtic realm, and according to the old sagas it is closely related to Brittany, Cornwall, Ireland and

western Scotland. Being located on the far western periphery of Britain, it might have survived to this day as a part of the "heartland" of the Welsh language. But suddenly, with the coming of the Normans, it was caught up in the cultural dynamo controlled from south-eastern England. The Normans and their followers transformed south Pembrokeshire. Since then, for almost a thousand years, the county has been undecided about whether to call itself English or Welsh. It learnt to live with its split personality, with the Welshry in the north and Little England in the south, and the invisible frontier of the Landsker in between.

Pembrokeshire felt, in the decades following the Second World War, that in spite of its confused past it did have a unique and proud identity. Local people were pleased to explain to others that theirs was "the premier county of Wales." Then the British Government decided that local government administration should be made less local, and in April 1974 the conglomerate county of Dyfed came into being. Pembrokeshire, kicking and screaming more furiously than any of the other Welsh counties, was exterminated. It was replaced by two local government districts called South Pembrokeshire and Preseli Pembrokeshire. Showing a total lack of sensitivity for language and culture, the bureaucrats decided that South Pembrokeshire should include most of eastern Pembrokeshire and a sizeable part of Mynydd Presely, while Preseli was designated to incorporate parts of the deep south such as Neyland, Milford and the Dale Peninsula. In the 1980's the situation was slightly rationalised. But during the twenty years or so during which Pembrokeshire did not formally exist, local people proved very reluctant to look on themselves as inhabitants of Dyfed. Now the Government, in its infinite wisdom, has realised that while Pembrokeshire may have been too

The new county of Dyfed, as designated in 1974 in spite of great public protest.

small in 1974, Dyfed is too large in 1995; and so Pembrokeshire has been re-created as a "unitary authority", much to the delight of almost everybody. The term "Pembroke-shire" has never gone out of local use, thanks to the gut feelings of the locals, the loyalty of the two district councils, and the continuous pressure exerted by the "Campaign for Pembrokeshire". This campaign has been ably assisted by local MPs and by the local press. In May 1996 the old county sees a political present-day reaffirmation of its historic identity. Hence the sub-title of this book.

Landscape and Character

The easiest way to obtain an impression of the character of a place (even a place as complicated as Pembrokeshire) is to look at the landscape and read its signals. This sounds simple enough, but as in the matter of history and culture the signals can be confusing. It is my task in the later chapters of this book to help the reader to interpret some of the signals, which usually take the

form of "fossil" landscapes and landforms, some of which are natural and others of which are man-made.

The landscape of Pembrokeshire is basically rural, but the county does contain a number of vivid and well-loved landscape types. Three of these are recognized in the separate sections of the Pembrokeshire Coast National Park. In the main section of the Park there is the spectacular beauty of the coastline itself, with its fierce ramparts of Atlantic cliffs separated here and there by wide sandy bays and narrow inlets. Then there are the bleak rolling moorlands of Mynydd Presely, whose flanks were naked and windswept until puritanical foresters began to clothe them with a dull cloak of conifers. Finally, there is the wooded secrecy of the Daugleddau estuary, whose tidal mudflats and steep oak woods are quite unknown to most Pembrokeshire people. But even if these are the "classic" landscapes which most visitors come to look at, we should not forget that there are infinite and subtle variations within them and transitions between them. Pembrokeshire even has its fair share of urban and industrial environments. Around the Milford Haven waterway long stretches of the Pembrokeshire Coast Path, designed to show the walker the best that Pembrokeshire has to offer, run through dusty streets and industrial installations where the smell of oil hangs heavy on the air. In places the craggy uplands reach the coast, and almost everywhere else farmland extends to within a few metres of the clifftops. More variety is found in the rolling gentle farmlands with their patches of woodland and moorland even at low altitude, their lush grassy fields bounded by leafy hedgerows, and their ancient buildings.

Perhaps the most striking landscape types can be defined as belonging to the north and south of the county. They arise, at least in part, from the cultural and linguistic

Carew Castle, one of the Anglo-Norman fortresses of "Little England beyond Wales".

characteristics mentioned above. In the north, which has for almost a thousand years been known as "the Welshry", the mountains are never far away. Moorlands and tors (upstanding rocks or crags) often provide a wild, harsh back-cloth in a landscape of little scattered settlements. Farms are small, and fields are bounded by bare hedges or rough stone walls. Churches, farms and chapels look Welsh, and they usually have Welsh names. In the south, we know that we are in the lowlands. The landscape is gentler and occasionally well wooded, with larger villages and towns. Farms are more modern and more profitable, and the pattern of life has closer links with England than with Celtic Wales. This is the "Little England" of the guide-books, the region of Anglo-Saxon place-names, Norman castles and tall battlemented church towers. Margaret F Davies, who made a special study of the historical geography of the county, recognized a "zone of frontiers" between these two regions, and pointed

out how closely geological, landscape, political, social and other boundaries coincide as they curve eastward and southward from St Bride's Bay to Carmarthen Bay. For something like a thousand years this vague zone of frontiers has been crystallized within the cultural landscape as the Pembrokeshire Landsker, a unique local phenomenon which has changed its character and its position several times. The Landsker still exists as a sharp language divide, and in the following pages we shall refer frequently to its past and present importance.

A further series of landscape types can be related to the halting progress of Pembrokeshire towards a balanced way of life in which modern trade and industry offset the traditional arts of fishing and agriculture. As mentioned above, the sea-trading era has left many traces in the landscape. Similarly, there are abundant relics of Pembrokeshire's coal era. The

Pembrokeshire anthracite field, the remote western extension of the South Wales Coalfield, enjoyed almost a century of moderate prosperity; we can still see traces of spoil heaps, pit-head buildings and machinery, railway tracks and quays in some rural localities. The waterway of Milford Haven was largely neglected by industrialists until the "new towns" of Milford, Pembroke Dock and Neyland were built in the nineteenth century. (Note that in this book I follow local tradition by referring to the town as Milford and the waterway as Milford Haven.) It was the age of the supertanker which, at long last, brought Milford Haven to the notice of the world in general and British industry in particular. Now it is Britain's major oil port, and its shores have been transformed by processing plants, storage tanks and jetties. Out in the waterway mammoth oil tankers ease themselves towards the oil terminals or slip quietly out to sea having disgorged their multi-million pound crude oil cargoes from all over the world.

Industry and Environment

The belated recognition of the qualities of the Milford Haven waterway, and the recent arrival of Pembrokeshire's oil-based "industrial revolution", can of course be welcomed from an economic point of view, but in the 1970's Pembrokeshire underwent a profound change in character which many local people still regret. The outer reaches of Milford Haven lie within the National Park, and inevitably there has been conflict between the interests of conservation and those of industry. There are many who still feel that large-scale industry is quite out of place in the sensitive environment of Pembrokeshire. In this gently undulating landscape it is difficult to hide oil refineries, and even more difficult to hide the 228 m stack of the Pembroke power-station and the rows of pylons which leave it

to march through the south Pembrokeshire countryside in close formation towards the east. More to the point, how appropriate is it to Pembrokeshire's "clean green" image for the county to play host to heavy industries which are responsible for atmospheric pollution on a quite gigantic scale? As we shall see in later chapters, the planning authorities are still trying to find a compromise between the interests of industry, the interests of the local farming and urban communities, and the interests of the tourists who flock in large numbers to enjoy coast and country during the summer months. Very often the jobs issue lies at the heart of the planning dilemma. Large and powerful companies like Esso, Texaco and National Power are used to having their way. The latter company, for example in its campaign to burn Orimulsion fuel in Pembroke Power Station, has become astute at using the "employment card" in the depths of an economic recession to encourage the government and the local authorities to push environmental considerations far down the list of priorities.

It would be naive to pretend that only large-scale industry affects a sensitive environment. Most of us live in towns, drive cars and use electricity without much thought for the environmental implications of our life-style. Even in Pembrokeshire, urban sprawl is an environmental issue. Sewage disposal methods and beach cleanliness are intimately related. Local people are highly supportive of the farming industry, but might be less so if they realised the scale and environmental impact of agrichemical use on the land. Tourism is welcomed by most people but makes a profound impact on the landscape, for example in large-scale caravan parks, theme parks and seaside developments. The assessment of environmental costs versus economic benefits is a difficult business, and no development can be totally benign. For example, recent proposals for windfarms in

The Texaco Oil Refinery, part of which is located within the National Park. Since this photo was taken the plant has been substantially enlarged.

Cars and caravans at West Angle Bay. Tourism may be good for the economy, but it can make a powerful environmental impact.

Pembrokeshire are seen by some as symbols of a new and bright pollution-free future, while causing others to suffer from apoplexy on the grounds that wind turbines can be seen and even heard. Since environmental issues have, in the last decade or so, come very much into the local news, Chapter 19 of this book looks at some of them in more detail.

A typical Victorian artists' impression of Pembrokeshire: cliffs near the Smuggler's Cave, Lydstep, after a storm. The vertical dimension is stretched, and clouds and rain add to the "Gothic" atmosphere. The modern guide-book image of Pembrokeshire is somewhat different!

Questions and Answers

At the very beginning of our examination of Pembrokeshire, questions, images and issues come crowding into mind. Does the county want to develop its Welsh identity or not? Does it see the National Park as a threat to economic development, or a boon? Does it want a modern industrial economy based on oil, or would it like to see the end of the oil industry sooner rather than later? What are the best policies for protecting the natural landscapes and the built heritage of the county? How should the agricultural industry develop so as to ensure a sound future? What will be the landscape and economic impacts of telecottages and the telecommunications revolution?

In the chapters which follow these and many more topics are explored in greater depth. Some of the chapters are historical, but always there is a conscious attempt to relate the events of the past to the landscape features of today. The chapters progress from an examination of the landscape's most ancient features to those which are most recent; but the approach is for the most part thematic.

Pembrokeshire still has a strong feeling of identity, and with this goes a strong feeling of unity among its people. Hopefully the pages which follow will serve to explain for a wide readership Pembrokeshire's unique historical tradition and its unique style of life. After the Government's ill-fated attempt to wipe it off the political map, the "premier county" of Wales once again exists. And that's official.

Chapter Two

The Natural Landscape

"As touchinge the forme and fashion thereof by the Topographicall discripcion yt is neyther perfect square longe nor rounde but shaped with diverse Corners, some sharpe, some obtuse, in some places concave in some convexe, but in most places concave and bendinge inwarde...

...the sea doth the like, dealeinge soe inkindely with this poore Countrey as that it doth not in anye where seeme to yield to the lande in anye parte, but in everye corner thereof eateth upp parte of the mayne...

...there are fine and sweete springes runninge in small little valleys, as if worne by their course, not deepe but broade, and shallowe, not headlonge or steepe, but allmost on playne ground..."

(George Owen, 1603)

Nowadays it may be unfashionable to describe anything as beautiful, but this is the word which describes, most simply but comprehensively, the natural landscape of Pembrokeshire. Forgetting for a moment the superficial paraphernalia of man's occupation of the land - his towns, his farms, his fields, his roads - one can look a little more closely at the forms and features of the landscape which have evolved, unseen by human eyes, over many thousands of years. These landforms are the foundations upon which man has scuttled about during the past few millennia, furiously erecting minute monuments to his own technical ingenuity. And make no mistake about it - they are

minute. The view of Pembrokeshire from a satellite, say 60 km above the earth's surface, is of a green and varied land without a trace of human habitation. Here the works of man are reduced to realistic proportions. The forces of nature are seen as the real creators of the Pembrokeshire landscape.

When we look a little closer, it is the variety of the Pembrokeshire scene which catches the eye. Even on the ground the most casual observer cannot fail to notice the landscape contrasts which appear on all sides: contrasts between the plunging cliffed coast of Pencaer and the gentle undulations of the Western Cleddau valley; between the heather moorlands of Carningli and the quiet woodlands of Cwm Gwaun; between the wide tidal estuary of the Daugleddau and the dry limestone plateau of the Castlemartin Peninsula. Other contrasts of many types rush to mind, for Pembrokeshire is a microcosm of Great Britain. Side by side there are small-scale illustrations of the types of countryside which elsewhere merge imperceptibly one with another over much greater distances. In other parts of Britain, the subtle changes of scene may defy recognition by all but the most acute observer; here in Pembrokeshire they are noticed and appreciated by visitors and local people alike.

The beauty of Pembrokeshire lies not just in the serenity of its deep foxgloved lanes, not just in the stark ferocity of its clifflines, nor in the tangled chlorophyll jungles which are its oak woods. Not even in the bleak wide purple vistas of Presely, or the famous wild Whitsuntide extravaganza of bluebells and pink campions on the island of Skomer, or the pastel shades of a Trefgarn autumn. For Pembrokeshire has all of these things, and infinitely more. It has the beauty of a many-sided character, a beauty of moods and seasons, of gales and calms, of seascapes and skyscapes as well as landscapes. And, above all, the landscapes are green landscapes, even in mid-winter; always there are green plants competing, thriving and then fading in a myriad of environments. The face of the old county has an instantly recognizable appeal which at the same time defies accurate description. Nevertheless, this chapter tries, even if inadequately, to describe just some of the landscape features which make up this enigmatic face of Pembrokeshire.

Rocks and Structure

The rocks of the county are to a large extent responsible for one of its most noticeable contrasts; namely that between the higher, bleaker lands of the north and the warm, wooded lowlands of the south. To generalize, the north is an area of immensely old rocks (between 2,000 million and 395 million years old), whereas to the south most of the rocks are much younger. Nevertheless, none of the rocks in Pembrokeshire are as young as those of south-east England; on the contrary, all of them are more than 295 million years old, classified as Palaeozoic and containing some of the oldest fossils in the British Isles. Many of the rocks of North Pembrokeshire are igneous in origin, made of basic earth materials, which have found

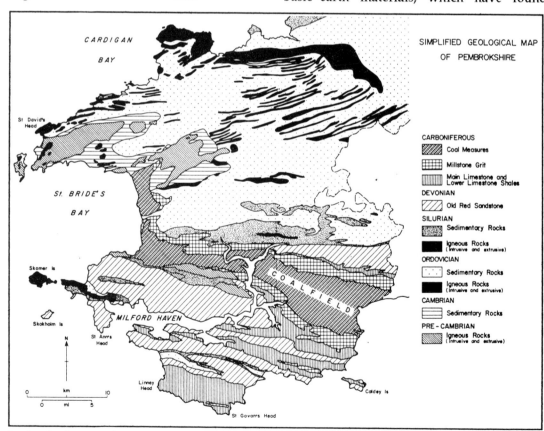

Geological map of Pembrokeshire, showing the main rock-types and ages.

their way in a molten state from the earth's interior to its outer crust largely by means of volcanic activity. The most prominent hill masses and carns in the north coincide with the outcrops of igneous rocks, for they have been more resistant to erosion than the layered sedimentary rocks (mainly of Cambrian and Ordovician age) around them. Examples are the massive dolerite carns of Carnllidi, Carn Treliwyd and Penbiri near St David's, which look for all the world like the stark ramparts of some gigantic distant mountain range; the long moorland ridge of Precambrian volcanic rocks which stretches westward from Mynydd Presely almost to the coast near Newgale, surmounted by the carns at Trefgarn, Plumstone and Roch; and the low smooth hills of whitish rhyolite along the coast road between Fishguard and Dinas. In the Presely uplands (always referred to by the locals, somewhat optimistically, as mountains) the carns of tumbled blocks which protrude from the generally smooth slopes are also of igneous rock. Carn Meini and Carn Alw, on the south-east slopes of the main Presely ridge, are thought to have been the sources of some of the bluestones of Stonehenge.

The oldest rocks in the north of the county are found around St David's, stretching from Ramsey Sound like abroad wedge into the centre of the peninsula, and around Roch, Hayscastle and the northern end of Trefgarn Gorge. Many of these rocks are volcanic ashes and lava-flows, but there are also more deep-seated igneous rocks such as granites and rhyolites; most are thought to be about 1,000 million years old. Somewhat unexpectedly, however, the oldest of all the rocks in Pembrokeshire are found in the south (around Benton, Johnston and Talbenny) amid rocks which are very much younger. Near Johnston, for instance, by taking just a few paces one can pass from Precambrian rocks which are well over 1,000 million years old to Coal Measures which are less than 300 million years old.

The "family of lions" at Maiden Castle, near the north end of Trefgarn Gorge. The rocks here are of Precambrian Age.

The geological map shows that the younger rocks of south Pembrokeshire are arranged quite simply in a series of more or less parallel strips, trending between W-E and NW-SE. This was described as long ago as the sixteenth century by George Owen, who in addition to his other accomplishments has been called the patriarch of British geologists. He traced the main outcrops of limestone and coal in considerable detail, and noticed that some outcrops repeat themselves. The following quotation shows that he was beginning to appreciate the principles of stratigraphy also:

...I found out two vaynes of lymestone to have their originale here in Pembrokeshire, and...theire Course holdeth eastward,... betweene both which vaynes of lymestone the coale is founde to follow, but not soe open as the lymestone in every place with the lymestone but in many places where the stone sheweth, the coale hideth himself & where the coale is founde, sometymes the lymestone lurketh underground, and in many places they are found neere together...

Hence, following in the footsteps of Pembrokeshire's Elizabethan geologist, it is possible to trace several outcrops of the bright red sandstones, pebbly grits and conglomerates of the Old Red Sandstone; the hard white and grey limestones of Carboniferous age; the younger buff and brown grits, sandstones and shales of the Millstone Grit; and the Coal Measures which contain the Pembrokeshire anthracite much valued by the early industrialists for its excellent heating properties and low ash content. Each of these rocks has given rise to its own particular landscape type. A careful look reveals that the bright red soils (used especially for arable farming north of Milford Haven, on the Dale Peninsula and on parts of the Castlemartin Peninsula) coincide with the Old Red Sandstone outcrops. The landscape is pleasantly undulating and varied, with frequent small wooded valleys and broad swelling interfluves.

Limestone stack on the south coast, not far from Flimston Castles.

The Carboniferous Limestone lands are sometimes so short of surface water that they make up Pembrokeshire's own small desert. The limestone area within the boundaries of the old Castlemartin tank range is a platform of wide open spaces, of white bleached grass and of stunted trees. There is generally a thin red soil, but close to the coast the white limestone breaks the surface. Near Barafundle Bay and Broad Haven there are pits, hollows and areas of bare "limestone pavement" reminiscent of more famous limestone terrains at Ingleborough and Malham Tarn. Elsewhere drifting white sand-dunes contribute to the desert image, as at Broad Haven and Tenby's South Beach.

In violent contrast, the lush well-wooded landscape of the centre of the county coincides with the broad outcrop of the Coal Measures and the Millstone Grit. The soils are heavy and cold, and have a tendency to waterlogging, so most of the fields are kept under grass for dairying and stock raising. Fields are small and hedges support a prolific growth of ground vegetation, shrubs and mature trees. The landscape here looks very much like the **bocage** of Brittany.

Inland there are very few clues to suggest just how complicated is the structure of Pembrokeshire, but the coast shows in fascinating detail how the rocks have been furiously tortured during geological time. In every bay, on every headland there are the signs of the intermittent massive upheavals of the land that have occurred over a period of 1,000 million years; rocks standing on end, rocks buckled and bent and twisted, rocks melted and fused and reconstituted, rocks shattered and fragmented to the state where individual beds become quite unrecognisable. Concerning the more general patterns on the geological map of the county, there are two main trends in the arrangements of the rocks. In the north the rock outcrops trend from WSW-ENE, whereas in the south the prevailing trend is WNW-ESE. These trends prevailing trend is WNW-ESE. These trends reveal the roots of two ancient mountain chains, now worn down so drastically by the forces of erosion that hardly anything remains of them. The rock outcrops of north Pembrokeshire show the course of an ancient Caledonian mountain chain, formed by the collision of the two ancient continents of Europe and North America some 400 million years ago. And in the south are the roots of the Armorican mountains, formed about 290 million years ago. Along a narrow zone in the centre of the county, stretching from St Bride's Bay through Haverfordwest to Tavernspite, the roots of these old mountain systems are in particularly close contact. But everywhere in the county the detailed pattern of rock exposures is related to the downwarps (synclines) and upwarps (anticlines) formed by the almost unimaginable forces released during these two main periods of mountain-building.

Coastal Contrasts

The varied magnificence of the Pembrokeshire coast, which led in 1951 to the designation of the Pembrokeshire Coast National Park, is due in large measure to its geological and structural diversity. The main features of coastal configuration can be simply explained as the result of long-continued erosion of rocks and structures of varying resistance. So the broad embayment of St Bride's Bay, with its long sandy beaches and crumbling cliffs, has been formed by marine attack along the broad syncline of the Pembrokeshire Coalfield, where the soft Coal Measures have been easily removed. The prominent peninsulas flanking St Bride's Bay to north and south exist in their present form because the igneous rocks of which they are partly made have proved much more resistant to wave attack.

These igneous rocks can be seen on the cliffs above Ramsey Sound, and on Skomer

Volcanic rocks exposed on the south coast of Skomer Island.

Island and around Wooltack Point in the south. Further out to sea, the wave-washed Bishops and Clerks and the gannet island of Grassholm are remote extensions of these same ridges of hard igneous rocks. The other main features of the Pembrokeshire coast can be related to geology in a similar way. The prominent peninsula of Pencaer, pushing bluntly northwards into Cardigan Bay, is made largely of intrusive and volcanic rocks of Ordovician age. The long branching waterway of Milford Haven and the Daugleddau shows how rivers and the sea have been able to exploit faults and synclines and soft rock exposures to create a winding main channel and many secret creeks and bays. Freshwater West Bay has been excavated by the sea along a line where a sharp upwarp has exposed broken and faulted rocks of many types. Saundersfoot Bay is a smaller relative of St Bride's Bay, having formed as a result of wave attack along the centre of the coalfield syncline. At a more detailed scale, many small bays and inlets coincide with soft sedimentary rocks or faulted zones; and headlands are made of harder igneous rocks or sedimentary rocks made resistant to wave attack by their massive and homogeneous nature.

With so many geological contrasts around the coast, little wonder that each stretch has its own characteristics, its own idiosyncrasies. Particular personal favourites are the coasts of the St David's peninsula, which I explored in minute detail over thirty years ago, in a bright, quiet early summer spent largely in the company of sea-birds and soft winds off the sea. Here the cliffs are immensely varied in colour and form. The north coast between Pencaer and St David's Head, for example, is a wild, lonely coast where rocks and sea are in unceasing and uncompromising conflict. Here there are no clean wide sandy beaches like those of St Bride's Bay; except for Aber Mawr and Abereiddi the small beaches are dark and menacing, and difficult of access. Here it is not golden sand and sunlight which catch the eye, but stark shadows on grey and black cliffs. Here all that matters is measured in the vertical dimension. The cliffs rivet the attention. If the eyes stray from them they wander up to the clifftop scrub of heather, gorse and stunted bushes; or down, far below, to the caves, fissures and stacks hewn by the waves from the resisting land. The sounds are the sounds of surf crashing over a chaos of massive fallen blocks and rock ledges, echoing in unseen caves; the cries of gulls, choughs and ravens; the rise and fall of wind buffeting against sheer rock faces and rushing through fine grass. The scents carried on the wind are of salt spray and blossoming gorse. Here there is peace, and beauty to be absorbed by all the senses.

Equally, many people fall in love with the coast between Porthclais and Solva, where the details have been etched by the waves into the subtle purples, reds, greens and greys of Cambrian sedimentary rocks dipping steeply seawards; or the high Old Red Sandstone cliffs which culminate in St Ann's Head; or the grey-white Carboniferous Limestone cliffs between Flimston and St Govan's where the waves have created a fantastic coastline dominated by vertical walls, ledges littered by collapsed blocks, caves, arches, blow-holes, stacks, chasms and caverns.

If one is temperamentally more attracted by the beauty which resides in peaceful things, there are the "inland coasts" of the estuarine Daugleddau, which make up a separate section of the National Park. Here, at high tide in Garron Pill or in the Carew River, there are no wide vistas; simply the quiet muddy river balanced between ebb and flow, the low rock cliffs and the smooth valley sides clothed by dense oak woodland. These are no ordinary oak woods. They are the last remnants of the Mabinogion forests, densely inhabited by twisted stunted trees which hide the ghosts of long-lost Welsh princes. The oaks, ashes and sycamores struggle for existence amid lichens and moss and brambles and climbing ivy - except where neat, well-ordered, alien coniferous woods have rudely replaced them. At low water everything is transformed; mud replaces water, rocks draped in steaming seaweed line the shore, and waders and waterfowl appear from nowhere to see what the ebbing tide has laid bare.

Platforms and Valleys

The relationships between geology and landscape are a little less obvious in inland Pembrokeshire, for here the agents of landscape destruction have gained the upper hand over millions of years of geological time. Much of the Pembrokeshire landscape appears extremely flat when viewed as a panorama. Near the coast the "erosion surfaces" are particularly spectacular, and the coastal flats cut across steeply dipping Carboniferous Limestone on the Castlemartin Peninsula are justly famous among geologists and geomorphologists. Around St David's also, the level waterlogged wastes of Dowrog Common, Treleddyd-fawr and the other moorlands are similarly easy to recognize. These coastal platforms have probably been fashioned partly by wave action at times of much higher sea-level, and the St David's carns must have stood above the water surface as islands, looking much as Ramsey Island and the Bishops and Clerks look today. Generally the coastal flats have surface altitudes less than 60m above sea-level, but there may be other surfaces at such altitudes as 120m, 180m, and above. Certainly there are extensive gently undulating areas to be seen well inland in Pembrokeshire, but their edges are difficult to find, and it would be misleading to describe this as a landscape composed of neat steps separated by old clifflines. However, at Dinas there is an old cliffline to the south of the A487 road, left high and dry together with its associated caves, cliff-face chasms and offshore stacks and skerries. In general, we can say that the Pembrokeshire land surface has been formed by the processes of wave action, slope degradation and river erosion. Over an immensely long period of time the primeval mountain masses have been worn down, slowly but surely, so that now the old upland is largely reduced to the status of a lowland. Most of the erosion responsible for the present-day landforms has occurred within the last sixty million years or so.

Apart from the past higher sea-levels relative to the land, there have also been periods of much lower sea-levels. The times of low sea-level within the last two million years have been linked to the events of the Ice Age (the Quaternary Period), when vast amounts of moisture were periodically extracted from the oceans and locked up in the major ice sheets of Antarctica, Greenland, North America and Scandinavia. But even earlier than this, Pembrokeshire experienced a prolonged period when sea-level was at least 30m lower than at present. At this time the ancient valley system of Milford Haven was formed, with streams draining a large part of the county flowing generally southwards and then westwards, sometimes independently of geology and sometimes exploiting and guided by weaknesses such as long fault-lines. The coast was well to the west of its present position. Since this time the magnificent waterway has gradually evolved; several times it has been flooded by the sea during the warm interglacial periods, and several times it has been drained as the glaciers advanced and sea-level fell to more than 120m below its present level. The red cliffs of the Haven, the broad amphitheatre of Angle Bay and the more irregular Pembroke River, the quiet creeks and rills up-river from Burton, have all had a long and complex history influenced above all by the violent changes of Ice Age sea-level.

The Ice Age

The natural landscape of Pembrokeshire was greatly affected by the Ice Age, with the greatest changes related to the work of glacier ice, ground ice, and water produced by the melting of ice and snow. On at least two occasions the county lay close to the southern margin of the largest British glacier, the Irish Sea Glacier. During the earlier of the two glaciations which have been discovered, this great glacier, nourished by the prolific snows of the northern and western British Isles, swept southwards (extremely slowly!) across Cardigan Bay, and then south-eastwards across Pembrokeshire. Even here it must have been over 1,000m thick, for the glacier had sufficient momentum to flow on up the Bristol Channel as far as Bristol and the Mendips. On its southern flank it

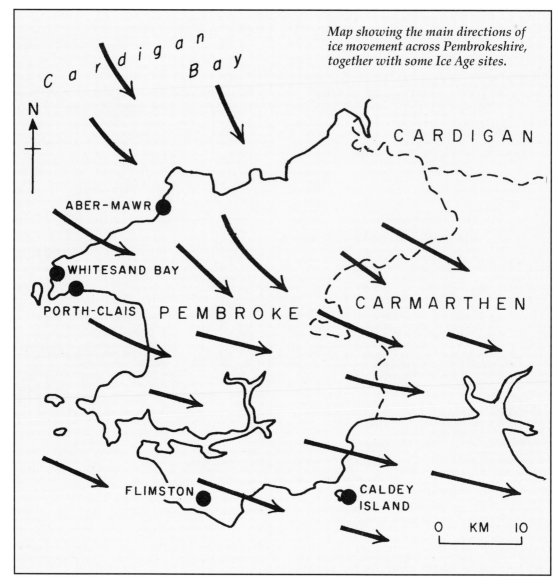

Map showing the main directions of ice movement across Pembrokeshire, together with some Ice Age sites.

reached as far as the Scilly Isles, 500 km from the snowfields that gave it birth.

At this time Pembrokeshire must have been completely submerged beneath a solid mass of glacier ice, pressing irresistibly on towards the south-east, removing mud and clay from the old sea-floor and soil, sand and loose bedrock from the face of the land. How much rock was eroded by the Irish Sea Glacier is difficult to say, for this last complete glaciation of the county occurred perhaps 450,000 years ago; most traces of it have long since been removed by more recent erosion and deposition. In the south of thecounty there is little trace except for "erratic" boulders carried by the ice from the St David's area and further afield, some of which have been used by enterprising locals as gravestones in the old churchyard at Flimston. In the north, however, there is one much more spectacular trace of this glaciation - the long, wooded Gwaun Valley and the little known series of deep valleys which join its western end. Cwm Gwaun itself cuts right across the uplands, isolating Carningli from the main mass of Mynydd Presely. It was cut by glacial meltwater flowing in tunnels beneath thick melting ice at a time when the Irish Sea Glacier was dying a slow, lingering death. The meltwater rushed westwards under enormous pressure, sometimes flowing uphill and carving a steep-sided valley which is occasionally over 50m deep. It escaped through the western series of connecting valleys into the upper basin of the Western Cleddau and thence southwards through the deep cleft of the Trefgarn Gorge. By far the most spectacular of these connecting valleys is the Nant-y-Bugail Valley, whose precipitous sides are in one place over 85m high. Perhaps more beautiful, but largely undiscovered, are the valleys of Esgyrn Bottom, Criney Brook and Cwmonnen, with their steep wooded flanks and their flat floors of thick, boggy peat. In autumn when the mist is rising and there are red dying leaves on the trees and dead white grass below, these quiet valleys also have the feel of magic about them.

Once again, more recently, the ice of the Irish Sea Glacier overwhelmed part of Pembrokeshire. About 17,000 years ago the glacier crossed the north coast and flowed almost as far south as Milford Haven; but this glaciation was not nearly as prolonged or powerful as its predecessors, and by the time the glacier reached Pembrokeshire its energies were almost spent. The ice changed the landscape hardly at all, but it did smooth the contours by dumping a spasmodic cover of till (once called "boulder-clay") especially in the north. On some of the moorlands near St David's and Fishguard this dark purple, sticky clay till was worked in clay-pits from medieval times until quite recently; it was described very accurately in 1599 by the ubiquitous George Owen. Here and there sands and gravels over 20m thick were laid down by meltwater steams.

Sometimes these sands and gravels have a hummocky surface, but more often they occupy the valley floors; they can be seen in gravel-pits at Trevayog, Tre-llys, Mathry Road and elsewhere. Occasionally the gravels contain shells dredged by the ice from the floor of Cardigan Bay and then re-deposited by meltwater.

Before, during and after this last glaciation the climate of Pembrokeshire was as severe as that of an Arctic tundra, and those areas not actually covered by snow and ice were subjected to intense frost shattering. The slopes of sharp, angular blocks in the uplands, and beneath many coastal cliffs, are the result of this process. In the uplands the coarser material is called **scree**, but on the coast, where it is often exposed in section, it has long been referred to as **head**.

At one or two coastal localities in north Pembrokeshire chance circumstances have led to the preservation of smoothed and ice-scratched bedrock and thick sequences of interglacial and glacial deposits; the most important of these are Abermawr and Poppit, both of which have been scheduled as Sites of Special Scientific Interest. Other interesting sequences of Ice Age deposits occur at West Angle, Druidston, and Porthclais, and Ice Age landforms made of sands and gravels are particularly widespread in the Moylgrove - Monington area. As with many of the other natural landscape features, the deposits and landforms of the Ice Age may not be particularly noticeable to the casual observer, but they are there to be seen by those who know what they are looking for.

Some Interesting Geological Sites

Those who are interested in geology and scenery are recommended to look at some of the publications recommended in the bibliography. The listed books and booklets contain considerable detail about particular sites, and there are also many ideas for "geological tours" of Pembrokeshire. However, for the non-specialist visits to the following easily accessible sites will provide first-hand information on the history of the Pembrokeshire rocks.

The magnificent rocky tor of Maiden Castle is made of Precambrian rhyolite about 1,000 million years old. It is situated above the northern end of Trefgarn Gorge, and can be reached after a short climb from Nant-y-Coy Mill. More recent rocks, this time of Cambrian age, can be seen on the coast at Porthclais not far from St David's. A short walk from the car-park at the head of the creek takes the visitor to the outer coast, where red, green, purple and grey Cambrian rocks can be seen in the cliffs. Rocks of Ordovician age are exposed in the Presely Hills, with igneous rock outcrops breaking the skyline as jagged carns or tors. The famous spotted dolerite of Carn Meini can be visited by following the eastern part of the "Golden Road" or Presely Ridge Track from Croesfihangel. Silurian rocks of several types can be seen in the fascinating cliff exposures on the beach at Marloes Sands. Here the strata are standing almost vertically in places, and there are many beautiful rocky stacks partly buried by sand on the beach. Rocks which are about 340 million years old can be seen at West Angle Bay, particularly in the little embayments to the north of the sandy beach. These rocks are Lower Limestone Shales and limestone beds of Carboniferous age, with individual strata again dipping so steeply that they appear to be on edge.

One of the classic localities for the examination of Carboniferous Limestone is the coastal stretch between Stackpole Head and the Green Bridge of Wales, which can be visited on days when there is no firing on the eastern part of the Castlemartin Ministry of Defence range. There are also excellent exposures on the cliffs of South beach, Tenby, immediately beneath The Esplanade.

The rocks of the Millstone Grit series are not particularly well exposed on the coast except in and around Waterwynch Bay, between Tenby and Saundersfoot. For the most part they are conglomerates, gritstones and sandstones somewhat similar to those of the Coal Measures exposed around the whole sweep of Saundersfoot Bay. The Coal Measures rocks, including occasional seams of coal, are often highly contorted and faulted; the Lady Cave anticline, south of Saundersfoot Harbour, is a superb geological site. Fascinating structures can also be observed at low tide in The Settlands, south of Broad Haven on St Bride's Bay.

Deposits dating from the Ice Age can be seen all round the coast. The oldest deposits (probably relating to the "early glaciation" referred to above) occur at the Witch's Cauldron near Ceibwr, and on Lydstep Headland. In both cases old glacial deposits have been turned into a sort of "concrete" by minerals precipitated from groundwater. Raised beach deposits from the last interglacial episode are best observed at Poppit on the Teifi estuary. Till and sands and gravels from the last glacial episode are easily seen from the beach at Druidston. Here, at the head of the bay, there is a great thickness of sticky chocolate-brown clay till containing sea-shells dredged up from the floor of St Bride's Bay by the Irish Sea Glacier as it travelled south-eastwards, and in the little valleys running inland from the beach there are hundreds of large ice-scratched boulders left by the ice when it melted away. At Trefigin, near Moylgrove, and at Penparc near Cardigan, sands and gravels were dumped by meltwater streams at the time of ice melting, about 13,000 years ago. Finally, the best site for viewing the frost-shattered scree formed at the end of the last glacial episode is the south face of Carningli, near Newport.

Chapter Three

Myths, Monuments and Mysteries

Since the end of the last glaciation, the impact of man upon the natural landscapes of Pembrokeshire has gradually increased, so that today the cultural features within the landscape tend to attract much of our attention. The tempo of landscape change has increased as man's technological expertise has advanced. Technological "generations" have become shorter and shorter. By looking at a variety of ancient cultural relics we can see that each succeeding generation has developed for itself the means, ever more efficient, of removing the landscape traces of its predecessors. But successive generations have had different territorial and economic demands, and in a region with landscapes as varied as those of Pembrokeshire this explains why many old features of the cultural landscape are so well preserved. There are fascinating relics of the prehistoric period to be found by those prepared to hunt for them among the shadows.

The Stone Age

The earliest known human occupation of Pembrokeshire occurred during the most recent cold stage of the Ice Age, over 20,000 years ago and at a time when sea-level was very much lower than it is now. Palaeolithic or Old Stone Age man hunted the tundra on the northern slopes of the (then dry) Bristol Channel. He occupied some of the old sea caves on the limestone cliffs of the Castlemartin Peninsula and also limestone caves further inland. Caves such as the

Priory Farm cave at Monkton were used, off and on, for thousands of years; and the evidence from Paviland in Gower and elsewhere shows that men belonging to the Aurignacian cultural group lived here during and after an "interstadial phase" when there was a temporary improvement of climate. We do not know whether man was forced to retreat from the Castlemartin Peninsula during the coldest part of the last glaciation, but archaeological finds of simple flint implements show that he was in residence again when the ice began to melt around 15,000 years ago.

Caves on Caldey Island and the mainland have yielded many finds of animal bones and teeth which show that Early Stone Age man had plenty of animal company. Among the animals were woolly rhinoceros, reindeer, giant ox, cave bear, brown bear, cave lion, glutton, wolf and wild boar. One fissure in the limestone cliffs at Daylight Rock, Caldey Island, contained so many bones of Ice Age animals that they must have been dragged there by hyenas. In addition to the animals mentioned above, there were remains of mammoth, giant deer, and horse; often the bones showed the teeth-marks of the feasting hyenas.

In the following Mesolithic or Middle Stone Age, which began about 10,000 years ago, some of the traditions of the Old Stone Age were continued; in particular, family groups in South Wales still depended on hunting and fishing, and followed a nomadic lifestyle. Some inhabited primitive shelters, but many of them still

A coastline with a long history of settlement: Deadman's Bay, near Marloes.

lived in caves. Gradually people were moving to other parts of the county, and finds of Mesolithic tools have been made at Nab Head, Benton, Newport, and Frainslake (near Castlemartin), in addition to the well-known cave sites of Pembroke and the Tenby - Caldey area. While Mesolithic man probably roamed more widely over the Pembrokeshire landscape than his predecessors, his impact upon it must still have been negligible.

During the Mesolithic period, which lasted until about 6,000 years ago, sea-level was rising by fits and starts. At the close of the last glaciation the sea was more than 100m lower than at present, but as the great ice-sheets of the northern hemisphere wasted away, more and more meltwater was returned to the oceans. Until about 9,000 years ago the rate of sea-level rise was about two metres per century; then after an "interruption" of about a thousand years during which sea-level may have fallen and then risen again slowly, the rate of sea-level

rise increased dramatically to about three metres per century. This was a real natural catastrophe, and the coastal lowlands of Cardigan Bay, St Bride's Bay and Carmarthen Bay were gradually encroached upon by the sea. The greatest inundations occurred when gale-force on-shore winds coincided with spring tides. Peatlands, marshes and woodlands were overwhelmed by the waves, sometimes during storms of such violence that tree-trunks were snapped off like matchsticks. In some of the "submerged forests" which are occasionally exposed at times of exceptionally low tides around the Pembrokeshire coast, the tree-trunks are seen to lie with a constant orientation, felled and then preserved in peat, mud and sand for over 7,000 years. Arthur Leach, Pembrokeshire's greatest amateur geologist, discovered the skeleton of a pig in the submerged forest at Lydstep. Across the poor beast's neck lay the trunk of a fallen tree. Leach and many other investigators have found flint implements among the remains of the submerged forest, together with stags' horns and many animal bones. Undoubtedly many of these drowned areas must have been the hunting-grounds of Mesolithic family groups, and probably many of their settlements, too, are now lost beneath the sea.

The submerged forests have frequently been described in the literature, from Giraldus Cambrensis in the twelfth century to George Owen in the seventeenth century and Arthur Leach and F J North in more recent times. According to Giraldus, a great storm at Newgale in the winter of 1171-72 "laid bare...the surface of the earth, which had been covered for many ages, and discovered the trunks of trees cut off, standing in the very sea itself..." For hundreds of years the people of Whitesands, Newgale, Lydstep, Amroth and Marros have collected firewood from the submerged forests; but recently great damage has unfortunately been done by souvenir hunters.

The rapid post-glacial rise of sea-level and the overwhelming of the coastal forests seems even after thousands of years, to retain a place in the communal sub-conscious. Lurking darkly amid the hazy half-remembered traditions of the Pembrokeshire coastal communities there are the stories of great floods; some of these stories date from the Iron Age or the early Christian period, but some may be much older. Who knows, for instance, where lie the origins of the story of **Cantref y Gwaelod**? The tale has a strongly Celtic flavour, but its roots may lie amid the tree-stumps and fallen trunks and branches of the Mesolithic forests lost in Cardigan Bay. Here, according to tradition, there lay a great tract of fertile country, cultivated, densely peopled and guarded by fine fortified towns. The land, called the Lowland Hundred (**Cantref y Gwaelod**), was defended from the encroachment of the sea by a strong embankment. Seithennin, the keeper of the embankment, was "one of the three immortal drunkards of Britain".

During a splendid banquet the immortal Seithennin became so drunk that he forgot to close the sluice-gates in the embankment, and the sea surged in to inundate the whole land. Most of the population perished, and the land was never reclaimed. It is said that traces of the walls and buildings can still be seen at times of low tide, or made out beneath the surface of the water when the sea is very calm. And sometimes, so they say, if you listen hard, you can hear the eerie sound of a church bell tolling in the dark depths......

Whether or not all this is true, there are many who know that the embankments of Cantref y Gwaelod still exist: during low spring tides, the **sarnau** of Cardigan Bay are exposed as long, stony ridges running straight out to sea. Sarn Cynfelin and Sarn-y-Bwlch are both more than five miles long, while Sarn Badrig (also called St Patrick's Causeway) stretches out to sea for no less than eleven miles. Modern research shows them to be lateral moraines constructed by

Pentre Ifan cromlech -- one of the most famous megalithic monuments in Wales.

the last outlet glaciers to flow westwards from the Cambrian Mountains, but who can blame our forefathers for not knowing that?

The first people who were really able to alter the face of the land we know as Pembrokeshire were the Neolithic farmers who arrived by sea some 5,000 years ago. They came by way of the Bristol Channel, probably sailing in simple skin and wattle vessels not unlike the Irish curragh or the Welsh coracle of today. They usually settled within sight of the sea, for example at Clegyrfwya near St David's. Here archaeologists have been able to make a reconstruction of a Neolithic house, showing it to have been built between two steps of rock with a wooden roof supported by eight timber posts. There was another Neolithic building on the same rocky hill, and there may indeed have been a real farming community here.

Probably they practised cattle-raising, but their food supplies must have been supplemented by hunting and by gathering fruits, roots and nuts. By this time Pembrokeshire was covered with an almost impenetrable jungle of deciduous trees and shrubs. In the most favourable areas the Neolithic communities are thought to have used shifting cultivation. In the broad lush basins of the Western Cleddau and Eastern Cleddau rivers they altered the damp forest of the Atlantic period by tree felling and selective burning, and their browsing animals slowed down forest regeneration by the removal of saplings. These processes continued into a time of drier climate after about 2,000 BC.

Cromlechau

The most spectacular achievements of the Neolithic folk were the megalithic burial chambers (**dolmens or cromlechau**) of various types, many of which can still be found in north Pembrokeshire. Among the best known are Longhouse near Mathry, Carreg Coetan Arthur near Newport, and Ffyst Samson near St Nicholas. Tombs probably began to appear in the Welsh countryside only when family groups had developed the arts of agriculture to the extent of remaining for several generations in one locality. Then it became the custom to build permanent structures as burial places and perhaps as monuments for the veneration of ancestors. The family vaults in present-day churchyards are not so very different. The main structure of each tomb was made by placing a huge "capstone" slab on top of upright stone pillars. The spaces between these pillars were filled with dry-stone walling, and then the structural core of the chamber was covered with stones or earth to form a substantial mound of cairn. Originally most "barrows", as they have come to be known, were elongated, with a large movable slab or portal at the entrance to the central chamber. However, over the centuries the natural processes of erosion, helped by farmers and tomb-robbers and amateur antiquarians, have removed almost all of the covering materials and have made the original shapes of these tombs difficult to discern. Nowadays there is little left to see of the remaining cromlechau except the grey lichen-encrusted pillars and the occasional massive capstone.

There are at least three different types of **cromlech**. The simplest is the "sub-megalithic" type of chamber, usually set in a hillside where the uphill edge of the capstone is supported on a bedrock ledge and the downhill edge held up by vertical pillars. The two cromlechau on St David's Head belong in this category, perhaps representing a rather lazy style of building which seems to have been common among the late Neolithic communities of St David's peninsula and Pencaer. Another cromlech built in a similar style is the King's Quoit at Manorbier. More complicated were the round barrows with polygonal burial chambers in the centre and access provided by a passage through the mound. The Longhouse monument is of this type, and there is a variation on the theme at Cerrig y Gof, near Newport, where the original round barrow had no less than five chambers or recesses set around its circumference. Most impressive of all were the large long-barrows built with pillars and capstones weighing fifteen tons or more, and with elaborate curved forecourts and portals. Paradoxically, these technically advanced monuments seem to have been built **before** the smaller and rather decadent hillside tombs referred to above.

One of the most famous examples of a megalithic long-barrow in the whole of the British Isles is the Pentre Ifan cromlech near Newport. Here three tall pillars provide delicate support for a capstone measuring almost 5m by 3m. At the entrance portal the capstone is more than 2m above the ground, and it slopes down towards the centre of the chamber. From the excavations undertaken at Pentre Ifan in 1936 it seems that the original barrow must have been over 39m long, 20m wide at its broadest, and at least 3.5m high. Pentre Ifan, like the other remaining cromlechau of Pembrokeshire, shows a mastery of a simple yet impressive technology, and there can be no doubt that such a monument must have been built and used with great ceremony.

It is perhaps not surprising, given their obvious antiquity and their impressive proportions, that some of the megalithic monuments have been linked with legends of giants and heroes such as Samson and Arthur. Early antiquarians also mistakenly attributed them to the druids, referring to the capstones as altars on which the priests performed human sacrifices. According to local tradition, Pentre Ifan is a great place for seeing fairies, who were themselves responsible for the building work.

Nowadays, sadly, we take a rather more sober view of the origins of Pentre Ifan and the other megalithic monuments of Pembrokeshire......

Between 5,000 and 4,000 years ago, the county was the home of a mixed population with different and distinct cultural traditions. There were still many groups of Mesolithic people living around the coastline, which by this time was in approximately its present position. Inland there were tribes of Neolithic farmers and herders, and there were other groups of Neolithic immigrants who seem to have followed a way of life along the coast which was not far removed from that of the Mesolithic groups. As a result of contact with each other and with influences from the outside world, these groups gradually merged and evolved their material culture. Trade became increasingly important, and Professor Emrys Bowen showed many years ago how the Pembrokeshire peninsula acted as something of a cross-roads between the coastal routes running S-N through St George's Channel and those running E-W across the seaway between Ireland and Wales. There was much trade in stone axes, and axe factories came into being in sites which had particularly favourable rock-types. There may have been axe factories in the Presely uplands, at least one manufacturing axes from rhyolitic tuffs, and another using the spotted dolerite derived from Carn Menyn and other nearby outcrops. Axes of these types are widely distributed in Pembrokeshire and elsewhere. They are referred to somewhat ambiguously, and since archaeologists like to use labels, as "Preselite" axes; however, no trace has ever been found of the supposed Presely axe factories.

At about the dawn of the Bronze Age, the Mesolithic and Neolithic peoples of Pembrokeshire were just beginning to come under the influence of the Beaker People and were learning the skills of metal-working. There was a new flowering of culture throughout south-west Britain, and the greatest remaining symbol of this culture is the famous Stonehenge monument in Wiltshire.

The Stonehenge Myth

Pembrokeshire has played a special part in the Stonehenge story since 1923, when the geologist H H Thomas proved that most of the remaining "bluestones" in the inner circle at Stonehenge come from the county. Furthermore, he suggested that the three main types of bluestone (namely spotted dolerite, rhyolite and volcanic ash) occur naturally close together only in a small area in the Presely uplands around Carn Menyn. Following these discoveries archaeologists evolved an elegant hypothesis to the effect that the bluestones, and other stones such as the altar-stone, were deliberately quarried and then transported some 300 km from

Part of the rocky tor of Carn Alw, on the north flank of the Presely upland ridge. Some of the Stonehenge bluestones came from here, according to geologists.

Pembrokeshire to Wiltshire. Some writers have argued that a sacred stone circle was first built somewhere in the Presely Hills, and later moved, lock, stock and barrel, to Stonehenge.

The hypothesis involves a great deal of imagination concerning land and sea routes, the "sanctity" of the Presely area, and the desire of the Stonehenge builders to use stone-types which had magical properties or with which they were already familiar from the stone-axe trade. In our minds this hypothesis has quietly turned into "fact". We all know the stirring tale of primitive men hauling the massive bluestones on sledges and then sailing them on rafts from Milford Haven along the Bristol Channel to the Avon valley, and taking them by sledge again, or on rollers, for the last triumphant part of the journey to the Stonehenge site on Salisbury Plain. This is all a part of our contemporary folk-lore, and when in 1954 a BBC experiment proved that the journey was indeed possible, the theory seemed confirmed. Novels such as the excellent *Bluestones* by Mary John have helped to entrench the theory even further.

Another angle on the Stonehenge Myth is that the monument is an astronomical observatory, built by a people with an intricate knowledge of the movements of the sun, the moon, the planets and the stars. Some authors insist that Stonehenge is itself a calculating or predicting device, and that it is linked geometrically with the source areas of the Sarsen Stones and the bluestones. This presupposes that one knows where all the stones have come from! It is argued, in a perfectly circular fashion, that if the Stonehenge builders were so aware of astronomical alignments and were so capable of mathematical precision in their building, then they must have found the transport of a collection of bluestones from Presely to Salisbury Plain a very simple matter.

Windswept grasslands on Mynydd Presely. The ancient Bronze Age "Golden Road" followed the crest of the upland ridge.

However, the "bluestone theory" has remarkably little archaeological or other evidence to support it, and it is only within the last 35 years that anyone has pointed out how flimsy the theory of human bluestone transport really is. For a start, there is no trace of a bluestone quarry at Carn Meini or anywhere else. In 1973 Geoffrey Kellaway of the Institute of Geological Sciences suggested, perfectly reasonably, that the Stonehenge bluestones may well have been carried to the innermost shores of the Bristol Channel by glacier ice. It has been known for many years that the great Irish Sea Glacier which overrode Pembrokeshire more than 400,000 years ago flowed south-eastwards up the Bristol Channel, carrying with it erratics and till eroded not only from Presely but also from Ireland, the Lleyn Peninsula and Galloway in Scotland. But only with the excavation of M5 motorway cuttings was it discovered that this glacier overrode the Somerset coast and deposited part of its load in the Bristol-Bath region. This being the case, it is now much more logical to assume that the bluestones (in reality from quite a wide variety of sources both within and outside Pembrokeshire) were, at the time of the Beaker culture, conveniently littering the countryside less than 50 km from Stonehenge. Indeed, we now know, as a result of recent archaeological investigations coupled with radio-carbon dating, that Presely bluestone boulders were being used in Stone Age burial chambers on Salisbury Plain at least 500 years **before** Stonehenge was built.

In an attempt to sort out the human/glacial transport problem, a team of scientists from the Open University undertook a comprehensive research project in 1988-91, concentrating upon an examination of rock samples taken from archaeological sites on Salisbury Plain and from rock outcrops in Pembrokeshire. After subjecting their samples to a wide range of analytical tests, they concluded that the Stonehenge bluestones (and the fragments of bluestones which have been broken up) had come from a wide range of sites. Most had come from the eastern part of Mynydd Presely, but other stones and fragments came from Mynydd Dinas, Carningli and other sites as yet unidentified. They concluded that the stones were so varied in origin and type that they appeared to be nothing more than an assemblage of glacial erratics, picked up and deposited by the ice of the Irish Sea Glacier.

The OU scientists could see no reason why Neolithic or Bronze Age men should have wandered all over North Pembrokeshire collecting stones from at least ten different sites to take all the way to Stonehenge. They also concluded that there was no evidence of Presely spotted dolerite being used preferentially by megalith builders either at Stonehenge or elsewhere. Thus there is infinitely more evidence to support the theory of ice transport than there is in support of the great contemporary myth of long-distance haulage by the Beaker people. However, old myths die hard, and since assorted learned professors have staked their reputations on the "human transport" theory, the arguments will continue for a good while yet ....

The Age of Metal Tools

The Bronze Age settlers who established themselves in Pembrokeshire between about 3,800 and 2,500 years ago seem to have made much greater use than their predecessors of the centre and south of the county. They continued and speeded up the process of jungle clearance, now with metal tools. It is thought that they depended less upon cultivation than the Neolithic people; but the cultural advances of this time may be seen as a sign of both increased trade and more stable settlement.

The most obvious of the traces left in the cultural landscape by the Bronze Age peoples are, like those of their Neolithic predecessors, made of stone. Such are the stone circles (of which the best preserved is Gors Fawr, near Mynachlog-ddu), the scores of standing stones which occur in the north of the county (as at Rhos-y-Clegyrn and Henry's Moat), and some smaller single-chambered tombs. Many of the round barrows of the Presely area and the south of the county date from this time. In some places (as on the flanks of Carningli near Newport) there are traces of Bronze Age circular enclosures and stone walls, and not far away, at Parc-y-meirw, there is a mysterious (and reputedly haunted) stone alignment also assumed to date from the Bronze Age. At Castell Garw there is a large "henge" monument, and at Meini Gwyr near Glandy Cross there is an embanked stone circle.

In recent years archaeologists have made great progress in their studies of Bronze Age Pembrokeshire. They have discovered a number of important "ritual complexes" containing burial sites, cremation traces, living huts, standing stones and lines of pebbles, and traces of circular timber structures. One of the most astonishing sites to be excavated is at Stackpole Warren, between the Bosherston Lily Ponds and Barafundle Bay, and another is at Longstone, near St Ishmael's. There are also hundreds of prehistoric hearths or "burnt mounds" all over Pembrokeshire, but especially numerous in the south of the county. They were probably used for cooking by seasonal hunting parties, but some of them may have been used in connection with prehistoric sweat lodges or saunas.

There are still a number of mysteries surrounding Pembrokeshire's Bronze Age. It has been something of a tradition to assume that most of the features still visible in the landscape are related to religious activities or to burials. However, at least some of the circular and rectangular stone enclosures near Newport appear to be domestic, marking hut sites and possibly animal enclosures or small cultivated plots. And can all the standing stones really all be associated with religious ceremonial? Some of them (for example the pair of "male" and "female" standing stones called Cerrig Meibion Arthur at Cwm Garw) may simply be crude fertility symbols. Bedd Morris, near Newport, has been variously described as a waymark, a memorial stone for a Bronze Age chieftain, a boundary marker, a phallic symbol, or a cattle rubbing stone! Maybe it has been several or all of these things in its time, and it still marks the boundary of the parish of Newport. More romantically, according to a local legend it marks the place where one Morris, who was in love with the daughter of the squire of Pontfaen, was buried after he was killed in a duel with a rival.

The most interesting mystery concerns the Bronze Age burial chambers of the county. Apart from the three massive mounds on the summit of Foel Drygarn, the barrows which covered the chambers were much smaller than those of the later Stone Age. Also, the impressive megalithic techniques used in the construction of cromlechs such as Pentre Ifan and Carreg Samson appear to have been forgotten or abandoned; the Bronze Age chambers were small box-like affairs with very small capstones, no tunnels or passages, and no impressive portals. Was there actually a technological regression going on at the time? Or were the Bronze Age or Beaker people of Pembrokeshire simply more nomadic than their predecessors, constantly on the move and preferring to make single graves rather than family vaults? Or did they simply have a ritual preference for cremations, which required only that small urns full of ashes should be placed in small and simple

stone-lined cavities? And why -- most intriguingly of all -- do the Bronze Age tribes of Pembrokeshire appear to have lost the ability to make wild and wonderful structures out of stone just at the time when Stonehenge (considered to be "the ultimate prehistoric monument") was being built in Wessex?

The Bronze Age was followed about 2,500 years ago by the dawn of the Iron Age. It came with the many groups of Celtic immigrants who followed the sea-trading routes northwards and westwards from Spain, France and the south-west peninsula of England. They spoke languages which were the forerunners of Welsh and Gaelic, and it was they who began to give Wales its imprint of Welshness. As they arrived the climate deteriorated, and the immigrant tribes had to contend with cool, damp conditions. Nevertheless, the density of their settlements in Pembrokeshire was greater than that of any of their predecessors and they must have been largely responsible for the removal of much of the virgin forest. They were also the first great fort-builders.

The Iron Age fort or defended settlement is easily the most striking relic of any of the prehistoric landscapes of Wales. Earth ramparts and ditches on clifftop headlands are commonplace on all the coasts of Pembrokeshire, as at Penpleidiau, Great Castle Head and St Ishmael's. Inland there are hundreds of defended sites, including the three great hill forts, at Garn Fawr near Strumble Head, at Mynydd Carningli near Newport, and at Foel Drygarn near Crymych. Those who are interested in "earth mysteries" claim that all three forts lie on a single ley-line. There are also smaller hill forts on spectacular rocky crags or tors at Carnffoi near Newport and at Carn Alw on the north flank of the Presely ridge. Many more forts, in less impressive landscape settings, are marked on the OS map as "raths" or "camps".

The hill fort on the summit of Carningli is a classic of its type. It covers an area of almost 10 acres, and takes maximum advantage of the defensive possibilities afforded by the craggy nature of an old volcanic peak. Steep rock faces, particularly on the south side of the summit, are used as natural defences, and on the other flanks of the settlement high stone walls (now ruinous but still visible) were thrown up to deter invaders. There are several defended enclosures on and around the summit, and below the steep scree slopes there are abundant traces of little boulder-strewn fields and paddocks, nowadays overwhelmed by bracken in the weeks of high summer. The outer enclosures were used for keeping animals, and the inner ones for the living quarters and store-rooms of the families who made up the tribe. Traces of the old hut circles can still be seen. There were a number of entrances into the fort, but the main one, which was heavily defended, was on the north-west flank.

The most impressive of all the defended settlements is the summit fort on Foel Drygarn, occupying the most easterly hill of the main Presely range. Its stone ramparts contain three enclosures, and in addition to the three prominent Bronze Age cairns (mentioned above) there are traces of many hut hollows and platforms to suggest a large population. As in the case of the Carningli fort, natural rock faces or cliffs have been used cleverly for defensive purposes, with man-made defences built only where necessary. There is another fascinating site on the St David's headland, where the stone-built defences of the "Warrior's Dyke" enclosed a compact settlement of perhaps a dozen round huts. The defensive structures, and traces of some of the hut circles, can still be seen. Beyond the main defences another stone wall may have defined the home territory of the Iron Age community, and in the valley between Porth Melgan and Carnllidi one can still see the stone walls of the original small enclosed fields. The finds from the settlement suggest that even in this barren, windswept locality there was a mixed farming economy in which stock breeding played a part.

A glimpse of the Iron Age can be seen at Castell Henllys, not far from Eglwyswrw, where a fortified site has been excavated and examined in some detail by archaeologists. In addition an attempt has been made to re-create the Iron Age environment through the construction of round-houses using authentic materials (local timbers, reeds from the Nevern estuary and wattle-and-daub). The thatched round-houses are surprisingly warm and spacious inside, and other smaller buildings, for storage purposes or for housing domestic animals, have also been reconstructed. The site (now owned by the NPA) is increasingly visited by school groups, and is open to the public during the summer months.

During the Iron Age the changing style of promontory fort and hill fort building shows that there were tribal rivalries in which raiding and open warfare were becoming more common. The earliest forts were protected only by single curved banks, but by 100 BC double- or even treble-curved embankments were characteristic. The embankments were probably faced with stone, topped with wooden stockades, and protected with a bristling array of pointed stakes; and sometimes they enclosed areas large enough to maintain beleaguered communities together with their livestock during long periods of siege. Examples are the promontory forts at Bosherston Pools, Flimston Bay, Greenala Point and the Deer Park at Martin's Haven. The Carn Alw hill fort is particularly interesting, since on its most vulnerable flank a complex "chevaux de frise" was built by the inhabitants; this was an extensive area of sharp stones and stakes set at an angle into the ground, pointing outward in such a way as to hinder mounted

Iron Age hillfort and Bronze Age burial cairns on the summit of Foel Drygarn.

warriors or foot soldiers. So far as we know, there is nothing similar anywhere else in West Wales. In case anybody should think that the Iron Age hill forts were crude affairs, it is worth pointing out that the Celtic tribes of pre-Roman times were just as aware as the Normans, over a thousand years later, of the niceties of defensive strategy. If one compares the plans of Iron Age forts with the plans of Norman castles, the similarities are striking. The deep ditch around the perimeter of the Iron Age defended site is the equivalent of the Norman castle moat. The outer defensive rampart is the equivalent of the stockaded or stone-built curtain wall. Gateways through the ramparts were always overlooked by vertical walls or banks from which the defenders could rain down boiling water, boulders, spears or arrows upon the enemy.

The Iron Age tribes knew all about the theory of the outer bailey and the inner bailey; the outer settlement platform at Carningli, for example, was probably used for stockading animals in times of trouble, but the defenders could also abandon it during a particularly fierce attack, and fall back upon the more heavily defended inner enclosure. If the inner defensive ditch and stockaded bank was breached, then the last line of defence was always on the highest point of the fort. In Norman times, an artificial mound or motte was sometimes built for this purpose, with a wooden fort or stone tower on its top. Next time you stand on the highest rocks of Garn Fawr or Foel Drygarn, remember that you are standing on the topmost battlement of a very ancient but nonetheless quite sophisticated military installation!

In stressing the importance of fortified sites in Iron Age Pembrokeshire and the ferocity of the Iron Age tribes, we are in danger of forgetting that huge strides were made during this period towards a more settled community. We now know a considerable amount about local economy, culture and society during the centuries before the birth of Christ. There are many superb field systems, for example on Skomer Island, which suggest that not only animal husbandry but also crop rotations were practised by people who had opted for a settled lifestyle. The greatest concentration of small defended sites in Pembrokeshire occurs in the area around Llawhaden and Gelli, and archaeologists have learned much about Iron Age life from the camps and enclosures at Woodside, Dan-y-Coed, Broadway and Holgan.

Stock rearing was very important for the local tribes, and archaeological finds include carbonised grain, rotary querns or hand mills, implements used in the spinning and weaving of wool, and tools for dressing and working leather. There was a hierarchical organisation of society, and the typical defended settlement may have consisted of a chieftain and his extended family, and servants or slaves up to about 30 in number. Bards (poets and storytellers) and druids (the religious leaders) also lived within fortified settlements. On the other hand the peasants lived in hovels scattered about amid the fields. There must have been considerable trading activity, and in some areas there were sufficient agricultural surpluses to allow some members of the community to develop their skills as potters, metal-workers or weavers. We know that Iron Age people had a great love of decoration and ornament, and this is reflected in the sheer exuberance of the ornamentation seen on the surfaces of swords, shields, chariots, flagons, cauldrons, torcs, helmets, trumpets and a host of other artifacts.

Many local historians have wondered about the religious beliefs of the Iron Age tribes and about the role of the druids. Much nonsense has been written about these mysterious men, and indeed many historians have interpreted the prehistoric remains of Pembrokeshire as druid sacred structures. However, the Celts do not appear to have had a uniform set of religious beliefs, and the druids presided over a series of cults involving the worship of more than twenty local gods. Some religious practices were bizarre and nasty, and there was certainly a "severed head cult" which was manifested in warfare as well as in sacrificial religious ceremonial. There is no doubt that the druids were revered as members of a priestly caste, and that they were mystics, teachers, healers, historians, scientists and even poets; but that is not to say that they were the guardians of some "lost wisdom". Since many of their crude religious ceremonies were conducted in oak groves and on pre-existing sacred sites they left few traces in the landscape. And we get little guidance as to the origins and functions of the druids from the gentlemen who march about in strange apparel at the National Eisteddfodau of the present day; they are the wonderful progeny of one Iolo Morgannwg, conceived early in the nineteenth century as part of his attempt to revitalize Welsh traditions in poetry and music.

During the Roman period (AD 43 - AD 410), which coincided broadly with the end of the Iron Age, Celtic tribal society in Pembrokeshire evolved largely unmolested. In this remote western peninsula only one possible Roman camp site has been discovered, but the Romans knew enough of the area to record its people as the "Demetae". Through the distant mysterious millennia before the birth of Christ, the many tribal groups of immigrants gradually coalesced into one people.

Chapter Four

The Welsh, their Saints and their Stories

Gradually the people of Pembrokeshire, and the landscape of the county, began to acquire the imprint of Welshness. The Celtic tribes grew, and their territories emerged during the long period after the departure of the Romans from Wales in AD 383. Complicated trading movements and folk migrations linked Wales and Ireland, and because of its strategic position on the busy seaways of

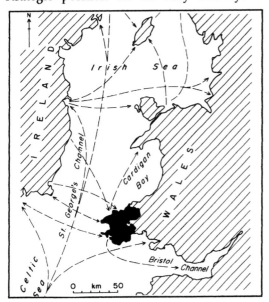

The trading and missionary routes of the Irish Sea and St George's Channel during the Age of the Saints.

the Dark Ages, Pembrokeshire at this time was one of the key areas in the development of Celtic culture. The early Christian missionaries brought with them a new faith

that was adopted first by members of the Romano-British community, and later by many of the Celtic princes and commoners.

The first Christians who came to Pembrokeshire found a community that was more Irish than Welsh. It appears that for several centuries South-West Wales was something of an Irish colony. Thousands of Irish settlers came across St George's Channel, and there is no doubt that they caused a great deal of trouble. There are ancient tales of Irish pirates and brigands pillaging, burning and stealing land from the native Welsh. At the time two Celtic languages were in use in the area -- Brythonic or Brittonic by the locals, and Goidelic by the invaders. The political situation in South-West Wales was for a time very confusing, but by the middle of the sixth century the kingdom of Dyfed had been established by the Irish. It was ruled by the mysterious Voteporix, who was variously described as "the protector" or as "the crazy king" of the Demetiae.

Whatever his virtues and vices may have been, Voteporix and his descendants resisted the advances of the Cunedda dynasty who were seeking to conquer territories far to the south of their heartland in North Wales, and they gave the area a cultural and racial imprint which has remained very different from that of North Wales to this day. They also established a tradition for erecting memorial stones to mark burial sites or to commemorate famous individuals. These "early Christian inscribed stones" can now be counted among the cultural icons of Pembrokeshire.

More than fifty inscribed stones dated to the period 400 - 700 AD are found in Dyfed, with the great majority in Pembrokeshire. Some are inscribed with Latin script, providing an echo of the Roman era. Others are marked with the strange Ogam alphabet, which was developed in Ireland for use on wood or stone, possibly in pre-Christian times. The script consisted of a series of short notches or grooves running at different angles and arranged in groups of five. There were 20 letters, and the script would be inscribed up one edge of the stone, along the top, and (if the text was long) down another edge. The most interesting stones contain both Latin script (always on a flat face, running either across the stone or along its axis) and Ogam script inscribed along an edge.

The Ogam and Latin inscribed stone in Cilgerran churchyard. The Latin script reads "Trenagussus, the son of Macutrenus, lies here."

Among the most famous of the "bilingual" stones are the Voteporix Stone found at Castell Dwyran on the Pembrokeshire- Carmarthenshire border,

the Cilgerran Stone, and the St Dogmael's Stone. The latter, which was used in subsequent centuries as a gatepost and as a bridge near the Abbey, was covered in whitewash and later broken in two; but it is reputed to be the stone which provided the key to the disciphering of the Ogam alphabet.

After 650 AD the use of the Ogam alphabet declined, and the later inscribed memorial stones featured ring crosses and simple ornaments which evolved on later and taller stones into complex and exuberant Celtic ornamentation.

The Celtic Saints

The saintly travellers who came to Pembrokeshire with the Christian gospel at the close of the Roman era made a profound impact upon society, culture and landscape. Their missionary activities probably began before AD 450. Gradually a network of religious cells was established through the area, based for the most part upon a belief in the spiritual benefits of individual withdrawal into the wilderness. Small churches were then established in remote localities, and were particularly common in Pembrokeshire. Here, as elsewhere, they seldom became nuclei for secular settlement; so small churches with Celtic dedications can still be seen around the wild rocky coastline, standing against the elements in splendid isolation.

Many of the Celtic saints and their disciples travelled back and forth across the Irish Sea and St George's Channel on their missionary journeys. These **peregrini** - as they are called by historians - used frail skin boats similar to the Irish curragh of today, and there is no doubt that the smaller Welsh coracle is another vessel which traces its ancestry back to these times. There can be no doubt either about the seamanship of the Celtic saints or about the seaworthiness of

The little church of St Govan, on the south Pembrokeshire coast. The building probably dates from the thirteenth century, but it stands on the site of an early hermit's cell.

their fragile craft, for well before AD 800 they had reached and established settlements in both the Faroe Islands and Iceland. They were, nevertheless, very much at the mercy of winds and tidal currents, for their sailing techniques were primitive and their knowledge of navigation limited. Where possible they used wide sandy bays, but often they must have been driven ashore by chance on to more precarious rocky landing-places. Where this happened, as John Barrett has pointed out, "...their first thought was a thanksgiving for safe delivery. So from the start, little chapels began to appear along our coasts, dedicated to the saintly leaders." Typical of the coastal chapels of this time were those at St Justinian's, St Non's, Cwm-yr-Eglwys and St Dogmael's. Many of these chapels have disappeared; others stand in ruins or have been replaced by later buildings.

The saintly skeleton found on the site of St Patrick's Chapel, Whitesands.

The little limestone chapel at St Govan's is perhaps the best-known symbol of this time of missionaries and monastic seafarers. It stands deep in a cleft in the white cliffs, approachable only by a steep flight of rough steps. The chapel, now restored by the National Park Authority, may have been a monastic cell as long ago as the fifth century; but probably only the rock-cut cell and the stone altar and bench date from this time. Most of the structure which we see today is no older than the thirteenth century. But it is a place shrouded in mystery. The holy well, which ran dry

during the present century, is said to have cured eye troubles, and as such the little chapel was a medieval place of pilgrimage. No one knows who St Govan really was. Possibly the chapel is named after one Cofen, the wife of a king of Glamorgan; or possibly after St Gobhan who was a contemporary of St David. Most popular is the theory that he was Sir Gawaine, one of the Knights of the Round Table who turned hermit after the death of Arthur. This is a nice idea, and there is another local legend that Arthur's sword Excalibur resides in the deep waters of the nearby Bosherston Pools. (The pools were not created until the end of the 18th century -- but why spoil a nice story?)

The most influential of the local Welsh saints were St David and St Patrick. As the fame of David (Dewi Sant) brought pilgrims flocking to this sacred corner of the western world, more and more beaches and small harbours were used by pilgrims and traders, and the beach at Whitesands was particularly widely used as a landing-place. Here the small chapel of St Patrick was established. Nowadays there is hardly any trace of it left, but it was excavated in 1924 and the skeleton of a young man was unearthed beneath the level of the old chapel floor. It is not known who he was, but he was certainly not St Patrick, for Patrick was apparently quite ancient but very much alive when he set off from here on his last voyage to Ireland.

Another saintly hero was St Brynach, an Irishman who had a considerable following especially in the north of the county. Before taking up saintly ways he was a tearaway adolescent; but after a visit to Rome he sailed to Milford Haven on a slab of rock, was almost seduced by a lusty princess, almost killed by a gang of thugs, and almost driven out of his mind by demons in the Gwaun valley. After a series of epic (and often hilarious) adventures, Brynach settled at Nevern, where he became a good friend of Dewi Sant. The great Celtic Cross in Nevern Churchyard is still known as St Brynach's Cross.

Dewi Sant and his Followers

Some of the early monastic cells in the county did attract settlement, and these grew into larger religious communities. Among these we can count Nevern, St Dogmael's, Penally and Caldey, but these never compared in importance with the community of Dewi Sant in the secluded valley of the River Alun. Like the others, the church of St David probably began as a monastic llan, about AD 520. However, as the reputation of the founder grew so did his church and the associated settlement, then called Menevia. Soon it was the most important ecclesiastical centre in South Wales, and it has remained so to this day . By its very presence the cathedral and its community have had a profound effect upon the course of events during the medieval period and later centuries.

The area round about the cathedral city has a wealth of tradition about the man himself and his followers. Legend tells us that Dewi was born during a great gale at a spot later to be named after his mother, St Non. He was baptized, possibly at Porthclais, by Elvis the Bishop of Munster, "who at that instant by divine intervention was landed there from Ireland". He was educated at Ty Gwyn, near the present city, but spent much of his missionary life far away from his monastery in other parts of the Celtic world. But he returned in his old age to Menevia, where he was visited by monks and disciples from other parts of Wales, Brittany, Cornwall and Ireland. The influence of his cult was so great that more than 100 churches and monasteries were established in his name. There is a jolly story about Dewi Sant and a heathen chieftain named Boia, who gave the famous

rock of Clegyr Boia its name. Legend has it that Boia's wife told her maids "to go to where the monks can see you and with bodies bare, play games and use lewd words". Although this display seems to have had the desired effect upon the monks, Dewi remained strong. As divine retribution against the family Boia's wife was driven to murder her stepdaughter and then went mad, while the chieftain and the rest of his household and camp were destroyed by fire from heaven.

When the saint died, probably on 1 March AD 588, a brilliant sun shone over his mourning and fasting disciples, and "Jesus Christ bore away David's soul in great triumph and gladness and honour. After his hunger, his thirst, and cold, and his labours, his abstinence and his acts of charity, and his weariness, and his tribulation, and his applications, and his anxiety for the world, the angels received his soul, and they bore it to a place where the light does not fail, and there is rest without labour, and joy without sadness, and abundance of all good things, and victory, and brilliance, and beauty..." These words, written in 1346, must be among the most beautiful in early Welsh literature.

There are other legends associated with St Justinian, who was David's friend and confessor. He retired to Ramsey to escape the lax ways of the mainland monks. But he had too many visitors, and prayed that the rocky causeway to the mainland would be destroyed. A giant axe appeared, and in an inspired piece of divine intervention chopped the causeway into a series of rocks called the Bitches. These rocks, submerged at high tide, force the tidal currents to run through them with great force and have been an effective deterrent to unwanted visitors. Poor Justinian was murdered by his own followers on Ramsey by having his head cut off, but showing great resilience he picked it up and then walked across the sound with it tucked under his

The Cathedral, Bishop's Palace and other buildings which lie within the Cathedral Close of St David's.

arm. He laid it down on the opposite shore before expiring, and at that site he was buried and his chapel was built. The present ruins of the chapel at St Justinian's are of much later date, but the saint's well can still be seen.

A rather more worldly tale of the early Christians is reminiscent of "the immortal drunkard" who precipitated the catastrophe of Cantref y Gwaelod. It concerns Pyr, the first abbot of Caldey who gave that island its Welsh name. According to a near-contemporary source, he came to a sad and soggy end. "One dark night this same Pyr in an unseemly drunken bout...wandered alone into the precincts of the monastery and fell into a very deep well. He raised a shout of distress, but when he was rescued from the water by the monks he was almost dead, and so he died that night."

The Celtic Way of Life

Although the saints and their settlements made a great impact upon the landscape of Pembrokeshire, probably of greater importance was the normal Celtic way of life, which gradually became based upon permanent settlement during the Dark Ages. As mentioned at the beginning of the chapter, the kingdom of Dyfed emerged as the forerunner of present-day Pembrokeshire. The kingdom was composed of seven districts or **cantrefi**: and in spite of the great political upheavals of the period 700-1093 there was a gradual progression towards an ordered society. A pattern of small scattered "homestead" settlements and fragmented holdings appeared in the landscape. The homesteads were built by tribal freemen, and they provided security and protection for large family groups. Some of the small hamlets of north Pembrokeshire originated at this time, and the prefix **tref** (township) is a common place-name element throughout the north of the county. Many of the isolated upland farms of Mynydd Presely must have been founded as **hafodydd** or dwellings used only during the summer cattle grazing season. The enclosure of many small rectangular fields bounded by stone walls or thick turf banks may date from this time, as must the creation of the dense network of trackways. Arable farming, with an increased use of oats, became more important, and the clearance of the remaining forest land continued at an accelerating pace.

Since most of the family dwellings of the Dark Ages were made of wood, few traces remain. Many families must have continued to use the peninsulas which had been fortified in the Iron Age, and other fortified hilltop sites must also have continued in occupation for centuries after the Romano-British period. There are very many settlement traces on the OS maps referred to as "raths", "camps" and "earthworks". They are often difficult to date, but many of them provided homes for the freemen of Dyfed and their families. Old field enclosures and hut groups on the island of Skomer, which may have been used in the Dark Ages, have been described in detail by Professor W F Grimes, and there may have been a sizeable community living in the old settlement and tilling the fields on St David's Head during the lifetime of the patron saint. On Gateholm, off the Marloes Peninsula, over a hundred rectangular huts set end-to-end or grouped around courtyards have been dated to the Dark Ages. There are a large number of oblong hut hollows (unfortunately not yet thoroughly excavated) on the grassy slopes of Sheep Island off the Angle peninsula. These, like the mysterious traces of ancient buildings on St Margaret's Isle near Caldey, may also be the remains of Celtic pre-Christian settlements long since abandoned and forgotten.

If it is difficult to interpret the landscape of these hazy times, there is no shortage of wordage on its history. It is not a purpose of this book to analyse the complicated internal conflicts which shook the kingdoms of Wales, nor to discuss the effects of the early wars with the English; but it is worth recording that some of the romantic memories of the Celtic Dark Ages were written down, probably in Dyfed, during the tenth and eleventh centuries. The outcome was one of the gems of European literature - *The Mabinogion*. Through the romantic poetry of its strange and complex tales there runs a thread of references to Pembrokeshire, and indeed much of the action of "The Four Branches of the Mabinogi", the best of the tales, takes place specifically in Dyfed. The first legendary king of Dyfed, named Pwyll, is supposed to have had his fateful encounter with Arawn, the king of the underworld, while hunting amid the beautiful oakwoods of Glyn Cuch near Newcastle Emlyn. We learn that his court was accustomed to meet at Arberth or Narberth. Pwyll's son Pryderi and his companions were forced to stay on the enchanted island of Grassholm for eighty years while travelling from Ireland to London. In another story Pryderi and all the people of Dyfed disappeared through the work of a magician; we are told of mice devouring the corn crop and of pigs being taken from Dyfed to Gwynedd.

Perhaps the most famous story is linked with the Arthurian legend, and occurs in the tale of Culhwch and Olwen. The great wild boar called Twrch Trwyth, having been attacked by Arthur and his knights, swam from Ireland to Dyfed and landed at Porthclais. To avenge himself on Arthur the great boar and his gang of seven attendant littler boars did enormous damage, "slaying what men and beasts were in Daugleddau" before Arthur caught up with him. There followed a furious battle in Cwm Cerwyn (not far from the summit of Presely) during which eight of Arthur's knights and several of the black boars were killed. The site of the legendary battle is located on the OS map as Cerrig Marchogion, which means "the rocks of the knights". Here the petrified remains of the fallen warriors appear as a litter of fallen rocks and lichen-covered crags on the misty mountain-side. Following this climactic struggle, the great black beast fled southwards to Laugharne and crossed the mouth of the River Tywi. After further battles in which the last of Twrch Trwyth's attendant boars were killed, he crossed from South Wales to Devon and Cornwall, with King Arthur still in hot pursuit. Eventually the monster swam off into the Atlantic, never to be seen again.

There are several other sites in Pembrokeshire associated with King Arthur. One such is the cromlech called Carreg Coetan Arthur in Newport; according to local legend only a hero such as Arthur could have lifted up the massive capstone and placed it on its supporting pillars. There is a Carn Arthur in the Presely Hills, not far from Carn Meini; and in the same area Bedd Arthur (Arthur's grave) is a strange elliptical arrangement of standing stones marking one of the many places where the great king is buried.

The Viking Sea-Rovers

The later part of the Age of the Saints was much disturbed by the raids of the Vikings, who had little respect either for the magical powers of the princes of Dyfed or for the holiness of St David's and other ecclesiastical centres. Roving far and wide from their bases in Ireland and Scotland in their magnificent long-ships, the Vikings terrorized the coasts of Pembrokeshire between AD 844 and AD 1091. St David's was burnt on no less than eight occasions during this period. Mathry, too prominent for comfort on its hilltop site, also suffered

greatly. We do not know which ports and harbours were used by the Vikings, but certainly there were a number of Viking coastal trading bases or "marts". There is a tradition that Milford Haven was widely used as a temporary base. In the year 877, for example, a chieftain called Hubba is said to have wintered in the Haven with a fleet of twenty-three ships and about 2,000 warriors. This had a considerable impact upon the local birth-rate.

Some authorities have believed that there was a substantial Viking settlement in the centre of the county around AD 1100, and indeed south Pembrokeshire people have some blood-group affinities with the Scandinavian races even today; but there is no reliable archaeological trace of either an inland settlement or of any colonies on the coast. There are very few Norse "finds" in the Pembrokeshire archaeological record; the best-known is a small lead brooch with a brass inset of a dragon, found on the shore at Freshwater West. Probably it dates from the tenth or eleventh century.

But there is much place-name evidence to prove that the Vikings were familiar with the Pembrokeshire coast and with some inland localities as well. There are at least twenty-one surviving place-names of Norse derivation, mostly linked with major coastal landmarks and islands, and it says something for the Viking imprint upon the local community that these names have persisted for a thousand years. Among these names are Fishguard, Skokholm, Grassholm, Ramsey, Skomer, Musselwick, Milford, Goodwick and Gosker. There would undoubtedly have been more were it not for the coming of the Normans.

Chapter Five

The Creation of "Little England"

It is difficult to decide just when Pembrokeshire began to be split into its two halves, the Englishry and the Welshry. It was suggested by Margaret Davies that a primitive settlement divide, a forerunner of the Landsker, split Pembrokeshire into two, even during the prehistoric period. She believed that the damp forests of central Pembrokeshire discouraged settlement, and that the western peninsulas and the Presely uplands provided more suitable sites both for agriculture and pastoral pursuits. From the maps of Neolithic and Bronze Age finds there certainly seems to have been a little-used belt of country approximately in the position of the Landsker zone, but Iron Age settlement traces are so widely distributed that it would be unwise to talk of any "cultural divide" at this time. Also traces of burials may survive best on the coast and in the uplands, because both have such stony thin soils that ploughing has been less intensive and has had less effect than in the centre of the county.

The map of Early Christian monuments and place names of Irish derivation shows a distinct clustering in northern and eastern Pembrokeshire, and we can speculate that this area (later to become the Welshry) developed a particularly strong cultural identity. However, Pembrokeshire during the period of Viking raids appears to have been a single Celtic community organized into **cantrefi** and **cymydau** and ruled by the princes of Dyfed. After about 950 AD the administrative units were governed according to the laws codified by Hywel Dda, one of the earliest kings with a real vision of a united Wales. In the year 1093 Pembrokeshire was, almost certainly, all Welshry. There was no Landsker and no Englishry.

The Coming of the Normans

The death of Rhys ap Tewdwr, the last Prince of South Wales, in 1093, precipitated the most important event in the history of settlement in Dyfed. The Welsh tribes of Deheubarth, weakened by their own internal dissensions, were no match for the Norman armies which arrived with expansionist designs from England. The army of Roger of Montgomery marched from Shrewsbury to Cardigan, and after establishing a castle there swept over Mynydd Presely and overran south Pembrokeshire before the end of the year. Pembroke was immediately established as the key strategic base of the Norman invaders.

However, the Welsh chieftains now had a common enemy, and repeated attempts were made to drive out the Normans. Temporary stockaded earthworks were constructed by both sides, but eventually the Normans consolidated their control over the southern part of the county as a result of a number of determined military thrusts. Gradually the land was parcelled out among the invaders; part of the native population was displaced, but those who remained were absorbed by the Anglo-Norman settlers and continued to practise the arts of farming under new management. Little England was already beginning to find its identity.

*Manorbier Castle, the least damaged of all
the castles of Pembrokeshire. (Studio Jon)*

During the first half of the twelfth century the stockaded earthworks evolved into more substantial motte and bailey forts, and later still massive stone castles took their place. In the north the Martin family came to Cemaes around the year 1110 and established a Marcher Lordship; it was administered initially from an older castle at Nevern, and after 1191 from the garrison town of Newport. Here William Martin built the strong stone castle which was to be his headquarters. Further south, major fortresses were established at Pembroke and Haverfordwest; and castles were thrown up at strategic points approximately four miles apart as a front line of defence against the Welsh, who continued in control of the northern and eastern parts of Dyfed. These fortresses, at Roch, Wiston, Llawhaden, Narberth and Amroth, are thought to have defined the early Landsker as a military frontier bounding the landward sides of

Anglo-Norman Dyfed. Probably the Pembrokeshire stone fortresses, like those of Ireland, were whitewashed and highly visible over considerable distances; the Normans used them as landmarks and as symbols of their military power, and to the infuriated Welsh they must have appeared as symbols of defeat and subjugation. The ancient lime-kiln in Cilgerran Castle was probably used for the manufacture of lime wash, and it may be that there were similar kilns in other castles as well.

It has often been claimed that the physical difficulties encountered in the northern part of Dyfed may have discouraged the Normans from attempting any large-scale settlement north of the Landsker. However, the Martin family appears to have settled happily enough at Newport, and it is more likely that administrative, rather than environmental, factors determined the boundaries of the early Anglo-Norman enclave. The real Landsker passed along the southern boundary of the bishop's lordship of Pebidiog (Dewisland) in the west and along the boundary between Cemaes and Daugleddau in the centre of the county. From near Llysyfran the medieval Landsker is harder to define, but it probably ran through the episcopal lordship of Llawhaden, along the northern boundary of Narberth and eastwards towards Whitland. Francis Jones, the Wales Herald Extra- ordinary, was in no doubt about the importance of this historical accident in preserving the "Welshness" of Dewisland and Llawhaden. Concerning Dewisland he wrote:

"It is the only part of Wales that has never been conquered by either the English or the Normans. Its inhabitants are the oldest free folk in Britain. The Normans, pious if nothing else, respected the property of the Church, so that Dewisland was spared the battles and sieges that accompanied the annexation of other parts of Pembrokeshire. No stone fortress was built on its soil; no alien garrison stood ward and watch over its inhabitants. The fact that it was the land of Dewi, the patron saint, proved sufficient to preserve it from the grasping hands of ambitious invaders. Here an agricultural folk passed tranquil days, for here the Cross was even mightier than the sword. While all the Norman castles are in ruins, the

Map of the administrative units, stone castles and earthwork castles of the thirteenth century.

cathedral of St David's remains an enduring monument to the arts of peace."

Nevertheless, the Welsh people of Dewisland and Llawhaden were very effectively under the control of Norman bishops and Norman knights in the twelfth century. At least eleven manors were established on the episcopal lands (for example at Letterston, Castle Morris and Pointz Castle), but there seems to have been no widespread immigration of Anglo-Saxons or any of the other racial groups who came in the train of the Norman invaders. The bishop retained one fortified residence, rebuilt in stone at Llawhaden about the year 1285, but his other residences, at St David's, Trefin and Lamphey, were unfortified.

Consolidation

During the twelfth century, when it was clear (outside the bishop's lordships) that Welsh labour was not going to be sufficient to maintain the manorial system, the Normans had to import many foreign workers to consolidate their control of southern Dyfed. English and Saxon immigrants were encouraged to settle, as were the Flemish immigrants introduced by Henry I about 1108. More Flemings arrived in 1111 and 1156. They were settled for the most part in Rhos and Daugleddau where they served as farmers and traders within the feudal system, as well as making up a part of the feudal armies. Many Flemish leaders rose to positions of eminence, and soon there were Flemish occupiers of the castles at Roch and Wiston. Anglo-Flemish villages and hamlets were established in Daugleddau on the southern foothills of Mynydd Presely up to an altitude of about 230m. These settlements can still be located by non-Welsh place-names on the OS map, as at Little Newcastle, Puncheston, Henry's Moat and Ambleston. Thus, by the thirteenth century, there existed in the centre of the county a

substantial non-Welsh settlement well to the north of the original fortified Landsker. It seems that the line of frontier castles, if indeed we can talk about a line at all, had ceased to have any military or economic significance within a few decades of its creation.

The impact of the colonial settlement upon the landscape of the Landsker zone was slight compared with the fundamental changes which occurred further south. Here Anglo-Normans introduced quite distinctive forms of landholding, settlement and farming. At least 120 villages and hamlets (many of which were on the sites of earlier Welsh settlements) were established in twelfth-century Pembrokeshire during this intensive phase of settlement. Most of the new villages and hamlets have Anglo-Saxon names like Hundleton, Hayscastle, Slebech, Rudbaxton, Johnston, Hodgeston and Picton. But there are also Flemish elements, as in Letterston (the tun of Letard the Fleming) and Wiston (the tun of Wizo the Fleming); and even south Pembrokeshire still has an abundance of Welsh place-names which have survived in spite of centuries of anglicization. Examples are Llangwm, Pwllcrochan, Manorbier (Maenor Pyrr), Rhoscrowther and Begelly.

In the Englishry the typical manorial village generally consisted of grouped farmhouses and cottages, clusters of burgage plots, a castle or fortified manor house, a well if there was no stream, and a church and parsonage. Later the church was given a disproportionately high, castellated tower, which served both as a watch-tower and as a last line of defence in case of attack by the "unquiet Welsh". Where possible the buildings were placed around a central green for defensive purposes, but often a village was forced by the dictates of site into an irregular outline. Great agricultural progress was made in the Englishry, where the dense alien settlement was organized on a feudal basis on the many new manors. Around the village were the open fields with their distinctive strip systems, which were gradually demarcated by earth banks and ditches. Traces of these strip field patterns still survive around many villages, for example Cosheston and Letterston. Where the enclosures had to incorporate elements of earlier "Celtic" field patterns they were irregular, but in the Englishry there are still traces of the original open fields (now subdivided) which may have been up to thirty acres in extent. The field pattern was interspersed with areas of woodland and moorland, some of which had common grazing rights.

In addition to the larger villages the medieval parish landscape incorporated a number of smaller hamlets, often founded beyond the boundaries of village lands in response to the growing population pressure of the thirteenth century. Settlements of this type have self-revealing names such as Carew Newton, Manorbier Newton and New House. Many single farmsteads appeared on the scene, cleared or assarted from woodland or scrub and held by tenants, often as a reward for military service. Examples are Bicton and Mullock near St Ishmael's.

Some of the immigrants arrived in Pembrokeshire by the sea route into Milford Haven, and now the great waterway assumed real strategic importance for the Normans, who needed it as a lifeline during many conflicts with the Welsh princes. Their defence system (although probably never planned in a co-ordinated way) was based upon the sea, and particularly upon the tidal waters of Milford Haven and the Daugleddau. Their early motte and bailey structures, and later their stone castles, show a distinct preference for easily defended bluffs overlooking tidal waters. Only four stone castles (Roch, Wiston, Llawhaden and Narberth) are inland, and as mentioned earlier these served originally as forward

defences against the Welsh raiding-parties in the Landsker zone. The major stone fortresses at Pembroke, Carew, Haverfordwest, Cardigan, Cilgerran, Manorbier and Tenby, and the other smaller fortresses, must have depended on many occasions during troubled times upon the transport of supplies and troops by sea and via the muddy tidal rivers of Milford Haven and the Daugleddau estuary.

The Anglo-Norman Towns

Later, as peace and harmony began to prevail and as agricultural surpluses began to flow from the prospering manors of the Englishry, Pembroke, Haverfordwest and Tenby developed into trading towns. By the thirteenth century sailing vessels were becoming large enough and seaworthy enough to make long trading voyages. Also, they could carry cargoes below decks where they were protected from both sea and weather. Sailing vessels were frequent visitors at each port, importing wine, salt, spices and luxury goods and exporting wool, hides, grain and herrings. All three towns acquired substantial numbers of wealthy merchants, and many small craft industries sprang up.

Many of the craftsmen were organized into guilds, which served to maintain prices, protect members and enhance standards of craftsmanship. The mercantile importance of Haverfordwest can be gauged from the fact that the mayor was granted the extra title of "Admiral of the Port", which survives to this day. Thus the ports of the south of the county began to prosper, and the full advantages of the sheltered waters of Milford Haven were at last realized. From this time onwards, the smaller ports on the rocky coasts of north Pembrokeshire were much less successful in comparison, although Newport did enjoy some prosperity as a market town and trading port.

Pembroke was the first important town to be established in the Englishry, and indeed it can claim to have been the first county town in Wales. It received its first privileges in the reign of Henry I (1100-35) and gave its name to the county palatine established in 1138. Even today it is a superb example of a Norman walled town. Its buildings are aligned along a single street on

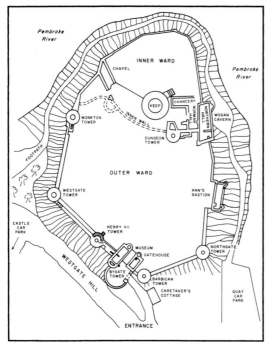

Plan of Pembroke Castle, showing the main defensive features.

a narrow limestone ridge which runs eastward from the castle, and the original community was protected by an embattled wall defended by several bastions and entered by well-guarded gateways. Some sections of the town wall are still intact, and within the medieval town there are several buildings whose white limestone masonry and projecting corbels attest to their age. But the crowning glory of Pembroke is its castle, dominating the western end of the town and controlling, as ever, the approach from the Pembroke River. It stands on a rocky promontory, its limestone walls rising almost

naturally from the grey-white cliffs of its base. The present castle was begun about the year 1190 by William Marshall. He built the round keep in the early inner ward, and the building was continued by his five sons until it was largely completed by about 1245. Although the castle has been damaged comprehensively and restored piecemeal during its turbulent history, it is still regarded as one of the supreme examples of an early medieval stone fortress. It is certainly the most spectacular castle in Pembrokeshire, and in the whole of Wales perhaps only Caernarvon and Harlech castles can compete in the magnificence of their sites and the strength and style of their buildings.

Beneath Pembroke Castle is a vast limestone cavern known as the Wogan. It is entered by narrow steps from the northern hall, and it has an exit to the river bank. Probably it was used by the castle inhabitants as a store-house and boat-house. In addition to the fortifications and interior buildings of the castle there are several other features of interest, including the Water Port in the south-west wall (where the piped water-supply was led into the castle) and the Mill Port which provided access to the flour mill and mill dam on the northern edge of the town. The mill was one of the earliest in Britain to utilize tidal power. The dam which impounded the mill pond was defended by a drawbridge. To the west of the town is the ancient Monkton Priory, established in the Dark Ages but with buildings (including a dovecote) whose remains date largely from medieval times. Like many other Benedictine priories, Monkton was "twinned" with the nearby Norman castle.

Pembroke, the proud stronghold and commercial centre of the early days of the Englishry, gradually declined because of its remoteness from the centre and the north of the county and because of the economic limitations of its own hinterland. As the strategic advantages of its site became less important the waterway of Milford Haven, which had been Pembroke's first line of defence, began to act as a real barrier to the aspirations of the town. Its port facilities were much inferior to those of Haverfordwest, and it began to lose more and more trade to its rival.

Located in the centre of Pembrokeshire, Haverford (as it was then called) received its first charter probably during the reign of Henry I, and this was renewed by Henry II in the later part of the twelfth century. The Anglo-Norman town, dominated by its impressive stone fortress and sited at the head of navigation and the lowest bridging point of the Western Cleddau river, expanded rapidly. At first it was entirely enclosed within its town walls; then, as the Englishry was developed and as Welsh raids from the north became less frequent, it spread through the adjacent parishes of St Martin and St Thomas, and later encompassed Cartlett and Portfield. Prendergast, to the east of the river, remained a separate village. During the Middle Ages the great advantages of site and situation became apparent. As the military functions of the castle declined the town came to depend more and more upon commerce and trade; the routeways which converge upon it demonstrate its success in generating business between the varied tributary areas of the Englishry and the Welshry. At the same time the town acted as a service, religious and administrative centre for a wide area and developed a variety of industries and trades; in the Middle Ages guilds of feltmakers, glovers, saddlers, tailors, carpenters and blacksmiths flourished, and later a guild of shoemakers appeared, capitalising upon the town's tanneries. Most of the later industries were located along the river banks, including three flour mills, two paper mills, two sawmills, a rope-walk, and a churn-works.

As the centre of the Flemish settlement of the Englishry Haverfordwest, with its port and markets, built up a considerable commercial tradition. To this was added, during the sixteenth century, the administrative functions of a county town at the expense of Pembroke; in 1543 a charter constituting it a county in itself guaranteed its continuing success.

Nowadays there are few traces of the medieval roots of Haverfordwest. The town walls have gone, but for occasional traces in gardens and back yards, and even the castle survives only as a battered shell frowning down from its leafy eminence above the main shopping centre. But the quays along the river bank remain, as do some of the ancient warehouses. The towers of the parish churches of St Mary, St Martin, St Thomas and St David (Prendergast) are all medieval, and St Mary's church at the top of High Street is renowned as one of the largest and finest parish churches in Wales. Down-river from the old quays are the sad ruins of a once-magnificent Augustinian Priory - one of many religious houses established by the Normans in their feudal lordships.

Of the other three Norman garrison towns in Pembrokeshire, only Tenby, on the outer coast, was fortified beyond the walls of the castle. In fact, it was given such substantial town walls that it is now regarded as one of the classic walled towns of Wales. There was a Welsh settlement (and a Welsh castle) here before the Normans arrived, but after the Conquest Tenby became one of the key sites in the defence of the Englishry. It was laid waste at least three times between 1153 and 1260 by the Welsh princes, but after that the Normans started to take serious measures to consolidate their power base, and a new town with a new street plan was built. During the later 13th century the castle was rebuilt as a larger stone fortress overlooking the sea, and a massive curtain wall was built around the town. It

Five Arches, Tenby. The old South Gate Tower has been considerably altered to meet the demands of modern traffic.

had four gates and towers, of which only the Five Arches Tower (the original South Gate) survives. The walls, made of locally-quarried limestone blocks, are still in a good state of repair, and contribute in great measure today to Tenby's summer traffic chaos ....

The Medieval World

We know a great deal about early medieval Pembrokeshire (a century after the Norman Conquest) from the writings of Gerald the Welshman or Giraldus Cambrensis. Gerald was born in 1147 in Manorbier Castle, the product of a marriage between a Norman knight and a Welsh princess. Because of his background he was uniquely placed to see the destiny of his country from both sides in those turbulent times. He was fascinated by everything around him, and was intelligent and well educated. He was trained as a cleric and diplomat and would have been Bishop of St David's had it not been for his own arrogance and the political intrigues of the day. He wrote two books, *The Itinerary Through Wales* and *The Description of Wales*, which contain fascinating details of the social customs, the economy, the politics and the folklore of his world.

Throughout his travels in Europe Gerald retained his great love of "Maenor Pirr", which he called "the pleasantest spot in Wales". He described the graceful character of the twelfth-century castle and manor with the following words:

"The castle...is excellently defended by turrets and bulwarks; and is situated on the summit of a hill extending on the western side towards the sea port, having on the northern and southern sides a fine fish pond under its walls, as conspicuous for its grand appearance as for the depth of its waters, and a beautiful orchard on the same side, enclosed on one part by a vineyard and on the other by a wood, remarkable for the projection of its rocks and the height of its hazel trees. On the right hand of the promontory, between the castle and the church, near the site of a very large lake and mill, a rivulet of never failing water flows through a valley, rendered sandy by the violence of the winds."

Apart from the Anglo-Norman castles and battlemented churches, and the traces of their abbeys, priories and friaries, there are many other features in the Pembrokeshire landscape which owe their origins to the Middle Ages. In the Englishry at least the distribution of villages dates back to this time, as does the basic road network and most of the features of the field pattern. The belt of large parishes across the country, stretching from Roch in the west to Amroth in the west, and coinciding with much barren moorland even today, is thought to coincide with the medieval **rhos** which separated the Welsh from the English. And everywhere, often in quite unexpected places, are the traces of medieval features in the domestic architecture of renovated halls and farmhouses. Some of the diagnostic features of these buildings are considered in a later chapter, but for the moment let us remember that the atmosphere of the Middle Ages is still a part of many Pembrokeshire towns and villages. Tenby and Newport have the feel of history about them. In villages like Llawhaden, Lamphey and Angle the visitor feels that he has strayed into another world: a medieval world of walled gardens and orchards, dovecotes, fishponds, mills, and tumbledown stone outbuildings.

The area around Carew and Sageston is a microcosm of the Anglo-Norman world of the middle ages. At the head of navigation on the Carew River there is a magnificent combination of millpond, corn-mill, castle and road bridge, seen as a unity from the picnic park on the north shore of the pond. At high tide the castle, now substantially repaired by the NPA, is reflected in the still waters. In the village centre there are old limestone cottages, their ages given away by their squat, square chimney stacks topped with slate ledges. In a garden there is a Flemish" round chimney standing in splendid incongruous isolation. There are ripe blackberries on the hedgerows in mid-July, and the air is heavy with the scent of newly cut hay. To the east there are some fine farm buildings at Sageston, but perhaps least affected of all by the passing of the centuries is the group of buildings around the fifteenth-century church at Carew Cheriton. The parish church with its massive tower and corner steeple, the high stone walls, the chantry chapel and the old rectory with its square corbelled tower are all splendid symbols of the Anglo-Norman heritage of Little England. If it were not for the early Christian Celtic cross at the roadside above the castle one might believe that the Welshry was a thousand miles away.

The Middle Ages came to an end with the reign of Henry Tudor (Henry VII), born in Pembroke Castle in 1456 and triumphant over Richard III in the Battle of Bosworth Field in 1485. Pembrokeshire played a crucial role in the demise of the wicked King Richard and the establishment of the Tudor dynasty. The young Henry, in exile in France, was advised by his mother and his court that the time was ripe for a move against Richard. He decided to launch his challenge from his home territory. Accompanied by a motley army of 2,000 French convicts and mercenaries of various nationalities, he landed at Mill Bay, near Dale, on 7 August 1485, flying the Tudor red dragon as his banner. He desperately needed the support of the local noblemen, and especially that of Sir Rhys ap Thomas of Carew Castle, who was the most powerful man in Wales. At first it seemed that Sir Rhys might remain loyal to the crown, but

Carew Castle, the home of Sir Rhys ap Thomas, who was in the late fifteenth century the most powerful nobleman in Wales.

then he decided to throw in his lot with the young pretender. His private army, which included 5,000 fully equipped horsemen, joined the march from Pembrokeshire to mid-Wales and thence to Shrewsbury. The red dragon banner, later to become the national flag of Wales, attracted thousands of men along the way, and the power of the Welsh contingent eventually encouraged various other disaffected noblemen to place their private armies at Henry's disposal. At the end of the fatal battle on Bosworth Field, legend has it that Sir Rhys was the man who placed Richard's muddy crown on the head of Henry Tudor.

Under the three powerful Tudor monarchs - Henry VII, Henry VIII and Elizabeth I - the kingdom became united as democratic institutions evolved and as the rule of law prevailed. The fact that the

Tudor dynasty was Welsh certainly helped to encourage respect for crown and parliament in Pembrokeshire, and with the advent of more peaceful times the castles began to fall into disrepair. At the same time fine farmhouses and mansions were built in the countryside and town houses, warehouses and civil buildings were constructed in the main urban centres.

The grand parting gesture of the Middle Ages was the last Great Tournament ever to be held in Britain, at Carew in the year 1507. It was organized by Sir Rhys ap Thomas, the Lord of Carew Castle, to celebrate the somewhat belated award of the Order of the Garter by King Henry VII. This legendary event, conjuring up in our minds images of King Arthur, Ivanhoe and Sir Launcelot, lasted for five days. It was attended by the aristocracy from all over Wales, together with hundreds of retainers. In addition to the tilting contests the young men took part in events such as wrestling, throwing the bar and tossing the pike. Other highlights included deer-hunting in the park and mass in Lamphey Palace chapel. Feasting continued every night in the Castle, accompanied by music, dancing and theatricals. It was quite a party. According to the historian Edward Laws, "although 1,000 men had spent five days in company, not one quarrel, unkind word, or cross look had passed between them". This was partly because the genial Sir Rhys, who presided over the proceedings, had the good sense to take innumerable precautions lest petty family rivalries should break out into real fighting and bloodshed. And so the chivalrous world of the Middle Ages quietly passed away....

Chapter Six

George Owen's Pembrokeshire

George Owen of Henllys (1552-1613) was one of Pembrokeshire's most famous sons and perhaps its most delightful character. We see him today somewhat hazily but certainly larger than life; to us he seems far more appealing that his illustrious contemporaries Sir John Perrot of Haroldston and William Philipps, the squire of Picton. Owen was neither a particularly powerful politician nor a particularly wealthy member of the gentry, but his fame rests upon the fact that he was an inveterate scribbler. He wrote furiously on all sorts of topics, and much of his manuscript materials has survived to this day. Most important of all are his writings about Pembrokeshire in general and about his beloved Cemais in particular. As a result of his magnificent *Description of Pembrokeshire* the county is the best documented of all the shires of Elizabethan Wales. There is no comparable achievement anywhere else in the Welsh literature of the time, and in the *Description* we have a unique record of Elizabethan life and manners. Owen's literary fame seems not to have spread very far during his own lifetime, but when the work was published in 1893 under Dr Henry Owen's editorship, it became freely accessible for the first time. The Welsh press referred to it as "an embarrassment of riches", and gradually its true worth was recognized. Somewhat belatedly, 280 years after his death, George Owen acquired a wide reputation as a scholarly antiquarian and an accurate and learned historian. At last he was seen as a man fascinated by the environment, the customs, the economic life and the life-style of his own times. Also, as we have seen in Chapter 2, he was thoroughly deserving of the title of "patriarch of British geologists".

Before we look at some of the themes from the *Description of Pembrokeshire* it should be stressed that George Owen was no more objective than anyone else in his assessments of history and of the scenario of late sixteenth-century Pembrokeshire. He does not seem to have been particularly well liked by the majority of his contemporaries, and Dr B G Charles, in his biographical portrait of the man, shows him to have been tough, determined and stubborn. He made many bitter enemies, but he was obviously well loved, too, for he fathered twenty-four children. Major Francis Jones has called Owen "a conceited, learned, litigious, biased, and wholly delightful individual". Much of his work was motivated by a desire to re-establish the past glories of the lordship of Cemais and to advance his own claims to the title of Lord of Cemais. His writings therefore contained much that was exaggerated or deliberately distorted, and his descriptions of Pembrokeshire localities and customs were very uneven. He described Cemais, his own home territory, in great detail: but other parts of Pembrokeshire (which he clearly knew almost as well) received almost cursory treatment. It is not surprising that he failed to keep up the early momentum of the *Description*, for even in its present form it is a monumental work.

The extracts on the following pages have already been published in *Elizabethan Pembrokeshire: the evidence of George Owen*. They do less than justice to the range

The old cattle pound on Barony land near Ffordd Bedd Morris, Newport. It was probably in use on this site in the days of George Owen. (John Havard)

of Owen's abilities as a writer, and it is a pity that there is no space to reproduce his descriptions of mountains and valleys, coasts and islands, hundreds and parishes, towns and villages. But the extracts do show something of Owen's affection of his county, his enthusiasm for poetic licence, his zeal for agricultural reform, his acute powers of observation, and his dry sense of humour. Much of what he wrote is very funny, and intentionally so. The extracts below are reproduced by kind permission of the book's editor, Dr Brian Howells. Together, they give us some fascinating glimpses of an Elizabethan world on the threshold of changing times. In 1603, when the *Description* was completed, the landscapes, manners and customs of the Middle Ages were finally giving way to a new order. But Owen described many survivals from medieval

times in his sections on agricultural practices, the use of various fuels, and the catching of fish, shellfish and wildfowl. In particular, his vivid and justly famous description of the game of cnapan showed it to be a survival of great antiquity.

The English and the Welsh

"The said county of Pembrokeshire is usually called Little England beyond Wales and that not unworthily, and therefore I think good to show my opinion why the same was so called. Mr Camden calleth it Anglia Transwallia. The reasons why it took that name may well be conjectured, for that the most part of the country speaketh English, and in it no use of the Welsh. The names of the people are mere English, each family following the English fashion in surnames. Their buildings are English-like, in townreds and villages and not in several and lone houses. Their diet is as the English people use, as the common food beef, mutton, pig, lamb, veal and kid, which usually the poorest husbandman doth daily feed on. The names of the county places are altogether English as Wiston, Picton, Haroldston, Robeston .... so that a stranger travelling from England and having ridden four score miles and more in Wales, having heard no English nor English names of people or of places, and coming hither to Pembrokeshire where he shall hear nothing but English ... would think that Wales were environed with England, and would imagine he had travelled through Wales and come into England again.

This shire is taken to be divided into two parts, that is to the Englishry and the Welshry .... The upper part of the shire, which I call the Welshry, is inhabited with Welshmen, the first known owners of the country, and are such as were never removed by any conquest or stranger that won the country. These are the people of the hundreds of Cemais, Cilgerran, Dewisland and part of Narberth, in which hundreds there are divers ancient gentlemen that to this day do hold and keep their ancient houses and descent from their ancestors for 400, 500, 600 years and more ...... But the countries of Roose, Castlemartin, Narberth and most of Daugleddy hundred, the bishop's lordships excepted, were wholly put to fire and sword by the Normans, Flemings and Englishmen, and utterly expelled the inhabitants thereof and peopled the country themselves, whose posterity remain there to this day, as may appear by their names, manners and language, speaking altogether the English and differeing in manners, diet, building and tilling of the land from the Welshmen.

What shall I speak here touching the constitution of the bodies of the people of this country must be understood of the general and common sort of people in the country ...... This kind of people I find to be very mean and simple, short of growth, broad and shrubby, unacceptable in sight for their personal service ..... so that of all the countries of Wales I find and speak by experience Pembrokeshire to be worst mannered ......

The gentlemen, serving men and the townsmen of this country are not so serviceable, comely and tall men ...... And of the common people of this country the Welshmen, whom the rest call the mountain men, are found to be the more personable, as men not so cloyed with labour as those that live by tillage. Generally, for the inclination of the people as well gentlemen, yeomen, rich and poor, they all embrace peace, quietness and neighbourly love, hating contentions, troubles, brawls and factions entreated after an offence received.

Country Life and Agriculture

.......this country of Pembrokeshire being almost enrivoned with sea, bare, open, and naked of wood and shelter, is more subject to extremity of storms and sudden tempests and sea, gusts of wind and hail than other inland countries are, and therefore there are few hedges or enclosures to be found, by reason whereof the husbandmen are forced to keep herds for their cattle and that in greater numbers than they themselves need ...... For I have by good account numbered three thousand young people to be brought up continually in herding of cattle within this shire, who are put to this idle education when they are first come to be ten or twelve years of age and turned to the open fields to follow their cattle, when they are forced to endure the heat of the sun in his greatest extremity to parch and burn their faces, hands, legs, feet and breasts in such sort as they seem more like tawny Moors than people of this land. And then with the cold, frost, snow, hail, rain and wind they are so tormented, having the skin of their legs, hands, face and feet all in chinks and chaps ..... that, poor fools, they may well hold opinion with the papists that there is a purgatory ..... And when they have redeemed their liberty out of this purgatory by attaining to twenty or twenty four years of age, then are they held in such continual labour in tilling of the land, burning of lime, digging of coals, and other slaveries and extreme toils, as while they live they never come in shape, favour or comeliness to be accounted among the number of personable men.

There was in times past in some parts of this shire, especially where gavelkind was, a custom used called rudwall custom, which was that no action of trespass lay for pasture in open fields out of enclosures ..... This custom seemed somewhat reasonable among the gavelkind men, for that at every descent the lands were shared and so the whole land of the country grew into small pieces, so that of necessity the owners must graze in common ..... And this custom, although it be almost abolished, yet remaineth the name and term thereof very usual among the common people, for that time of the year after harvest when all the neighbours' cattle run together in the common fields they call 'rudwall time' ......

This commodity of corn is the chiefest that bringeth in money to the country, being a country more apt for tilling than for breed, the soil being naturally dry and fit for the plough work, but this differeth much in some part of this shire from other.

The chiefest corn land in Pembrokeshire is the hundred of Castlemartin as that which yieldeth the best and finest grain and most abundance, being a country of itself naturally fit and apt for corn, having lime, sand, weed of the sea, and divers other principal helps to better the soil where need is. This country yieldeth the best wheat and greatest store, being found by experience to be better of yielding in the mill, and maketh the bread fairer than any other wheat of the shire. The next to Castlemartin for good store of corn is Roose, an open and plain country without much wood or enclosures. This although it may

not compare with Castlemartin, is the next good soil and yieldeth great abundance of wheat, barley and other grain ......

Next cometh in course the hundreds of Narberth and Dewisland. Which to prefer to their tillage I cannot well discuss, for although Narberth have the better land and better means of mending as lime, sand, seaweed, stone marl, yet by reason the country is woody and enclosed the inhabitants convert more of their land to pasture than Dewisland doth or can do, the country being all open champion and dry land ..... Dewisland [is in] many parts thereof very fruitful for corn, especially barley, but it is accounted oaty and not so fine as that of the other parts, which I take to come by the negligence of husbandmen in sowing of bad and oaty seed, for I have not seen better or finer land nor grater store of corn than I have seen growing about Saint Davids.

The second and next commodity that this county selleth is cattle, as oxen steers, bullocks, heifers and kine of the country breed, which of late years is greatly increased more than in times past as a commodity that particularly yieldeth profit with less charge to the owner, but generally not so commodious for the commonwealth as tillage, by reason it procureth depopulation and maintaineth less people at work. This trade of breeding cattle is used much in all parts of the shire, but most in the Welsh parts and near the mountains where their land is not so apt for corn and where there is large scope of ground.

The third commodity that helpeth this shire to money is wool, whereof there is great quantity yearly sold, beside that which is spent in the country for their necessary uses of clothing. The country aboundeth with sheep more at this present than heretofore, and yieldeth great profit with little charge, for in this country they feed not their sheep with hay in winter, as is used in divers parts of England, but let them get their living out themselves. Yet in some part of the country they might house them by night, which they do to keep them from the fox and for making of dung for their land more than for any other cause, for fodder they never bestow on them, for in this country the snow never covereth the ground for any long time and therefore they are sure always of feeding. The sheep are but small of body and the wool coarser than the English wool...but the flesh of these muttons is found to be very sweet in taste, wholesome and good meat...

The fourth principal commodity that this country yieldeth is butter and cheese, whereof there is greater store made now in this shire than in times past and the same is uttered, especially the butter by sea, but this may not be known; so is the cheese to the countries adjoining, and sometimes to Ireland for provision of the Queen^s garrisons there.

The manner of tilling the ground in this shire is in two sorts. The Englishmen use most sowing of wheat, rye, barley, peas and beans. The Welshmen, being the worse husbands, apply more to tilling of oats, and some cause there was which caused this in former times, which now being taken away the Welshmen are become the better husbands.

Now ..... I will speak somewhat of the natural helps which are found in the country to better the land to make it more fruitful and apt to bear corn and grass.

The chiefest thereof I reckon the lime, for that it is most commonly and most used ..... This limestone, being dug in the quarry in great stones, is hewn lesser to the bigness of a man's fist ..... and being hewn small the same is put into a kiln made of walls six foot high, four or five foot broad at

Lime kilns on the shore of Solva Harbour.
The use of such kilns was described in detail
by George Owen.

the rim but growing narrower to the bottom, having two loopholes in the bottom which they call the kiln eyes. In this kiln first is made a fire of coals or rather culm (which is but the dust of the coals) which is laid in the bottom of the kiln, and some few sticks of wood to kindle the fire. Then is the kiln filled with these small hewed pieces of limestones and then, fire being given, the same burneth ..... and maketh the limestones to become mere red fiery coals, which being done and the fire quenched, the lime so burned is suffered to cool in the kiln and then is drawn forth through these kiln eyes, and in this sort is carried to the land where it is laid in heaps. And the next shower of rain maketh it to moulder and fall into dust, which they spread on the land, and so sow wheat or barley therein as the time of the year requireth ..... This trade of liming hath been more used within these thirty or forty years than in times past and it destroyeth the furze, fern, heath and other like shrubs growing on the land and bringeth forth a fine and sweet grass and quite changeth the hue and face of the ground and hath greatly enriched those that used it.

The next and chiefest kind of mending of the land is the clay marl, so called for the difference between it and the sea marl. This kind of marl is digged out of the earth where it is found in great quantity and thought to be in round great heaps and lumps of earth as big as round hills, and is of nature fat, tough and clammy, and must be cast and set on the ground very thick in small pieces close one by another, so thick that it must cover all the ground.

The fourth kind of amendment that this country yieldeth is the sea sand, which is found in many places but not on all parts of the sea coast. This is found in Newport, Dinas and about these parts and the people knowing these places do use upon spring tides, or after great tempests of the sea, at which time the sea will cast the same in more abundance together into great heaps, and lay it out of the high tide mark, and there hence fetch it in sacks on horseback and carry the same three, four or five miles and cast it on the land, which doth very much better the ground for corn and grass...

As for the sea weed, or woad as some call it, which is very weeds growing underwater in the sea upon rocks and stones, and with tempest of the sea is torn and cast ashore with the wind and tide, and under the high tide mark may be gathered and cut off the stones, the same is used of many rather as muck or dung, serving but for one year only ..... This kind of ore they gather and lay it in great heaps, where it heateth and rotteth and will have a strong and loathsome smell. The same being so rotten, they cast on the land as they do their muck, and thereof springeth good corn, especially barley.

It is a saying among the countrymen of the continuance of these aforesaid amendments that a man doth sand for himself, lime for his son, and marl for his grandchild...

Markets

There are three market towns in Pembrokeshire, viz Pembroke, Haverfordwest and Tenby, the second whereof, being seated in the midst of the shire and most convenient for trade, is greatly frequented of the country people, and therefore is the greatest and plentifullest market of the shire, and is kept once every week on the Saturday, wherein methinketh the town is very backward in their own profit in not suing for another market in the middle of the week, which would turn to the great good both of the town and country. Also they have but one fair in the year, whereas if there were more purchased from His Majesty it might be beneficial both for town and country. This market of Haverfordwest is thought to be one of the greatest and plentifullest markets, all things compared, that is within the Marches of Wales, especially for the plenty and goodness of victual, as namely for beef, mutton, pork,

The old farmhouse at Garn, not far from Llanychaer in the Gwaun Valley. (Robert Evans)

bacon, veal, goose, capon, kid, lamb, rabbit, turkey, and all sorts of wildfowl in their season, that it is a marvel to many where the victuals that are there to be seen at noon should be shifted away ere night, and for fish it passeth all others in Wales, without any comparison both for plenty and variety.

Pembroke market is also on the Saturday, and Tenby on Saturday for victuals and on Wednesday for corn. These two towns for their markets are much inferior for plenty of victuals and corn to that of Haverfordwest by reason those towns are seated, the one very near the lower parts of the shire and

An old drawing of Narberth Market in the eighteenth century. It would not have looked very different in Tudor times.

much hindered by reason of a ferry on the one side, and Tenby seemeth, as it were, a town running out of the country and stayeth on the sea cliff, by reason whereof they stand not so commodious for resort of people, which maketh less trade and utterance in their markets. But both these towns, being seated in a more fruitful soil than Haverfordwest is, for goodness of victual are nothing inferior if not better than Haverford, and so for goodness of corn, and for fish especially Tenby, where is a daily market thereof, passeth Haverford market ....

There are also markets of victuals used in St Davids and Newport, not worth the speaking of, partly for that they be so small and bad, but especially for the abuse for that the same is used every Sunday before service, even about sunrise. There hath been in times past divers markets used in divers other places, and by reason of the poverty of the towns and unaptness of the places altogether decayed, as at Cilgerran, Fishguard, St Dogmaels's, Rosemarket, Wiston, Llawhaden, where, by report of ancient men, markets have been kept in old time.

The Gentle Game of Cnapan

I cannot overpass a game used in one part of this shire among the Welshmen both rare to hear, troublesome to describe, and painful to practise ..... This game is called cnapan and not unfitly, as shall be shown. The game is thought to be of great antiquity and is as followeth.

The ancient Britons being naturally a warlike nation did, no doubt for the exercise of their youth in time of peace and to avoid idleness, devise games of activity where each man might show his natural prowess and agility, as some for strength of the body by wrestling [and] lifting of heavy burdens, others for the arm as in casting the bar sledge, stone or hurling the bowl or running, and surely for the exercise of the part aforesaid this cnapan was prudently invented had the same continued without abuse thereof. For in it, besides the exercise of bodily strength, it is not without a resemblance of warlike providence, as shall be here after declared.

Plays would oftentimes be by making of match between two gentlemen, and that at such holiday or Sunday as pleased them to appoint the time and place, which most commonly fall out to be the greatest plays, for in these matches the gentlemen would divide the parishes, hundreds or shires between them, and then would each labour to bring the greatest number and would

The gentle game of Cnapan in full swing in Tudor North Pembrokeshire. This artist's impression is quite accurate in most details.

therein entreat all his friends and kinsmen in every parish to come and bring his parish wholly with him, by which means great number would most usually meet. And therefore against these matches there would also resort to the place divers victuallers with meat, drink and wine of all sorts, also merchants, mercers and pedlars would provide stalls and booths to show and utter their wares. And for these causes, some to play, some to eat and drink, some to buy, and some to sell, others to see and others to be seen (you know what kind I mean) great multitudes of people would resort besides the players. They contend not for any wager or valuable thing, but for glory and renown - first for the fame of their country in general, next every particular to win praise for his activity and prowess, which two considerations ardently inflameth the minds of the youthful people to strive to the death for glory and fame, which they esteem dearer unto them than worldly wealth.

The companies, being come together about one or two of the clock after noon, beginneth the play in this sort. After a cry made, both parties draw together into some plain, all stripped bare saving a light pair of breeches - bare headed, bare bodied, bare legs, and feet, their clothing being laid together in great heaps under the charge of certain keepers appointed for the purpose, for if he leave but his shirt on his back in the fury of the game it is most commonly torn to pieces. And I have also seen some long-locked gallants trimmed at this game, not by polling but by pulling their hair and beards ..... This kind of trimming they all do bestow freely without asking anything for their pains.

The foot company thus meeting, there is a round ball prepared of a reasonable quantity so as a man may hold it in his hand and no more. This ball is of some massy wood as box, yew, crab or holly tree, and should be boiled in tallow for to make it slippery and hard to be held. This ball is called cnapan and is by one of the company hurled bolt upright into the air, and at the fall he that catcheth it hurleth it towards the country he playeth for. For goal or appointed place there is none, neither needeth any, for the play is not given over until the cnapan be so far carried that there is no hope to return it back that night, for the carrying of it a mile or two miles from the first place is no losing of the honour so be it still followed by the company and, the play still maintained, it is oftentimes seen the chase to follow two miles or more in the heat of course both by the horse and foot.

The cnapan being once cast forth you shall see the same tossed backward and forward by hurling throws in strange sort, for in three or four throws you shall see the whole body of the game removed half a mile and more, and in this sort it is a strange sight to see a thousand or fifteen hundred naked men to concur together in a cluster in following the cnapan as the same is hurled backwards and forwards.

If the cnapan happen to come to the hands of a lusty hurler he throweth the same in a wonderful sort towards his country, further than any man would judge the strength of the arm were able. If it happen to the hands of a good footman he presently singleth himself and runneth and breaketh out of the body of the game into some plain ground in the swiftest sort he can which, being perceived, all the company followeth, where the good footmanship of all the company is plainly discerned, being a comfortable sight to see five or six hundred good footmen to follow in chase a mile or two as greyhounds after a hare, where shall see some gain in running upon his precedents, some forced to come behind those that were once foremost, which greatly delighteth the beholders and forceth them to follow likewise to see the pleasure of the chase. And thus the one seeketh to win honour by his footmanship until he be overtaken by a better runner or encountered by one of the scouts which will not fail to meet with him, and when he seeth himself

near surprised or that his breath or legs fail him, he hurleth the ball forward towards his country, with a great violence, and perchance it lighteth to some of his fellows, who carry the same as far again which, notwithstanding, is not given over as long as the main body is anything near at hand: and when the ball happeneth to one of the contrary party it cometh back again as fast.

It is strange to behold with what eagerness this play is followed, for in the fury of the chase they respect neither hedge, ditch, pale or wall, hill, dale, bushes, river or rock or any other passable impediment, but all seemeth plain unto them wherein also they show such agility in running, such activity in leaping, such strength and skilful deliverance in hurling, such boldness in assaulting, such stoutness in resisting, such policy in inventing, such skill in preventing, as taking them out of their game they are not able to perform or invent half the prowess or devices shown in the same, a thing much noted of men of judgement.

The horsemen have monstrous cudgels of three foot and a half long, as bit as the part is well able to wield, and he that thinketh himself well horsed maketh means to his friends of the footmen to have the cnapan delivered him, which being gotten he putteth spurs and away as fast as the legs will carry. After him runneth the rest of the horsemen, and if they can overtake him he summoneth a delivery of the cnapan, which should be thrice by law of the game, but now they scarce give it once till he be struck. And if he hold the cnapan it is lawful for the assailant to beat him with his cudgel till he deliver it.

The best of foot troops also will follow the horse, who are so well trained by the often exercise of the game, as that when the horsemen miss to fetch up the cnapan the foot will often times recover the same and will in heat of chase follow the cnapan when it is out of sigh and past hope...You shall see gamesters return home from this play with broken heads, black faces, bruised bodies and lame legs, yet laughing and merrily jesting at their harms, telling their adversaries how he broke his head, to another that he struck him on the face and how he repaid the same to him again, and all this in good mirth, without grudge or hatred. And if any be in arrearages to the other they store it up till the next play and in the meantime will continue loving friends.

This play of cnapan seemeth to be an ancient exercise described to us Welshmen from our first progenitors the Trojans ....."

Cnapan and Rugby Football

There has rightly been some speculation as to the accuracy of George Owen^s description of the game of cnapan. After all, our George did have a tendency to exaggerate in order to impress his audience. But there seems to be no doubt that the game was widely played in various parts of Pembrokeshire, and that it was not specifically restricted to the Welsh-speaking districts. Of the annual cnapan occasions listed by George Owen the first, on Shrove Tuesday, was held on the sands of Traeth Mawr, Newport, between the

Cnapan territory. The Nevern estuary, the ancient borough of Newport, and Carningli mountain beyond. (Studio Jon)

parishioners of Newport and Nevern. The second was on Easter Monday at Pont Gynon, between the parishes of Eglwyswrw and Meline, and the third at Pwll Du, Penbedw, on "Low Easter Day". The biggest games, involving over 2,000 players, were held at St Meugans in Cemaes on Ascension Day and on Corpus Christi Day, involving the men of Emlyn and the men of Cemaes.

From the above description we can see that cnapan was a handling and passing game quite unlike the primitive football games played in many other parts of Britain. There were three categories of players: the "sturdy gamesmen" who were the equivalent of modern forwards, the "scouts" who were the equivalent of the three-quarters, and the "fore-runners" who seem to have had blocking duties rather like those of some players in American football games. After stoppages the game was restarted by throwing the ball into the air as in the modern lineout, and there were prolonged episodes of mauling, rucking and primitive scrummaging. The skills of passing, tackling and evasive running with the ball were greatly admired, and it is clear that fresh players were brought into the fray at crucial times to replace those who were tired. There seems to have been some awareness of defensive and offensive tactics, although with up to 2000 players involved in each game the tactics could not have been very sophisticated!

It is not known when the game died out in Pembrokeshire, but it is probable that no games have been played at the venues described by George Owen for well over a century. The last cnapan game was played in the Llandysul area of Cardiganshire on 13th January 1922. Little is known about the rules on that occasion, but it is reported that the goals were eight miles apart at the churches of Landysul and Llanwenog. The disorder and unruliness at this famous game became so great that it was transmuted, in the following year, into a Sunday School Festival full of peace, joy and brotherly love.

In recent years the game of Cnapan has been revived in Newport, with an annual contest between players from the adjacent parishes of Newport and Nevern competing for a fine wooden trophy. (In reality, anybody who feels like joining in is allowed to do so, and the teams are selected more or less at random!) Male and female players have pitched in with great gusto, and at the time of writing Nevern has won the trophy six times and Newport four times. There have been various TV programmes featuring the game, and at the Gateshead Garden Festival in 1990 there was even a cnapan international match which the Welsh players (from Newport) won by a substantial margin since they were the only ones who knew the rules. Sadly, at the time of writing the contests have had to be discontinued, largely because of the near-impossibility of obtaining insurance cover for cnapan players and organizers in a world which does not fully understand the joys of the old game.

A small group of cnapan enthusiasts continues to argue that cnapan is the real forerunner of rugby football, and that the game which is now so famous worldwide started not at Rugby School in 1823 but at Newport in Pembrokeshire some time in the fourteenth century ......

Chapter Seven

War and Peace

The three centuries which followed the death of George Owen proceeded quietly enough in Pembrokeshire -- a remote rural backwater largely by-passed by the great events of Britain and Europe. But occasionally local events came to the attention of the outside world, as during the turbulent years of the Civil War, or during the farcical "last invasion of Britain" near Fishguard in 1797. This latter event was the main local manifestation of the Napoleonic Wars. Later, the continuing friction between Britain and France also made an impact on the county, leading eventually to the building of various powerful forts designed to protect the Milford Haven waterway (and the Royal Naval Dockyard in particular) in case of foreign attack. This chapter examines the historical and landscape impacts of these turbulent episodes.

However, we should also remember that the military campaigns of the period were -- as far as Pembrokeshire was concerned -- relatively short-lived. The great events of state made but a small impact upon the majority of Pembrokeshire people; news travelled slowly in the days before newspapers and railways, and most people lived out their lives on the land blissfully unaware of what was happening on the mainland of Europe or even in Westminster. News of the Battle of Waterloo or the Battle of Trafalgar probably reached the ears of the poor peasantry weeks or months late, and then only if sons or relatives were involved as soldiers or seamen. It is useful, therefore, while examining the impact of intermittent conflict on the local scene, to draw attention,

as a counterpoint, to a number of more peaceful topics. For example, we should consider the way in which the countryside changed quietly but inexorably with agricultural reform and with the growth of small industries using agricultural products. The fishing industry was also developing quietly around the coast. Ultimately the farmers, the fishermen and the millers of the period 1600 - 1900 did more than the statesmen, the soldiers and the sailors to give Pembrokeshire a landscape something like that which we know and love today.

The Civil War

The Civil War of 1642-8 made but a minor impact upon the Pembrokeshire landscape, for the county was spared the most vicious and destructive of the military campaigns. But some of the results of the fighting can still be seen by those who know where to look, and several of the famous events of the later part of the war took place in the area. For the most part the Welsh-speaking section of the county was loyal to the King, but many townsmen and some squires in south Pembrokeshire embraced the Parliamentary cause. In 1644, the royalist Earl of Carbery (of Golden Grove, in Carmarthenshire) attempted to reduce Pembrokeshire, but he was repulsed by Rowland Laugharne of St Bride's, who was "one of the ablest tacticians thrown up during the unhappy conflict". Laugharne, the Parliamentary leader of the day, took Tenby, Haverfordwest and Carmarthen. This stirred the Royalists to replace their leaders

*Llawhaden Castle, not far from the scene of
the "Colby Moor Rout" (Robert Evans)*

in West Wales, and during a determined assault they recaptured Haverfordwest and Carmarthen. However, Tenby and Pembroke held out as a result of the superiority of the Parliamentary fleet. It controlled the waters of the Haven, relieved the beleaguered garrison of Pembroke, and was able to support various land operations.

The tide was turning against the Royalists, and as troops were withdrawn to England Laugharne again took most of Pembrokeshire and the town of Cardigan as well. In 1645 Charles Gerard returned and made good these losses for the Crown, but by this time much of Wales was alienated from the Royalist cause by the insensitive

military control of the King's armies and by the plundering of the countryside. When Laugharne turned to the offensive again there occurred the most famous local battle of the Civil War, on a patch of moorland between Wiston and Llawhaden. Here a Royalist force of about 1500 men, including 450 on horseback, were routed by a force of 750 Parliamentarians, largely as a result of Col Laugharne's superior battlefield tactics. Laugharne lost just two soldiers, but 150 Royalists were killed and 700 taken prisoner. This was Laugharne's greatest hour, later termed the "Colby Moor Rout". It was 1st August 1645, and the decisive Parliamentary victory signalled the beginning of the end for the Royalist cause in Wales.

During this first phase of the Civil War the focal points of the armed campaigns were the old medieval fortresses, now hopelessly out-of-date from a military point of view and quite inadequate to withstand a battering by heavy guns. Nevertheless, they were used and strengthened, and they served to hold off attacks from lightly-armed forces and even to resist prolonged sieges. The castles at Tenby, Pembroke, Haverfordwest, Roch, Cardigan, Laugharne, Carew and Picton all figured prominently in the ebb and flow of the complicated military campaigns of 1643-5, changing hands frequently.

The so-called "Second Civil War" of 1648 made a much greater impact upon the castles of Pembrokeshire. The fighting began because of a variety of dissensions and partly because of disappointment and resentment against the disbanding of the Roundhead army. The local Parliamentary commanders, who had served their cause well, were disappointed with the rewards paid for their efforts. Mayor John Poyer of Pembroke refused to give way to a new governor, and he was joined in his rebellion by Colonel Rice Powell and Major-General Rowland Laugharne. All three had previously been staunch Parliamentarians. Powell and Laugharne joined the Glamorgan Royalists. Their army of about 8,000 men advanced eastwards through Carmarthen into Glamorgan, taking Swansea and Neath on the way. They were defeated by a smaller but highly trained Parliamentary army under Horton at St Fagans on 8 May 1648, although the renegade leaders managed to escape back to Pembrokeshire.

But the net tightened. Cromwell had had enough, and he decided on a show of strength in South Wales. He advanced with Horton into Pembrokeshire, taking Tenby on 31 May and capturing its chief defender, Powell. Poyer and Laugharne, with their garrison, were established in Pembroke, protected by the town walls and the great stone fortress itself. Cromwell decided to starve out the garrison, for he had only his light artillery with him and could make no impression on the defences. He sent to Carmarthenshire for shot to be made in the iron furnaces there, and he ordered his big guns to be sent by sea from Gloucester. Various attempts to scale the town wall failed. The big guns arrived and finally opened fire on 11 July, and after a seven-week siege Poyer was forced to surrender. He and Laugharne joined Powell in captivity. The three renegades were taken to London, where they were tried by court martial and sentenced to death. As a gesture of clemency it was decided that only one of them should die. According to legend they were asked to draw lots, but they refused. So three slips of paper were given to a child, one of the them blank and the others bearing the words "Life given by God". The child gave a slip to each of the prisoners and the hapless Mayor Poyer received the blank one. He was shot at Covent Garden by firing-squad.

Now the castles of Pembrokeshire had seen their last military action. They had proved an unexpected nuisance to Cromwell during the 1648 rising, and he ordered them to be destroyed. He commanded that towers should be blown up and lengths of curtain wall demolished. He seems personally to have ordered the destruction of several of the towers and wall sections of Pembroke Castle. Tenby and other fortresses also suffered sadly as a result of his edict. Within days of the surrender of Pembroke, Cromwell wrote to the mayor and corporation of Haverfordwest leaving them in no doubt as to his intentions. He demanded that they "forthwith demolish the works, walls and towers of the said Castle, so as that the said Castle may not be possessed by the enemy, to the endangering of the peace of these parts. We expect an account of your proceedings with effect in this business by Saturday, being the 15th of July instant." There followed a menacing footnote: "If a surprising that the county was visited by the Plague or Black Death in 1651-1653.

The worst affected areas were in and around Haverfordwest, but people died in all the villages to the south and east, and the plague also spread to Dewisland and the Newport area. The "sickness" which struck Haverfordwest in 1651 was the greatest calamity ever to affect the town, for it reduced the finest trading centre in South Wales to acute poverty and distress. The Black Death was probably brought to the town by sailors, and it spread like wildfire. The parish of St Martin's was most sorely infected, and two pest houses were established; one of these was used by the "tarr-coats", men who wore grotesque tarred coats as a primitive form of disinfectant and who collected and buried the corpses and tended the sick. Other premises were secured where comfort could be given to the inflamed and bloated bodies of the dying. The disease killed in three days; hardly anybody who caught it survived.

Roch Castle, where Cromwell is reputed to have been almost killed by a javelin thrown from the battlements.

So many people died or fell ill that the town's markets and fairs were stopped, and the local Guilds complained that their trade had come to a standstill. Some fairs were relocated outside the town. An attempt was made to isolate the townspeople, and the High Constable of Dungleddy issued a warrant preventing anybody from entering or leaving the built-up area. The Mayor complained that the townspeople would starve if food could not be brought in, and common sense prevailed. Food was sent in from all over Pembrokeshire, and received at the Red Gate at the bottom of Holloway.

speedy course be not taken to fulfill the commands of this warrant, I shall be necessitated to consider of settling a garrison." The threat was enough, and the municipal authorities set to work with their explosives to such effect that the castle was largely destroyed. To this day only the sorry remnants of the walls of the once-great fortress remain, although some rebuilding work was undertaken in 1779 and 1820 to provide a solid and secure County Gaol.

The Plague

At the end of the war Pembrokeshire was in a miserable state, and food was in such short supply that the authorities feared rebellion. Bands of robbers ranged across the countryside, and the Parliamentarians forced harsh financial penalties upon all classes of people. With low public morale, poor standards of hygiene, and agriculture badly damaged by the war, it was perhaps not

However, fear stalked the streets and the stench of death was everywhere. Many people moved out into the countryside. Out of the town's population of 3,000, more than half locked up their premises and fled; in May 1652 about 990 poor people were recorded as on the verge of starvation, and when it was all over about 500 of the inhabitants had died. One who died was an eccentric and garrulous old woman referred to in the borough records as Widow Howells, who made a thorough nuisance of herself in the midst of all the chaos. The great hero of the Plague was Rev Stephen Love, the Puritan Rector of St Thomas. He travelled all over the county collecting money and food for the plague victims, visited all the houses where people were ill or where deaths had occurred, and spent much time in the "pest-houses". He won the respect and admiration of everybody; and although he survived the Plague he was worn out by his exertions and died in 1656. Other heroes were Thomas Davids the Mayor and Ben Price the Surgeon, who worked tirelessly for the town as they saw their own families and friends die.

Farming and Fishing

The effects of the Civil War and the Plague were soon past, and Pembrokeshire returned to more tranquil times with agriculture and trade occupying most of its inhabitants inland and with an important herring fishery at many centres around the coast. In 1700 the gentry were still in control of the large estates which had evolved from the manors of the Middle Ages, and they consolidated and improved their properties. However, more free farmers, tenants and peasants were able to benefit from agricultural advances, and the merchants of the main towns grew rich through the improved marketing of larger and larger agricultural surpluses. As in the time of George Owen, arable farming was important in the south of the county, and Castlemartin and Rhos continued to produce good crops of wheat, barley and oats. On the St David's peninsula the main grain crop was oats, while in the eastern and northern parts of the county landlords and tenant farmers devoted more attention to livestock farming. Sheep were plentiful everywhere, and there were large surpluses of wool, some for export in the form of raw fleeces and some for feeding the local woollen mills. As far as the coastal communities were concerned, there was a growing market for salted herring stored in barrels and shipped out of ports like Tenby and Fishguard.

On the land the old open-field style of farming was gradually giving way. As the larger landowners increased the size of their estates more and more of the county was affected by enclosures. However, as late as 1774 there was still much unenclosed land even though farmers knew which land belonged to them and which areas belonged to their neighbours; a traveller in the county wrote that the lack of fences "... is a circumstance attended with much inconvenience, both to the owner of the lands and to the traveller. There being no common sheep herd, all the horses, sheep and even poultry are staked at the end of a line to the ground, in order to prevent mutual trespass; the consequence being that the ropes frequently cross the high road and entangle the horses' feet of the unwary traveller." But gradually the open fields were divided, fenced or hedged, as landowners cooperated to ease some of their land management problems. The landscape of open fields and strips around nucleated villages and hamlets gave way at last to a landscape of smaller enclosed fields, separate farmsteads and consolidated farm buildings.

Over a period of 300 years or more, farming also became more efficient as new methods of crop rotation and animal husbandry were introduced. Some of the wealthiest families in Pembrokeshire were renowned for their farming innovations; these included the Cawdors of Stackpole, the Kensingtons of St Brides, the Scourfields of New Moat and the Allens of Cresselly. Lord Cawdor, for example, showed great enterprise in land reclamation, draining several hundred acres of "wasteland" at

Castlemartin Corse and turning it into high-quality arable land which later became the most productive corn land in Wales.

But eighteenth-century innovators were frustrated by the slow rate of change and by the reluctance of Pembrokeshire farmers to accept scientific methods. Arthur Young, on a visit to Pembrokeshire in 1776, described the normal Pembrokeshire crop rotation as "plough grassland for fallow and lime; wheat; pease and barley; barley or oats; oats; leave to grass and weeds for five to seven years, but few sewing clover." Farms at the time were often no more than a few acres in extent, and most of them had an annual income of less than £100. Many farmers kept cows, which were bred mainly for meat, and milk production was so small that most milk was consumed on the farm or used for butter and cheese. There were plenty of sheep but few goats in the upland areas. Oxen were still used, particularly on the heavy land, for ploughing and hauling carts. Charles Hassall, who was a land agent with a great interest in agricultural improvement, wrote in 1794: "The inhabitants of this county are not forward in receiving improvements in agriculture. I mean the middling and lower orders of them. A general prejudice seems to pervade the people against anything new or differing in respect from the old and beaten track in which they and their forefathers have trod..." Other observers were particularly disturbed by the lack of progress in the Welshry, where conditions were often harsh and where efficient land management was most necessary. Even the agricultural societies founded in the later eighteenth century failed to make any great impact north of the Landsker.

However, Pembrokeshire was by no means unique in demonstrating some reluctance to accept agricultural reform, and under the leadership of the powerful landowning families farm productivity --

and farm incomes -- gradually increased. The agricultural societies played a significant role in the process of education. The earliest one in the county was the Society for the Encouragement of Agriculture, Manufacture and Industry, formed by William Know in 1784. Later the Pembrokeshire Agricultural Society was formed, partly because of the personal zeal of King George III, who campaigned ceaselessly for new crops, new breeding programmes and better methods of husbandry. As described by Derek Rees in his book *Rings and Rosettes*, this society has worked hard ever since on behalf of local agriculture.

A typical small Pembrokeshire cottage with only two rooms. A cottage such as this may have started life as a "ty unnos".

The land enclosures may have been good for agriculture in general and for the landowners in particular, but they were most unwelcome to the poorer farming classes. They traditionally made use of the commons and of the unenclosed estate lands, and the enclosures effectively shut many of them out of the farming economy. As the rural population grew thousands of people were forced to take to the roads. Squatting became a real problem, and landless peasants built their miserable shacks wherever they could find space, preferably where there was shelter and water, and on land which they still assumed to be common land. However, the majority of their squatting sites were owned, or at least claimed, by the big landowners; whole groups of cottagers were evicted, and serious riots often resulted. Many poor people falsely believed that if they could clear wasteland and build a cottage (known as a **ty unnos**) in a day and a night, so that smoke could be seen issuing from the chimney next morning, then the cottage became their freehold by law. It was also believed that the marks made by an axe thrown from the cottage door to north, south, east and west would define the area of land included in the new freehold. While the rich became richer, the poor became poorer, and as we shall see in the next Chapter, trouble was inevitable.

On the Pembrokeshire coast, and within the Milford Haven waterway, many families and even whole communities depended upon the harvest of the sea for their livelihood. Although there were rich fishing grounds off the Pembrokeshire coast and out in the Celtic sea, deep-water fish were not caught on a large scale because of the limitations of fishing boats and trawling equipment. Most of the cod catch was obtained through deep-water line fishing. Mussels, lobsters, crabs and mackerel also featured in the local fishery, and the villages of Dale, Angle and Lawrenny were famous for the oysters and cockles harvested from their tidal mud-flats. But Pembrokeshire was blessed in particular with a sizeable herring fishery, and it was upon the humble herring that the local fishing economy was largely based.

Fishing vessels were built at many of the little shipyards around the Pembrokeshire coast, and they were operated out of virtually every small port. Herring fishing was conducted from Abercastle, Porthclais, Cwm-yr-Eglwys, St Bride's, Angle and many other creeks and landing beaches; but the largest herring fleets were based at St Dogmaels, Newport, Lower Town Fishguard, Solva, Dale and

Tenby. There are few records to tell us how large these fleets were, but we can assume that at some places up to twenty boats were involved in the fishing industry around the open coast. There was a separate industry inside Milford Haven which exploited the shoals of herring which preferred these quiet waters; for this fishery the main ports were Llangwm, Lawrenny, Pembroke and Burton. There were even some herring boats operating out of Haverfordwest. Other fishing smacks came all the way from Brixham during the Milford Haven herring season, and some of the Brixham fishermen returned, like old friends, year after year.

The herring fishery was conducted throughout the year, but the peak season was the summer. Each fleet had its favourite fishing grounds, usually within sight of the Pembrokeshire coast. When the catch was landed the herring would immediately be cleaned, because it was a fish that rotted quickly. Some would be dried or smoked, but most would be salted and packed down in barrels. Many members of the community would be involved in this task, during which time the quayside would be transformed into a babbling chaos of fishwives and fishermen, small children, elderly relatives, and seagulls wheeling, screaming and swooping for scraps. The barrels of salted herring would be stored in little warehouses and then, when a full load was assembled, packed onto a cargo boat and sent off to Bristol, Swansea or some other South Wales port for sale to local merchants. Some of the catch was disposed of in Pembrokeshire, and especially in the main towns.

Records of salted herring exports are scanty, but in the early eighteenth century a thousand barrels of salted herring per year were exported from Fishguard and Newport alone. At least 100 cargoes per year left Pembrokeshire ports, and the peak of the industry occurred around 1750. Later on, overfishing and possible changes of climate and ocean currents led to the disappearance of the herring shoals, sometimes with such suddenness that whole communities were plunged into despair.

The disappearance of the herring shoals from Tenby is explained by an old tale about a beggar. In the seventeenth century the local herring fishery was prosperous, and was based upon certain very rich fishing grounds not far offshore. All seemed to be well. But then a poor deaf and dumb beggar was falsely accused of acting as a spy for a pirate who was operating in Pembrokeshire waters, and he was beaten so seriously by a local citizen called Leekie Porridge that he almost died. Before he dragged himself away from Tenby the old man silently cursed the town, and from that moment on the herring left the fishing grounds and the industry went into an irreversible decline.

Another community which made its living from fishing was Llangwm, and for very many years Black Tar was full of small tarred boats and salty gossip as local families went about their fishy business. The men spent long hours out in the estuary, fishing for herring, cockles, shrimps, oysters, sewin and salmon. Mostly they used small open rowing-boats, and some of them used an ancient "compass net" fishing technique when fishing for sewin and salmon. Since the compass nets were often used in the hours of darkness and in appalling weather, many men were drowned within a mile or two of home. The women of Llangwm were a tough breed, and according to legend the whole village was organized on matriarchal lines in a tight, almost closed society with its own dialect. The women were in total control of the sales of fish and shellfish, and there were no big merchants or middle-men to take

A group of Llangwm fisherwomen, pictured in Tenby around the year 1890. They sold herrings, shrimps, oysters and cockles. This trade was carried on for at least 150 years, and ended inside the present century.

their "cut". Several times a week the women would load up their panniers and baskets with fresh herring, oysters, pickled cockles and mussels, and set off in little groups on foot for Haverfordwest, Tenby and Pembroke. Sometimes they would walk 50 km in a day. In the towns, and on the highways of Pembrokeshire, they were a common sight, quite recognizeable in their colourful tweed dresses, flannel shawls and aprons, and black felt hats. In each town they would set themselves up in the market-place and dispose of their load, haggling with regular customers over a few miserable pennies before returning home to Llangwm with their empty baskets in the hours of twilight or darkness.

The Llangwm fisherwomen became quite famous in the latter years of the nineteenth century because they were by then something of an anachronism; they were regularly photographed and featured on post-cards, and Mary Palmer, the toughest and most famous of these colourful characters, was even interviewed for the *Daily Mirror* newspaper.

In the main river estuaries the sewin and salmon catch was important even at the time of George Owen, and it became commercially more important as time went on. In addition to the strange compass netting technique used in the Llangwm and Hook area, seine net fishing was common in the Teifi Estuary and on Newport Sands. With this technique a long net with floats was fixed to the beach at one end and then carried out to sea and back to the beach by four men working in a black-tarred rowing boat. The net would then be hauled in to the beach from both ends. With luck, the net would trap salmon and sewin making their way along the shore towards the river mouth, and huge catches were sometimes made. There is a wonderful old photograph of Teifi fishermen at work, resplendent in their bowler hats, around the year 1880. At

that time there were 30 such nets in use in the village of St Dogmael's alone, and possibly over 100 nets in the whole of Pembrokeshire.

The other fishing technique employed for salmon and sewin fishing further up the main rivers was coracle fishing. The coracle is an ancient craft made by stretching skin, calico or canvas over a frame of bent laths. It is very light, being made to hold but one person, and can be carried across the back of the fisherman. It is remarkably manoeuvrable in the hands of an expert, and it is ideal for fishing in shallow rivers with strong and variable currents. Coracle fishermen would work in pairs, with a net strung between their frail craft. Probably in the eighteenth century there were several thousand coracle-men fishing in the rivers of West Wales. By the middle of

An old photograph of a fisherman carrying a Cleddau Coracle. It had a squared stern and flat bottom, and lacked the sweet curves of the Teifi and Tywi coracles.

the last century numbers were greatly reduced, but there were still over 300 coracles in use on the Teifi alone, mostly based at Cenarth and Cilgerran. There were also large numbers on the Tywi at Carmarthen, at St Clears on the Taf, and at Haverfordwest and Blackpool Mill on the two Cleddau rivers. Every river had its own peculiar design of coracle; for example, the Teifi coracle had gentle curves and straight sides, while the Tywi coracle was characterised by its "pinched waist" and the Eastern Cleddau coracle by its flat bottom and flat back end.

The old fishing industries of Pembrokeshire have left relatively few traces in the landscape, but when all of them are taken together we can see that they provided a livelihood for many thousands of local people over the centuries. They ensured the survival of many small coastal communities, and provided the pool of skilled mariners, boatbuilders and other craftsmen which was needed for the other seafaring and industrial activities examined in more detail in Chapters 9 and 11.

The Drovers

Between the medieval period and the middle of the nineteenth century Pembrokeshire figured prominently in the overland trade in livestock. Mostly this was a one-way trade, with herds of cattle, sheep and pigs (and even flocks of geese) being driven along the network of drovers' roads towards the Welsh borderland and beyond to the fattening pastures, markets and fairs of central and southern England. Many of the "great herds of black cattle" from the Castlemartin peninsula and other parts of the county ended up in Smithfield Market in the heart of London. The livestock were delivered by farmers to the drover and his helpers in one of the collecting centres. Haverfordwest was the main centre in

Pembrokeshire, but there were others at Eglwyswrw, Boncath, Crymych and Whitland. Here the animals were shod before setting off along one of the traditional routes eastwards. Cattle could be driven at a rate of up to twenty miles a day, but pigs travelled only about six miles a day; the journey from Pembrokeshire to London could take almost two months. Many of the resting-places along the route had inns to house the drovers - hence the frequently encountered inns named "Drover's Arms".

The drovers' routes kept clear of the main highways as far as possible; thus they avoided the payment of tolls on the turnpike roads and avoided coach traffic and town centres. Some routes involved considerable river crossings by the livestock droves. Traces of the old drovers' roads can still be seen, particularly in the north of the county where they have been preserved from the assault of agriculture in the quiet hills of Mynydd Presely. One particularly well-preserved route runs across the upland ridge near Cwm Garw and past Carn Goedog; the deep rutted tracks made by thousands and thousands of hooved feet are still prominent features in the moorland landscape. But few of these droving routes have been used during the past 150 years, for the coming of the railways effectively destroyed the droving trade.

Nowadays there is a tendency among historians to romanticise the drovers and their trade. It is all too easy to think of the "Welsh cowboys" as inhabiting a world of camp-fires and rosy sunsets, with hard days on the trail followed occasionally by hard nights on the town. In reality the droving trade was tough and cruel, involving terrible suffering on the part of the animals. Alexander Cordell catches the atmosphere strikingly in his novel *The Fire People*:

"...in the reviling shouts of the drovers the cattle ran; bucking, shouldering, leaping upon one another in a melee of flying bodies and dust. And their hooves beat a rhythmic thunder to an accompaniment of cracking whips and a shrieking of cow and heifer. Barging, leaning, horning, the mad pack came, and the night was filled with the agony of the passage: whips curled and flashed against the moon: men stood at out-stations with braced legs and cracked their flails in the faces of the beasts to maintain the herd; Welsh collies raced through the bordering heather, barking and snapping at their heels, others lay like quivering arrows in the grass, waiting for the command that would send them into battle.... And after the cattle came the sheep and these numbered more than two thousand; a crawling, maggotty mass that blanketed the common. Fringed with racing dogs and shepherds, they followed the mad stampede... In the vanguard ran the fittest, in the middle the majority flock, and at the end of the heaving mass fell the foot-rot stragglers, the old ewes, the blind rams baa-ing pitifully in their limping, staggering pace, for to fall meant death; this they knew by instinct. And the killing shepherds walked in file behind them with blood-stained crooks and gullet-knives, and behind them was a donkey-cart filled with carcasses..."

Seen in their proper context, the drovers played a considerable part in the agricultural trade of Pembrokeshire. The export of animals on the hoof helped to sustain the farming economy through difficult times, stimulating improvements in stock breeding programmes and also bringing cash into the economy from the outside world. Indeed, the origins of the local banking system can be traced to the droving trade. But in the middle of the nineteenth century it declined quickly, in part because of rising public concern about the cruelty involved but most of all because the new railway network made it possible to transport huge numbers of live cattle and sheep from the marts of Haverfordwest or Whitland to the slaughter-houses of London or Birmingham in twelve hours or less, in good condition and at very low cost.

The Last Invasion of Britain

The "Last Invasion of Britain" was more of a farce than a threat to national security, but it is still very much part of local folklore. And at the time (1797) it caused great alarm, not only in Pembrokeshire but in Westminster also. Britain was at war with revolutionary France, and there was some expectation that the French might make some attempt to attack the south coast of England. Even as far west as Fishguard a fort was built on the headland overlooking the harbour just in case of an assault from the sea.

The invasion arose out of a French theory that forces landed in Ireland and Britain might provoke a widespread "peasants' revolt" of the poor against the rich. It was planned that 15,000 troops should land in Ireland, and 1,400 near Bristol or in Cardigan Bay. As it happened, the Irish invasion never took place, and the Bristol expeditionary force was forced by unfavourable winds to sail round the tip of Pembrokeshire towards Pencaer. The four ships of the expedition carried a motley and undisciplined force of ex-convicts and grenadiers under the command of an American named Colonel Tate. Tate was no great leader of men, and he must in any case have been somewhat confused by the complex details of his military instructions.

The ships were sighted off St David's on 22 February 1797, by Mr Williams of Treleddyn, who decided that they were French in spite of the fact that they were flying English flags. Soon the alarm was raised, and by the time the ships reached Fishguard Bay the Fishguard Fencibles were ready for them. A single shot from the fort warned off the French naval commander, Castagnier, and he withdrew his vessels

An old picture of a Fishguard Fencible, one of the local heroes who frightened away the French invaders of 1797.

Cawdor (who had studied military tactics but never been involved in conflict) assumed overall command of his motley army of 575 volunteers. The army was made up of members of Lord Cawdor's Yeomanry Cavalry, the Cardigan Militia, Captain Ackland's Pembroke Volunteers, the Fishguard Fencibles, and a party of Royal Navy sailors. The local force reached Manorowen, but after almost walking into a French ambush on Carnwnda, Cawdor withdrew to Fishguard and Goodwick for the night of 23 February.

Meanwhile the French force of 1500 men was showing its true colours. Tate himself seems to have been remorseful at his involvement in the invasion, his officers were rebellious and angry at having been abandoned by the ships, and the men were undisciplined and rowdy. Tate needed transport and food for his men, and sent out foraging parties in all directions. As the day wore on the invasion turned into a fiasco. Small groups of soldiers wandered far and wide, making no attempt to hide their movements. They looted all of the farms they came across and slaughtered calves, sheep and poultry for food. A number of local people and French soldiers were killed or injured in isolated incidents throughout Pencaer, for the locals were united in their opposition to the invader; there was never the slightest chance that a "peasants' revolt" would be the outcome of the action.

As luck would have it, in January a Portuguese coaster had been wrecked on the nearby coast and there was hardly a farmhouse in the vicinity which did not have a plentiful supply of Portuguese wine. Soon both soldiers and officers were drunk and even less capable than they had been when sober. On Thursday evening Tate was forced by his officers to write a surrender note. Following a stern reply from Lord Cawdor, the surrender terms were signed by various officers on Friday morning, 24th

eastwards out of sight of Fishguard. This was just as well, since the fort was now entirely without ammunition! The day was uncommonly hot for the time of year, and the sea was calm, so after some deliberation Castagnier and Tate decided that the expeditionary force should be put ashore immediately, at the foot of the inhospitable cliffs of Carreg Wastad. During a calm moonlit night all the men and supplies were ferried ashore, and by morning everything had been carried up the cliffs. Soon Tate had established his headquarters at Trehowel Farm, Castagnier and his ships had left for home, and French troops were in charge of Carnwnda rocks, the highest point in the area. From this point on, the successful military exercise deteriorated into farce.

There was no trained body of professional soldiers to oppose the French, and for a while the local military leadership was in a state of panic. However, the defences were soon organized, and Lord

February 1797, on the small table that stands in the bar of the Royal Oak inn. Tate probably signed the agreement later at Trehowel Farm, and during the afternoon the French troops (less twenty-five or so who were recovering from the effects of alcohol and eating uncooked poultry!) marched down to Goodwick Sands to lay down their arms. They were later taken to Haverfordwest and imprisoned for a while in the castle and in the churches of St Thomas, St Martin and St Mary. The great invasion was over.

Inevitably, various incidents connected with the invasion have entered into local folk-lore. One story concerns the local women dressed in "scarlet mantles and round hats" who crowded the hills on the Fishguard side of Goodwick Sands, looking from a distance like soldiers. Tradition has it that Lord Cawdor had them march round a rocky knoll, giving the enemy the impression of a seemingly endless line of troops and striking terror into their hearts. There is probably little truth in this, for Tate had almost certainly decided to surrender before most of the local women had appeared on the scene as spectators or volunteers.

All good stories need a hero, a heroine and a villain. Lord Cawdor was certainly the hero of the moment, for he took decisive control of a situation that was threatening, on the first day of the Invasion, to get out of hand. But the local heroine was one Jemima Nicholas, "a tall stout Amazon masculine woman who worked as a cobbler in Fishguard." She marched out with a pitchfork and captured twelve Frenchmen in a field near Llanwnda. When asked later how she had managed it, she reputedly replied "Why, I just surrounded them!" She herded her prisoners into the guardhouse in Fishguard and then went back for more. She died in 1832 at the age of eighty-two, and today her tombstone stands at the front of Fishguard church. It bears the noble inscription:

In memory of
JEMIMA NICHOLAS
of this town.
THE WELSH HEROINE
who boldly marched to meet
the French Invaders
who landed on our shores in
February 1797.

Our friend Jemima appears not to have been a particularly romantic figure, but the story of the invasion was not entirely devoid of romance. There is a charming story of two young ladies named Anne Beach and Eleanor Martin, who fell in love with, and eventually married, two of the French prisoners who were professional soldiers. The girls were hired to bring food to the prisoners who were at first herded into St Mary's Church in Haverfordwest and later incarcerated in the Golden Prison just outside Pembroke. With the two romances flourishing under almost impossible circumstances, the young lovers devised an escape plan. Each day the girls carried in the shin-bones of oxen and horses among the food supplies, and these were used by 31 of the prisoners for the excavation of a sixty-foot tunnel under the prison walls. The food baskets were used by the girls to carry out the excavated soil. Again with the help of the girls, the prisoners escaped under cover of darkness, stole Lord Cawdor's yacht from the Pembroke River, later commandeered a trading brig near the mouth of Milford Haven, and eventually made it to St Malo. The two girls married their French heroes, and (so far as we know) lived happily ever after.

The villain of the piece was James Bowen, who had been a servant at Trehowel Farm on Pencaer but had been dismissed by his master, Mr Mortimer, and transported for horse-stealing. It is uncertain how he came to be involved in the invasion, but probably he found his way by chance to Brest, and was enrolled there by Tate as a guide before the departure of the troopships. Perhaps he hoped to use the expedition as an opportunity to return home and regain his freedom, or perhaps he was bent on vengeance against his local community and against his old employer in particular. Whatever Bowen's motives, it must have been largely due to his presence that the French landing was made at Carreg Wastad, on a piece of the coastline with which he must have been very familiar. In addition, he must have encouraged Tate to use Mortimer's farmhouse as his expedition headquarters. Probably, had it not been for Bowen's presence on board Tate's ship, the last invasion of Britain would not have taken place near Fishguard at all.

The Protection of the Haven

The first attempts to fortify the Milford Haven waterway came during the reign of Henry VIII, when two simple forts (East Blockhouse and West Blockhouse) were built near the Haven entrance. These forts were probably manned during the Spanish Armada scare of 1588, and during the Civil War of 1642-1648. Also during the Civil War the Royalists built an armed encampment and gun emplacement at Pill, near Milford.

During the nineteenth century, with the great investment in the new towns of Milford, Neyland and Pembroke Dock, the Haven became a harbour of great strategic importance (see Chapter 10 for more detail). There was continuing trouble on the continent of Europe, and as Napoleon persisted with his military adventures he was increasingly perceived as a threat by the British government. After Nelson defeated the French fleet at Trafalgar in 1805, the government realised that the margin between victory and defeat was a narrow one. There were particular fears about the growing strength of foreign fleets on the high seas. After 1814, therefore, in parallel with

the building of the Royal Naval Dockyard at Pembroke Dock, elaborate plans for the defence of the waterway were put in hand. Lord Palmerston, as Foreign Secretary and later as Prime Minister, was instrumental in bringing these plans to fruition; later, as the foreign threat faded into insignificance, the fortifications came to be known as "Palmerston's Follies". So far as we know, none of the forts ever fired a shot in anger.

The first large building project was near the Dockyard itself. Paterchurch Fort (later replaced by a Battery) was built near the present Carr Jetty before 1831. Between 1844 and 1857 the Defensible Barracks were built (to hold a garrison of 500 men), together with two martello towers to protect the waterfront where ships were launched and fitted out. The Barracks were not defended by gun emplacements, but were surrounded by a deep dry ditch with a massive revetted wall. Both the Barracks and the martello towers are still largely intact, and the tower at the eastern edge of the Dockyard is now open to the public.

Further down the Haven no less than seven impressive new forts were built (partly by convict labour) between 1850 and 1870 at Dale Fort, Popton Point, Chapel Bay, South Hook Point and Hubberston, and in the waterway itself on Thorn Island and Stack Rock. The strongest of the forts, at Popton Point and Hubberston, were designed to hold garrisons of more than 200 men, and they were each armed with about thirty heavy guns. The Hubberston Fort, on the outskirts of the built-up area of Hubberston, is now in a ruinous state, but it is nonetheless a hugely impressive structure. The garrison was housed in a bomb-proof D-shaped barracks set back from the coast, while the gun emplacements were directly above the headland. There were casements for eleven heavy guns, with the others in batteries. The magazine for shells was below the casements, and the powder magazine was cut

Martello Tower on the edge of the Pembroke Dockyard, part of the last line of defence in the Milford Haven Waterway.

into solid rock. There were plans to defend the landward approaches to Milford Haven too, and a number of promising sites were selected for new forts. However, only two of these additional forts were ever built - at Fort Scoveston and on St Catherine's Island, Tenby. In all, the forts could accommodate a total garrison of about 1,900 men, defending the Haven with all the modern weapons of the day. The cost of constructing the defences was about £1 million, which was a considerable sum in those days.

The Milford Haven forts are fascinating to military historians, not only because of the defensive building techniques used in their construction but also because of the armaments involved. More than 220 heavy guns were placed in the forts, and they were carefully positioned so as to provide the safest possible "shield" for the waterway in general and for the Dockyard in particular. All guns were located so that their "swept areas" overlapped with those of the guns located in adjacent forts. There were four lines of defence. The first covered the Haven entrance; the second involved South Hook, Stack Rock and Chapel Bay batteries; the third involved Hubberston and Popton Point forts, with a floating battery located in mid-channel; and the final defences were located on the flanks of the Dockyard itself. The armaments included 18 ton guns, 25 ton guns, guns firing 7 inch and 9 inch shells, and rifled muzzle-loaders (reputed to be the ultimate weapons of the day) using pallister shells.

Some of the forts are now in ruins, but they are well worth looking at in any case, Others have been preserved and are put to good use. The Thorn Island fort (built between 1852 and 1859) is used as an hotel; Dale Fort is a popular field studies centre; Part of the Defensible Barracks is used as a golf club house; the South Hook Point fort was used by the Esso Petroleum Company from 1960-1983 since it lay within the refinery boundary; and the Popton Point fort was used as the headquarters of the BP Angle Bay ocean terminal before becoming the base for the Field Studies Council's oil pollution research unit. St Catherine's Fort in Tenby was used some years ago, even more exotically, as a private zoo.

Early Industry

Later in this book (in Chapter 11) we will look at the activities associated with Pembrokeshire's little "industrial revolution." For the most part these arose out of the exploitation of mineral resources. However, we should not forget that long before the days of mass production and steam engines there were small-scale industrial activities going on all over the county. They contributed in no small measure to the growth of the economy in the three centuries which are under review in this chapter. In the towns (for example in Haverfordwest, Pembroke and Tenby) there were tanneries and rope-walks, glove-making workshops, hatters, tailors, cobblers, potters and candle-makers. In the coastal communities of Solva, Newport and Fishguard there were coopers, net-makers, boat-builders and sail-makers.

The valley of Cwm Cych became quite famous as a centre of wood-turning. There were carpenters and masons all over Pembrokeshire, and typical rural or cottage industries included clog-making, knitting, lace-making, basket weaving, and the carving of wooden bowls, spoons and ladles. Most of these industries were very small, employing half a dozen people or less, and many of them maintained the old traditions of the Middle Ages, particularly through an insistence on long apprenticeships. In some of the towns the old trade guilds, established in the Middle Ages, survived until the present century.

People have known how to use water power to drive mill wheels ever since Roman times. Probably the Celtic tribes were using water power for various purposes in the Age of the Saints, and there is ample evidence to show that the Vikings operated water-driven corn mills alongside fast-flowing streams. But the Norman invaders were the first people to organize a systematic exploitation of Pembrokeshire's water power resources. Every Anglo-Norman village grew corn, and the corn had to be milled, so every village also had its water mill. Almost always the mill was owned by the lord of the manor and operated by a miller who paid for the use of the premises by paying rent or tithes. For example, the ruinous "castle mill" adjacent to Newport Castle is still owned by the Lady Marcher of Cemaes; it was unusual in that it was actually driven by water released from the castle moat. Other "castle mills" can still be seen at Carew and Manorbier.

As the centuries passed, and as the farming community created larger and larger agricultural surpluses, more water mills were built to cope with the increasing demand for flour. One of the best known is Blackpool Mill, not far from Canaston Bridge. The corn mill at Felin Isaf, St David's, is thought to have operated more or less continuously for

500 years. Literally hundreds of Pembrokeshire farms had their own small mills. Nowadays the only traces we can find of them are infilled millponds, sections of mill races, rusting waterwheels and tumbledown buildings. Some very simple mills were used for crushing and chopping furze or gorse, which was used as an animal feedstuff. Others were used for crushing bones to make bone-meal. As the demand for timber beams and planks increased with the growth of the urban population, saw-mills began to replace the old (and very labour-intensive) saw-pits which had previously been scattered about the countryside. In Haverfordwest there was one saw-mill at Crow Hill and a larger one downstream at Cartlett, below the New Bridge.

Although most of the Pembrokeshire mills depended upon water power to keep their wheels turning, other forms of natural energy were also used. The corn mills at Carew and Pembroke, for example, were quite sophisticated tidal mills. They operated in conjunction with barrages built across tidal inlets. These barrages had sluice gates built into them; twice a day the flooding tide would be allowed to fill the mill pond, and at high tide the sluices would be shut in order to hold back the water. Later on, when the tide had fallen on the outside of the barrage, the water would be released past the mill wheels, driving the mill machinery. These mills were much more reliable than the little water mills built on the banks of streams and rivers, since they were unaffected by droughts, neighbourly disputes and river diversions for irrigation. It is not surprising, therefore, that both the Pembroke and Carew mills were large and successful enterprises; the former was demolished after the Second World War, but the latter (called the "French Mill" possibly because its millstones came from France) has four storeys and most of its machinery is still intact. It is now in the care of the NPA.

Windmills were not common in the county, possibly because the frequency of gales was too great for the primitive structures to cope with. There are records of at least eight windmills used for milling corn, of which two were in Tenby, one in Dale and two in St David's. Many years ago one of the St David's windmills was dismantled because, according to the locals, "there was enough wind for one but not for two!" The survivor was the windmill at Twr y Felin; even without its blades the tower is still obviously that of a windmill, and it is still a prominent landmark. A most peculiar windmill was built adjacent to the Rosebush slate quarry around 1880, probably to pump water; but it lasted for only a few years before running out of control in a gale and smashing itself to pieces. Animal power was also used on very many farms for milling purposes. Primitive "horse works" were widespread, especially on farms which did not have access to fast-flowing streams. There is a fine example of a horse-works behind the farmhouse on Skomer Island. And it is as well to remind ourselves that until at least 1820 treadmills operated by convicts were still used for certain primitive processes in Cardigan and Haverfordwest gaols ....

Finally in this chapter, we should remind ourselves of the importance of woollen mills not only in the landscape but also in the economic and social history of Pembrokeshire. Rough cloth was certainly being manufactured here before the arrival of the Normans. Later there were many small mills making rough cloth in the Middle Ages, both for local use and for export. It is thought that the arrival of Flemish immigrants was of great importance for the development of the industry, for they brought with them a range of skills new to Wales. As we have seen, George Owen was in no doubt about the value of the woollen industry in Elizabethan times, and there is much evidence to show that the county was then the main centre of Welsh woollen cloth

Blackpool Mill on the Eastern Cleddau.

particularly good, there were little "strings" of mills located one after another on a single stream; for example, there were five mills on a single stream near St Nicholas. Mostly the mills were family affairs employing no more than four persons; they made tweeds, knitting yarn and flannel for sale in local markets and fairs. The tweeds and flannels were sold on the roll by the yard, and were used for making all manner of clothes including vests and night-shirts. According to tradition, the best way to keep a youngster healthy through the winter in the good old days was to impregnate a Welsh flannel vest with goose grease, put it on him or her in the autumn and not take it off till the spring.

manufacture. The industry continued to develop in the following centuries, but in the 1700s its relative importance declined as better quality cloths began to be produced in the Welsh borders and elsewhere. There are not many traces of the older generation of woollen mills left nowadays, but at Pandy (near Llannerch, in the Gwaun Valley) there is a fascinating old ruin where water power was used to drive the drop-hammers of a typical pandy or fulling mill. In the 1700s local weavers would have brought their cloth here for soaking in a urine mixture and for beating to bind the woollen fibres together; this was the final stage in the manufacture of the Welsh flannel which so many of the older generation love to hate.

After 1800 the woollen industry received a boost with the invention of machinery for carding and spinning, and many new woollen mills were set up in Pembrokeshire. Nobody knows how many there were, but in 1850 there were certainly several hundred. They were all driven by water power, and they were nearly all small and remote, being located for the most part in narrow valleys with fast-flowing streams. Here and there, where conditions were

Towards the end of the nineteenth century the import of mass-produced woollen cloth from the big mills of Yorkshire and elsewhere effectively killed off the local woollen industry. By 1900 there were only about 30 working woollen mills left in the county; mostly they produced traditional and complex Welsh tapestry designs which did not compete directly with the mass-produced fabrics. But the competition was still very tough, and gradually the mills were forced to close. One of the largest of the twelve mills near Narberth was the Lan Mill, which once had 40 power looms in operation. At Gelli, near Llawhaden, there was a factory with about 20 looms, but unfortunately it was destroyed in a fire in 1938. Today there are only two mills left, at Tregwynt and Middle Mill. As their owners would be the first to admit, they owe their survival at least in part to the presence of a local tourist industry; but when it comes to design and marketing some nifty footwork is required in the difficult economic conditions of the 1990's. Things have changed on a quite unforeseen scale since the simple days when the people of Pembrokeshire looked to their local water mills for the flour and the cloth which they needed to keep themselves fed and warm.

Chapter Eight

Religious and Social Awakening

During the period 1600 -- 1900 the landscape changed in a host of subtle ways with the changing fortunes of agriculture, with the rise and fall of the great landowning families and the minor gentry, and with the great religious revivals which swept across Wales. The foundations of the modern transport system were being established, and the development of the railway network in particular, in the later 1800's, had a huge impact upon agriculture, trade and population mobility. New ideas came flooding into Pembrokeshire, partly because political and social campaigners could travel more freely than ever before and partly because of the increasing availability of news-sheets, news letters and newspapers. In both town and country more and more people were learning to read and write, and the nonconformist leaders did much to heighten "social awareness". Peasants and poor tenant farmers began to seek political and social reform, and a host of great causes began to exercise the minds of local people. In the first half of the nineteenth century new legislation came flooding in, partly as a result of public protest; some of it was accepted by the common people, and some of it was not. The Rebecca Riots in Pembrokeshire arose directly out of the hardship and frustration experienced by poor farmers and peasants, and an increasing (and often naive) belief in the ultimate triumph of right over wrong. The modern period was being ushered in, and in the following paragraphs we examine some of the themes of greatest importance for landscape change.

The Religious Revivals

While life in town and country developed quietly during the seventeenth and eighteenth centuries the established church made relatively little impact. But from about 1730 onwards there was a series of "evangelical explosions" throughout Wales, collectively known as the Methodist Revival. As elsewhere in Wales, this revival made a considerable impact upon Pembrokeshire life and landscape. The roots of nonconformity go back well into the seventeenth century, for the "Green Meeting House" (now Albany Chapel) in Haverfordwest was founded in 1638 and maintained a faithful congregation even during the time of persecution prior to the 1689 Toleration Act. There were groups of Quakers and other dissenters in the other towns also. And while the nonconformists slowly built up a following, another impetus for the intense religious experience of the 1730s was provided by the "educational revival". In this respect Pembrokeshire was particularly fortunate to have received the patronage of Sir John Philipps of Picton Castle, who as a leading member of the SPCK founded several schools entirely at his own expense. By 1712 a visitor was able to report that "Pembrokeshire, though it be one of the smallest counties in South Britain, out vies most of the largest counties in the number of Charity Schools." Sir John played an active part in the founding of the famous "Circulating Schools" of Griffith Jones, which did so much to encourage adult literacy and the survival of the Welsh

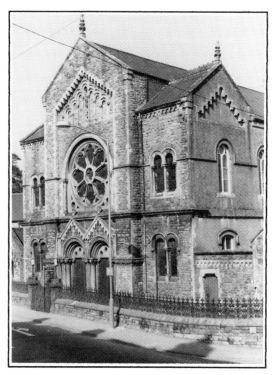

The fine facade of Bethesda Chapel in Haverfordwest.

"College" where teachers were trained and where many hundreds of local youngsters received part-time education over a period of about a hundred years.

The religious movement gathered momentum. Griffith Jones made himself rather unpopular with authority (frequently requiring the support and protection of his brother-in-law Sir John Philipps) by his insistence upon itinerant evangelism. His bishop complained that he was "going about preaching on week days in Churches, Churchyards, and sometimes on the mountains to hundreds of auditors". These activities were not only frowned upon but actively discouraged by the established church, which signally failed to appreciate the spirit of evangelism which was now abroad in the countryside. Griffith Jones was a powerful preacher, and one of his converts, Daniel Rowland, also took up the life of an itinerant evangelist in 1735. In the same year Howel Harris began independently to preach beyond the confines of his native Breconshire, and in 1738 William Williams joined the evangelical campaign. These three were the first real leaders of the Methodist Revival. Rowland was one of the most famous of all Welsh preachers; Harris was above all a tireless itinerant organizer of religious societies in all parts of Wales; and "Williams Pantycelin" was the poet and hymn-writer whose music became as powerful a factor in the religious revival as the sermons of his contemporaries.

language through the medium of religious instruction. By 1760 there were twenty-three charity schools in Pembrokeshire with a total of 837 pupils and there must have been thousands more who received some teaching in the Circulating Schools. It is estimated that over a period of about thirty years more than 150,000 Welsh people of all ages were taught to read by the itinerant teachers.

One of the great local benefactors was Madame Bevan of Laugharne, who devoted much of her personal fortune to the support of the Circulating Schools. One of the best-known of the movement's teachers in north Pembrokeshire was John Jenkin of Nevern (also known as "Shion Crydd Bach" or John Little Cobbler), who had a reputation as a poet, man of science and even as a conjuror who could summon up evil spirits. On College Square in Newport we can still see the buildings used as Madame Bevan's

Intense religious experience was felt in Pembrokeshire as elsewhere and the county had its own great revivalist in Howell Davies. However, because the greater part of the evangelical campaign was conducted through the medium of Welsh, its impact upon English-speaking south Pembrokeshire was less marked than in the north. Conversely John Wesley himself appears to have made a greater impact in "Little England", and he did little preaching north of the Landsker during his various visits to the county. He visited Haverfordwest on fourteen different occasions between 1736 and 1790. He recorded his first visit thus: "I rode over to Haverfordwest. Finding it was the Assize Week, I was afraid the bulk of the people would be too busy to think about hearing sermons. But I was mistaken; I have not seen so numerous a congregation since I set out of London; and they were one and all deeply attentive. Surely some will bring forth fruit." By the time of his visit of 1772 he was able to write "There is a considerable increase in this Society, and not in number only. After preaching on Wednesday evening, we had such a meeting as I have seldom known. Almost everyone spoke, as well as they could for tears, and with the utmost simplicity: and many of them appeared to know "the great salvation", to love God with all their heart."

Within fifty years of the beginning of the Methodist Revival the Pembrokeshire landscape was dotted with chapels. Generally these were built in the towns and villages, although some served as the centres for scattered rural societies and were built in isolated spots just like the original small Celtic churches of a thousand years before. Most of these chapels were built without the support of the local gentry; with the exception of the Bowen family of Llwyngwair (Newport) they remained loyal to the established church. In Haverfordwest the Moravian church dates from this time (1773) as does Wesley Methodist chapel (1772), Tabernacle (1774) and Bethesda (1789). Ebenezer chapel (1817) and Hill Park Baptist chapel (1885) followed after a while, and many of the chapels of Haverfordwest and other parts of the county were extensively restored or rebuilt during a later religious awakening in the period 1870-90. At this time Welsh nonconformity was at its height, and the villages and towns of Pembrokeshire were enlivened by active religious societies whose congregations far surpassed those of the established church.

In style the new chapels were very different from the older churches with their stone exteriors, their arched windows and their medieval battlemented towers or simple bell-cotes. They were functional buildings, paid for by the subscriptions of ordinary folk rather than with the endowments of landed gentry. They were constructed on a simple rectangular plan with sparse furnishings and, as often as not, an unprepossessing facade. There were exceptions, like the fine chapels of Tabernacle and Bethesda in Haverfordwest and Hermon in Fishguard, but often these are later rebuildings by larger and more prosperous congregations.

The new chapels were the homes of Baptists, Wesleyan and Calvinistic Methodists, Congregationalists, Moravians and Presbyterians, and their sheer density on the ground still causes amazement. In Haverfordwest, for example, there is a distinct cluster of churches and chapels on the old western edge of the town, with three large medieval parish churches and six substantial nonconformist chapels providing total accommodation for several thousand worshippers. In addition to the chapel buildings themselves, many of the nonconformist societies built school halls and large vestries adjacent to their places of worship, for Sunday School and week-night activities have always been a strong part of local nonconformist tradition. In the towns few of the chapels were built on sites large enough for graveyards, so burials were performed in the parish graveyards on the outskirts of the towns; but in the countryside many chapels have their own adjacent graveyards, as at Jabez in the Gwaun Valley and at Bethesda near Llawhaden. Often the chapels have magnificent biblical names: Hermon, Tabor, Zion, Bethel and Tabernacle crop up time and again.

Caersalem Baptist Chapel, located in Cilgwyn, near Newport.

But while the face of town and country changed as a result of the Methodist Revival, society was changed even more by the inspired preaching of the evangelists. Wynford Vaughan-Thomas said "the Church could not possibly hold such enthusiasts. The final break ..... was devastating for the Church of England when it came. The new Methodist church took with it great numbers of the Welsh people. The chapel, not the church, now held the loyalty of the people. The Church stood for the gentry, the landowners, the alien traditions of England and Toryism. The Chapel sprang from the people. It was democratic in form, radical in politics, and Welsh in thought and speech." The chapels acted as the new social centres, and they provided new leaders. In the Welsh-speaking areas the language acquired a new status. "But," said Wynford, "there were losses too. Wales after the revival was a sterner place. The dancers, the fiddlers, the

carefree interlude players, the laughter in the ale-houses died before the strict admonition to men that their first duty was to save their souls from Hell."

Ironically, under the rule of the new preachers and deacons the "non-conformists" were themselves required to conform to strict codes of behaviour and to subscribe to a rigid set of beliefs. These beliefs owed more to the Old Testament than the New, and those who strayed from the straight and narrow were liable to suffer harrowing humiliation at the hands of the fearsome men who cast evangelical thunder and lightning from their pulpits on the Sabbath. One particularly savage tradition, which became a part of eighteenth- and nineteenth-century chapel life, was the public "casting out" from the congregation of, for example, young unmarried women who became pregnant; sometimes girls were literally beaten down the aisle with sticks, bibles and hymn-books

Below: The ramparts of Manorbier Castle,
one of the centres of social life in the Middle
Ages and still in a good state of repair. It is
open to the public during the summer months.

Above: The ruins of old farm buildings on
Skomer Island.   The farm was once a
substantial "yeoman farm" with superb
outbuildings.

and driven out screaming through the chapel doors. Loving forgiveness was a commodity in short supply, reserved mostly for those who were faithful members of the chapel family.

Another tradition which became a part of chapel life, particularly in the Welsh-speaking districts, was the **pwnc**. This was an annual celebration of the scriptures, in which whole chapters from the Bible were memorised and then recited by the congregation in a strange, repetitive, hypnotic harmonized chant. Dating from a time when literacy was rare and bibles in short supply, the pwnc was partly an educational device and partly a means of strengthening the bonds which held the chapel congregation together. The pwnc is still held in some chapels in Pembrokeshire - a thing of beauty to those involved but almost beyond the comprehension of those who belong to another culture.

The Social Scene

During the Eighteenth Century the Pembrokeshire gentry were at their most powerful. It should be remembered that the population of the county, although growing rapidly, did not rise above 50,000 until about 1800, and many areas were very sparsely populated. The population of Haverfordwest, the largest town, was not much more than 2,000. The professional class, comprising lawyers, clerics, merchants, bankers ands so forth, was numerically not very strong; and the "lower orders" of society, comprising small farmers, cottagers, servants and labourers, lived hard and precarious lives. The gentry were dominant socially. economically and politically, and they also controlled local justice, administration and education. The great religious and educational upheavals described in the paragraphs above occurred in the face of stiff opposition from the majority of the gentry, who rightly saw

greater literacy, greater freedom and greater political awareness as a long-term threat to their cosy world.

And it was indeed a cosy world. There were few peers in Pembrokeshire, but there was otherwise a strict hierarchy of baronets, knights, esquires and gentlemen. The status of each family was measured in acres, but pedigree was also important, and there was a complex network of patronage and mutual support which maintained the power of the few (probably no more than one per cent of the population belonged to the gentry) and ensured the subservience of the many. There were shifting alliances beteen families; an obsession with "good" marriages; and a constant desire on all sides to move upwards in the social scale. this was the sort of world so acutely observed by Jane Austen in her wonderful novels. There was a constant jostling for position, and family feuds were common which sometimes erupted into violence during parliamentary elections. David Howell, the historian of the Pembrokeshire gentry, talks of a system maintained by a recognition of the "social pretensions and boundless self-esteem of the lesser gentry families."

There are many intriguing glimpses of Pembrokeshire gentry life in Richard Fenton's *Historical Tour Through Pembrokeshire*, first published in 1811 and recently reprinted by Dyfed County Council. We read of their concerns as managers of vast tracts of land, of their petty jealousies, of their political ambitions, and of their social priorities. Much of their life was given over to pleasure or recreation. They had large financial resources, and a great deal of time on their hands since most of the estates were actually run by stewards. Young men in particular were educated at public schools and many went on to Oxford. Popular pursuits were fox-hunting, fishing, billiards, shooting, horse-racing, and gambling. Some young gentlemen went off on the Grand Tour of the Continent. Young ladies were taught the accomplishments of needlework, playing the piano, singing, and writing poetry. Many of the members of the most powerful families spent the winter and spring away from Pembrokeshire, perhaps in London or Bath, on a gay round of concerts, operettas, balls, house parties, and concerts. Pleasant hours were whiled away in clubs and coffee-houses. The wealthiest families took up winter residence in southern France or Italy.

As the powerful families became more powerful, many country mansions were demolished and replaced by even grander houses. In their magnificence, the mansions of Stackpole Court, Lawrenny, Orielton and Slebech came to rival the old fortified residence of Picton Castle. By about 1790 there were other, more modest, mansions dotted all over the Pembrokeshire landscape. But by this time the real world was beginning to catch up with the gentry, for social pretensions had driven many of them to lifestyles which were ultimately not sustainable. Their incomes from agricultural sales and tenant rents could not go on rising for ever, and much of the land on which the gentry based their wealth was not actually of very good quality. The merchant class was growing in size and influence. The common people resented the flaunting of wealth, and began to organize themselves (with the encouragement of the religious and educational reformers) to fight against injustice. So the smaller gentry began to decline, and as the century drew to a close this decline spread further and further up the social ladder. Bankruptcies, property sales, estate amalgamation and litigation increased, and old families with good pedigrees were brought to their knees.

Some faught tooth and nail to delay the inevitable demise of their family estates. One such was John Laugharne, the eccentric squire of Llanrheithan (near Solva) who was the last man in Pembrokeshire to keep a jester on his staff. Over a decade or so, culminating in 1751, he was involved in a series of adventures involving raids, posses, arrests, sieges, seductive young ladies, horrible sisters, private armies, escape attempts from prison, and court cases which kept the good people of Dewisland thoroughly entertained. Indeed, some of the incidents in his ultimately fruitless campaign would not have been out of place in Dodge City or Tombstone.

Protest and Progress

It has often been said that the French invasion killed all sympathy in Wales for the French Revolution and removed any possibility of a revolt of the local peasantry against the ruling classes. This may be so, but South Wales at the onset of the nineteenth century was a region of discontent. There was great hardship among the poorer people of the towns and villages of the coalfield; the suppression and exploitation of industrial workers eventually led to attempts to organize labour representation, and although trades unions became legal after 1824 the discontent boiled over in the terrible clashes in Merthyr in 1831 and the Chartist encounter in Newport (Gwent) in 1839. There were many other clashes in the industrial areas.

There were problems on the land too. Agriculture was passing through a depression, and the rural population was increasing rapidly. There were complete harvest failures in 1816 and 1817, and more or less continuous rain through the summers of 1837 and 1838. The large landowners were enclosing vast tracts of land in West Wales, and pushing the limits of cultivation higher and higher into the hills. There was a serious riot in the Maenclochog district in 1820 against the enlosures of common land in the surrounding hills. Life was hard for the small farmer and the agricultural labourer;

rents were soaring, agricultural prices were falling, and there was great resentment against the new Poor Law legislation which broke up families and condemned poor people to a prison-like existence in the hated Workhouses.

Although the people of the rural areas were slow to organize protest, the demands for better political representation and for social justice did spread into the countryside, and when the first Reform Bill failed in 1831 many rural peoople were involved in rioting in Carmarthen and in noisy demonstrations elsewhere. The abolition of slavery, the new tithe legislation, and the reorganisation of local government in 1834 all helped to heighten public awareness of political issues. Livestock sales seized up and butter was so cheap that it had to be sold to chandlers for use as "a common grease."

The Rebecca Riots

As far as the starving peasant farmers and their families were concerned, survival was a more important matter than penal reform and anti-slavery legislation. The gentry , widely hated aready as exploiters of the rural poor, now became closely involved in the turnpike trusts. Life became even harder for tenants and landless people as new turnpike roads were built out in the countryside and as greater stringency was exercised in the collection of tolls. In West Wales there were many small trusts, each one controlling a part of the road network and operating its own toll-gates but not necessarily using its income to improve the muddy and pot-holed roads.

In the area between Narberth and St Clears most of the roads were owned by the Main and Whitland Trusts. In 1839 the

A famous illustration, from a journal of the time, of Rebecca rioters assaulting one of the Pembrokeshire turnpike trust gates.

latter trust decided to erect new toll-gates on its roads, which were in a very poor state of repair. One of the gates was at Efailwen in the foothills of Mynydd Presely. The gates were brought into use just as the lime-carting season was about to begin. This was the last straw for local farmers, who had suffered extreme hardship because of a succession of bad harvests.

On the night of 13 May, scarcely a week after it had been opened, the gate at Efailwen was destroyed and the toll-house set on fire. The gate was re-erected and provided with seven special constables for its protection, but on the night of 6 June 1839 a mob of about 400 arrived on the scene, drove off the constables and smashed down the gate and the toll-house. All were disguised; some wore women's clothes and had blackened faces. A week or so later another mob, similarly disguised, smashed down another new gate at Maes-gwyn north of Whitland. On 17 July, this time in broad daylight, a crowd of "black-faced women" again smashed the Efailwen gate, and the leader was referred to as "Becca". Whoever she was -- and she was probably Thomas Rees, a pugilist who farmed at Carnabwth in the parish of Mynachlog-ddu -- Rebecca won a remarkable victory, for the riots were followed by an order from the Whitland Trust for the dismantling of the four new gates. So the legend of Rebecca and her daughters was born.

In 1842-3 there was more rioting over the toll-gates, and this time it started at St Clears. Here, near the junction of roads owned by the Main and Whitland Trusts farmers, cattle drovers and other travellers had to pay tolls twice within a mile as a result of a new gate built to prevent toll avoidance. In November and December 1842 the gates in St Clears were destroyed by Rebecca and her daughters on three occasions. At Pwll-trap in Carmarthenshire the destruction of the gate was accompanied by a little pantomime which frequently thereafter became a part of the rioting. Approaching the gate, Rebecca would say in Welsh: "My children, this gate has no business to be here, has it?" The reply would come, "No, it has not!" Then the "children" would ask what should be done with it. On receiving the reply that it should be destroyed, Rebecca's daughters would remove the chain and cut off the gateposts.

Now the rioting spread like wildfire. There was no shortage of men inclined to play the role of Rebecca, and no shortage of followers. Gates were destroyed at many places in Pembrokeshire, for example at Prendergast in Haverfordwest, Narberth, Robeston Wathen and Whitland. On one famous occasion (11 September 1843), the town of Fishguard was occupied by Rebecca and her daughters, who destroyed the toll gates and toll houses with the support of the whole population and with no opposition from the forces of law and order.

The violence spread further afield, with gates being destroyed in the Teifi and Tywi valleys and eventually in the semi-industrial area of south Carmarthenshire. Local militiamen, professional troops and special constables were pressed into service to quell the rioting, and eventually the open riots were replaced by greater secrecy and by more sinister activities on the part of Rebecca and her daughters. Soon they transferred their attention to other grievances besides the toll-gates, and at the culmination of the rioting in 1843 matters occasionally got out of control and the original objectives of Rebecca were largely forgotten. In the country north-west of Llanelli a gang led by Shoni Sgubor Fawr and Dai'r Cantwr represented the lunatic fringe of the movement. David Williams, one of the historians of the Rebecca Riots, wrote "By day the countryside seemed quiet, but at night fantastically disguised horsemen careered along highways and through narrow lanes on their mysterious errands. They developed uncanny skill in evading the police and the infantry, and although their mounts were unwieldy farm horses, they also succeeded in outwitting the dragoons."

Although a number of "Rebeccas" and their daughters were captured, tried and even transported to the penal colonies of Tasmania, the riots which began in Pembrokeshire achieved their objectives, for a commission which met in 1844 resulted in legislation which removed many of the turnpike grievances. By their somewhat grotesque activities, Rebecca and her daughters gave a jolt to authority and made their own life on the land a little easier to bear.

Emigration and Immigration

When we concentrate on Pembrokeshire affairs we are in danger of losing sight of some of the great events affecting the destiny of Europe and America. The "parting shot" of the last glacial episode was The Little Ice Age, during which the world came dangerously close to the brink of another full-scale glaciation. Between 1500 and 1900 the northern hemisphere climate deteriorated, culminating around 1750 and around 1850 in periods of harsh snowy winters and cold rainy summers. In the high valleys of Scandinavia and the Alps the glaciers advanced, and in the lowland parts of Europe the spectre of famine was never far away from the peasants and poor tenant farmers who had to eke out a living on the sodden cold land.

Gradually, as the rural population expanded, conditions of "acceptable hardship" were replaced by conditions of unremitting misery and even starvation. The

population of Iceland was halved. In Ireland the Potato Famine of the 1840's resulted in 1.5 million deaths and sowed the seeds of the social resentment and unrest which have continued to this day on that unhappy island. Death stalked the hovels and rural cottages of Norway and Sweden. One of the consequences was "The Great Emigration", one of the largest folk migrations to affect Europe prior to the terrors of the Second World War. Hundreds of thousands of people left the land and moved to the towns and cities and to the burgeoning industrial centres where coal and iron were bringing unimaginable wealth to the few at the expense of the many. In South Wales some were pulled to the coalfields and the iron towns by the prospect of work and improved living conditions; far more were pushed from the countryside not only by the social conditions which led to the Rebecca Riots, but also by the horrors of failed crops, rotting potatoes and dying animals.

Hundreds of families decided to make a complete break, and to sail off to the virgin lands of the New World. As the demand for emigration built up, improvements in sailing ship design made the prospect of trans-Atlantic travel less daunting than it had been. Ship-owners built new passenger vessels or converted old cargo ships to take passengers, and before 1850 a thriving trade built up, with passages to the New World widely advertised through handbills, newspapers and posters. More and more families set their sights on America, saved up their pennies to pay for their tickets, and sailed off into the sunset from Aberystwyth, Cardigan and Fishguard. Even small ports such as Newport and Solva participated in the trans-Atlantic passenger trade. The emigration built up to a peak around 1880-1890, and many Pembrokeshire people were involved. But by that time steamships had replaced the old sailing vessels, and the cheapest passages were being offered on big passenger ships sailing from Liverpool. Smaller vessels took people from Cardigan to Liverpool for trans-shipment; the standard all-in fare was about £3.

While thousands of local people left Pembrokeshire during the Nineteenth Century, thousands more came into the county, attracted by the prospect of jobs at Milford, Pembroke Dock and the other growing towns. Many of the men who brought their families with them were miners, iron workers and builders; others were labourers or navvies needed for the work on the railways. They came from Ireland, England, Scotland and from even further afield, adding to the already rich social mix of the old county.

The Coming of the Railway

The old communications network of Pembrokeshire was transformed by the arrival of the railway in Pembrokeshire. The iron rails, and the strange vehicles that ran upon them, were welcomed by thousands of local people as reducing the power of the Turnpike Trusts and the hated "toll farmers". The most significant developments occurred between 1850 and 1866, and the rail network was further extended during the later decades of the century, allowing both passengers and cargo to reach the growing urban centres of Cardiff, Bristol, Birmingham and London with comparative ease.

In Westminster, there was a seemingly endless succession of Acts of Parliament designed to enable hundreds of railway projects to go ahead. Many of them failed. But throughout West Wales there were crowded meetings of businessmen, investors and landowners as railway fever spread far and wide. Surveyors trudged across the Pembrokeshire landscape,

appearing in remote hamlets with their assistants and their strange instruments. Maps were drawn, legal agreements were signed, and then the navvies moved in. Many of them were Irish and English, but thousands of Welshmen were also attracted by the prospect of good money in exchange for hard work. The navvies moved from one railway project to another; the gangs or teams were fiercely independent and close-knit, protecting their territories from outsiders. They worked prodigiously and drank hard, and there were frequent weekend brawls involving groups of Englishmen, Irishmen and Welshmen. In one episode, on 13 October 1874, an Engishmen was killed after a drunken brawl with three local men at one of the Maenclochog Railway work camps. The three men were arrested and charged with murder. At the trial in Haverfordwest, the local jury released all three, obviously believing that since the dead man was only an Englishman the crime was not really very serious. As the railway lines snaked their slow and painful way across country, these work camps would be set up and used for a few weeks at a time, bringing total disruption to the host community but a great deal of trade to local shopkeepers and innkeepers.

The South Wales Railway reached Haverfordwest in 1854, and was extended to Neyland by 1856. South of the Haven the rail link from Whitland to Pembroke Dock, via Tenby, was completed in 1866. Milford was given its own rail link in 1863. In the north of the county the railways were built at a much slower pace. The earliest line was the Narberth Road and Maenclochog Railway which reached the Rosebush slate quarries in 1876. This line, then known as the North Pembroke and Fishguard Railway, was extended to Fishguard in 1899, but it was destined to fail. This was hardly surprising, for it ran through very difficult country (with steep gradients) in the Presely Hills, and it could not compete with the

The railway station in Rosebush -- an oil painting from 1887. (Gareth Williams)

new line built from Clarbeston Road via Letterston to Fishguard Harbour in 1906. In that year there were four main rail termini in the county, and the railway network was quite substantial. It included the lines of the Saundersfoot Railway in the south-east, and the line transporting slate from the quarries in the hills below Mynydd Presely. Later on (1929) the Hook Colliery Railway was also added.

The extraordinary story of the North Pembroke and Fishguard Railway, and the little settlement of Rosebush to which it gave birth, is worth recounting. The railway, which started life as the Narberth Road and Maenclochog Railway, was constructed between 1872 and 1876 between Clynderwen and Rosebush to export slates from the Rosebush slate quarries. The driving force between the whole project was the owner of the quarries, Edward Cropper, who was more visionary than entrepreneur. His line somehow attracted sufficient passenger traffic to Rosebush station in the wild Presely foothills to encourage six years of development. Artificial lakes were dug

out and stocked with fish, a coach service to Fishguard was inaugurated, stables were built adjacent to Rosebush station, and extensions to the value of £30,000 were carried out in the quarry. The "Precelly Hotel" was built to accommodate tourists, and twenty-six cottages were built for quarry workers. Sir Hugh Owen, the local squire, provided signposts for the tourists and built a gymnasium for the nearby Maenclochog school. By 1880 the population of Rosebush had risen from four families living in squalid conditions to a total of 179. The slate quarry was thriving, but its good fortune did not last long.

After a series of financial escapades Rosebush was linked to Fishguard in 1899 by a line which enjoyed only a short period of prosperity. It was taken over by the GWR which determined, as part of its plans for the development of Fishguard Harbour, to run down the difficult (and badly constructed) line through the uplands and to concentrate instead upon a link from Clarbeston Road to Letterston junction. After 1906 all the boat trains used the new main line, and the North Pembrokeshire branch became just one more of the vast network of branch lines run by the GWR. The Rosebush slate quarries closed around 1900, and apart from intermittent passenger services the line was little used. The track was lifted in 1914 as part of the war effort, but re-laid again by 1923. Now the GWR itself attempted to attract tourist traffic to the Presely Hills, but no more than 50-100 passengers per week could be induced to use the line. For a while the local rabbit trade kept the line alive, but passenger services ceased in1937. In the Second World War the track was used by the RAF for bombing practice. In 1949 the last goods train ran on the North Pembrokeshire branch, and in 1952 all the track was lifted.

Today Rosebush still retains an air of fascination. The little settlement, dominated by its abandoned quarries, still inhabited, and still served by the Precelly Hotel (now called Tafarn Sinc), is a fascinating relic of the county's industrial past. The row of quarrymen's cottages is still in excellent repair. Many of the homes have traditional cement-washed slate roofs, and some have colour-washed outside walls in pastel shades. Nearby is the site of the old railway station, and across the track is the solid memorial erected in honour of Edward Cropper, the Hon Mrs Owen and J B Macaulay, all of whom were involved in the establishment of the settlement. The old lily-ponds are still there, and the multitude of planted conifers, rhododendrons and other exotic shrubs gives a hint of what the place could have become if circumstances had not combined to plot its downfall.

Away from the village the sweep of the old railway line can still be followed, running through the coniferous plantations which are gradually covering the floor of the broad Rosebush depression. Even further away one can still trace the cuttings, embankments, stations and halts of the railway, for example at New Inn, Puncheston, Beulah and Letterston, and the course of the track is marked on O S maps.

The economic impact of the railway companies upon nineteenth-century Pembrokeshire was considerable. Their new lines were connected in part with confident and grandiose schemes typical of the mid-Victorian era. As we will see in the next chapter, Isambard Kingdom Brunel was personally involved in a number of these schemes, providing both the vision and the engineering expertise required to bring them to fruition. So Neyland was conceived as the terminus of the South Wales Railway and as the great trans-Atlantic port; the Pembroke Dock line was built as an essential component in the development of the Royal Naval Dockyard; and the line to Fishguard Harbour was completed, in the face of great engineering difficulties, because the GWR was determined that Fishguard should win its battle with Liverpool to attract the big new passenger lines which were appearing on the trans-Atlantic routes. Of course the visions were seldom turned into reality; neither Neyland nor Fishguard succeeded as trans-Atlantic ports, and other planned developments (including a new harbour at Aber-mawr and a branch line to serve the Nolton-Newgale Coalfield) failed to happen, partly because of the economic problems which plagued the small railway companies of the day.

But by the end of the century most of the people of Pembrokeshire had access to the railway not only through the main stations but also through the smaller stations and halts such as Crymych, Letterston, Puncheston, Clarbeston Road, Saundersfoot and Lamphey. These stations provided an excellent and regular passenger service and also allowed the export of raw materials and manufactured products, including slate from Rosebush, bricks from Templeton and Goodwick, butter-churns from Haverfordwest, silver-lead ore from

Llanfyrnach, pig-iron from Saundersfoot, and of course coal from Kilgetty, Stepaside and other mining communities in the centre and south of the county. Pembrokeshire's industrial revolution would not have occurred had it not been for the growth of the rail network. But the coming of the railway had dramatic social consequences for the rural communities of the county, for over a period of 25 years a whole new world was opened to them.

The Tithe War

The Tithe War of the 1880's had important repercussions throughout Wales and further afield in England. Its root cause was, as indicated above, the poverty and over-population of the rural areas, with small tenant farmers (many of them non-conformists) living close to the breadline and finding themselves forced into the payment of tithes to their local Anglican clergy. In the 1880's there was an agricultural depression. But it was the "religious" dimension that now came to the fore, since few people identified with the church. In 1885 and 1886, within the space of twelve months, there were two General Elections in which the disestablishment of the Anglican Church became a major issue.

Trouble had been brewing up since the 1700's, when disputes between the clergy and the lesser squires of Pembrokeshire were common. For example, in 1749 the belligerent vicar of Llanrheithan beat up the local squire for refusing to pay his corn tithes! Things deteriorated further in 1836, with the legislation which required the payment of tithes in cash rather than in kind. Tithes also went up by as much as thirty per cent. In some parishes tithes were collected even though there was no resident priest and even though the local church was in ruins! In such circumstances the issue of tithes became one of great church - chapel animosity.

In the period 1886-1891 there were many ugly confrontations between Pembrokeshire farmers and the agents, bailiffs, police contingents and auctioneers responsible for the collection of tithe dues and for the disposal of debtors' property. Clergymen, through no fault of their own, were frequently abused and ostracised. Nobody was killed, but there were many injuries. Some of the early trouble was in the parishes of Llangolman and Maenclochog, and there were tithe "strikes" where the clergy would not agree to a remittance of tithe payments. In Llanhowell near St David's the vicar, Rev John Evans, had great difficulty in arranging an auction to recover unpaid tithes, and when it did go ahead the auctioneers were pelted with rotten eggs and had to abandon the proceedings. A stuffed effigy of the vicar was paraded back and forth by an angry crowd. In Llangolman in 1890 the church windows were smashed with stones four times. "Distraint" sales were held, and the auctioneers, bailiffs and police involved in the of recovery of unpaid tithes were subject to abuse, harassment and even physical assault. There were ambushes in lonely places, and a welter of prosecutions for assault and disturbances of the peace came before the magistrates. But often the offenders were let off with nominal fines, and it became clear that the magistrates and many members of the County Council were more sympathetic towards the farmers than they were towards the church.

The demonstrations and riots led to the introduction of new legislation in 1891 which shifted the tithe burden from tenant farmers to their landlords. Small farmers who owned their own land were not affected by the new law, but Parliament introduced new tithe exemptions related to the "annual value" of land, and many owner-occupiers found their burdens greatly reduced. As the century drew to a close the storm waves of political and social upheaval rolled away and left a state of relative calm.

Chapter Nine

Seafaring and Life by the Sea

The influence of the sea pervades every part of Pembrokeshire, and as mentioned in Chapter 1 the sea has to be considered as one of the great "themes" of the county. Because of its very irregular coastal outline, and especially because of the presence of the ancient drowned river-system of Milford Haven and the Daugleddau, no part of the county is more than 15 km from the sea. In addition, the wide variety of coastal environments provides literally hundreds of good landing-places for vessels of all types, ranging from muddy creeks and narrow tidal inlets to open sandy beaches, and from sheltered rocky coves to splendid natural harbours like Solva and Milford Haven.

A typical two-masted ketch. Vessels similar to this carried the lifeblood of Pembrokeshire's coastal communities for hundreds of years.

Pembrokeshire people have always lived in rare intimacy with the sea; only one Pembrokeshire town (Narberth) is located away from tidal waters, and the visitor is just as likely to find families with long seafaring traditions in Haverfordwest or Llangwm as in Solva, Fishguard, Milford or Tenby. Even in the 1700s and early 1800s the land traveller from England could only reach this remote western peninsula after a long and wearying road journey; no wonder, then, that the sea has always been Pembrokeshire's great highway. We have already (in Chapter 7) looked at the old fishing industry of Pembrokeshire, and in the paragraphs that follow we examine some of the other manifestations of the county's maritime tradition.

Coastal Trading

The seventeenth and eighteenth centuries were exciting ones in the lives of the Pembrokeshire ports. Coastal trading developed rapidly, and storehouses and lime-kilns as well as stone quays and jetties were constructed wherever there was a need for the export and import of goods and wherever coastal conditions were suitable. The road network of the county, and of the rest of South Wales, was quite inadequate to cope with the long-distance transport of bulky loads, and almost everything was moved by sea. Such roads as there were in the coastal districts converged on the nearest small port. Manufactured goods became more and more prominent as items in the shipping registers, and minerals such as coal, limestone and slate became important as the value of the woollen trade gradually declined.

A beached trading vessel being unloaded at Parrog, Newport, around 1920. Such scenes were familiar in many of the ports and harbours of Pembrokeshire. (John Havard)

Coastal trading in George Owen's day had been organized and financed by the local gentry and the merchants of the main towns, to an increasing extent after 1650 local farmers, fishermen, townspeople and joiners shared in the ownership of small vessels. They shared, too, in the profits as their ships traded in a vast range of commodities with an ever-increasing number of British and foreign ports. For example, in 1603 almost all of the overseas trading contacts were with Ireland and France, but a century later there were many links with Spain, Portugal, Holland, Germany, and ports across the Atlantic. Whereas in 1603 most of the coastwise shipments were to and from Bristol, Barnstaple, North Wales and South Devon, the port books for the later part of the seventeenth century show that the number of trading links had increased and diversified greatly. The volume of trade was substantial; for example, in 1680 alone there were no less than 793 shipping movements in and out of Pembrokeshire ports. In addition, there must have been many more movements which were deliberately or "accidentally" omitted from the port books and registers.

Shipbuilding

There was thriving local shipbuilding industry, and by about 1800 small vessels were being built at thirty or more coastal sites. Only in a few places (such as Fishguard, Newport and Lawrenny) were there proper shipyards, and most vessels were simply constructed on temporary slipways on the beach just above high water mark. But there was considerable local craftsmanship involved; some of the ships' timbers were cut in the county, and sails, fittings and ropes were generally made by local craftsmen. Most of the early vessels built were ketches and sloops (fore-and-aft rigged) of less than twenty tons and often less than forty feet long; but in the later part of the eighteenth century larger sloops of twenty to forty tons were being built, as well as schooners and square-rigged vessels of 100 tons or more.

Most of the memories of those ship-building days have been dimmed with time, but many of the old "shipyards" can still be located by reference to old maps and through conversations with the older inhabitants of coastal communities. On an old map of about 1856 "shipyards" are shown at Whalecwm (Cosheston), Lawrenny and several other sites in the inner reaches of Milford Haven. There are some details of the shipyard at Cosheston in the writings of Florence Howell, one of the literary sisters who lived at Blackpool Mill and Whalecwm. The shipbuilding business there was owned by David Morgan and Thomas Howell. Many ships were built to order for Liverpool ship-owners, and it was the custom in the late 1800s for the ships' captains to stay at Cosheston during the final stages of building in order to supervise the details of fittings, rigging and sails. Up to thirty men and boys were employed at the yard, and there was an apprenticeship of seven years. Local oak was widely used, and the ships' seams were caulked with "oakum and pitch". The larger ships took two years or more to build, and they were launched down the greased slipway with due ceremony, often by the new owner's wife. This was followed by a launch dinner: "a fine spread on the mould loft; and that night we had singing and dancing until the early hours of next morning". Then came the fitting-out process, with the erection of the masts, the construction of the superstructure, the fitting of the rigging and the making up of sails. Then, again in the words of Florence Howell's old shipwright, "......when she was ready for sea, everybody on the place went aboard, and the Minister

come, and we had a service aboard the new ship, prayers and singing and a short sermon. After that, we went ashore, her crew up anchor, her sails was hoisted, and down the Haven she sailed. We watched her till she was out o'sight, on her road to the sea."

Wrecks and Rescues

The Pembrokeshire coast may appear beautiful to the average tourist, but it was full of terror for mariners in the days of sail before 1850, and afterwards as steamships became more and more numerous upon the western seaways. Nobody knows how many ships have been lost on the cliffs, shoals and reefs of the coastline, but there are thousands of recorded shipwrecks. Maritime historian Tom Bennett, who has made a special study of the Pembrokeshire coast, has described at least 500 wrecks in his various publications.

Some idea of the excitement of Pembrokeshire coastal life during the era of sea-trading can be gained from the old port books and from contemporary ships' logs and other records; but some people enjoyed more excitement than others. Several remote coastal communities indulged in wrecking activities, and the historian Richard Fenton (writing in 1811) tells us that Llanunwas, near Solva, "had the reputation of hanging out false lights to decoy the wandering mariner in order to benefit from his misfortunes". Ships driven on to the rocky coasts during storms were rapidly relieved of their cargoes, often with the energetic help of the local customs officers. Several coastal localities have names connected with flotsam and jetsam, or with particular shipwrecks, or with smuggling. For instance, we have Brandy Bay and Dutch Gin near St Bride's Haven, Driftwood on Ramsey, and Ogof Tobacco near Solva.

There are numerous Pembrokeshire tales to compete with *Whisky Galore*. A report of 1668, concerning the fate of the cargo vessel **Amity**, reads: "The ship being at anchor in Ramsey Sound was by a violent storme put from her anchors and nothing to be expected but death, the men deserted her and went ashore on Ramsey Island in their boats: the ship ran ashore near St David's Head where the country people were soe barbarous that they staved the wine casks in so much the master saved not anything considerable only some fruit which we indemnified." As we saw in the last chapter, the failure of the French Invasion of 1797 was due in no small measure to the abundance of Portuguese wine discovered by the motley army in the farmhouses of Pencaer following a recent shipwreck. When the iron trading ship **Loch Shiel** was wrecked on the rocks of Thorn Island near Angle in 1894, cases of whisky were washed up on local beaches inside and outside the Haven. Many people risked their lives in trying to recover them; and it is ironic that while all of the passengers and crew of the vessel were rescued, at least

three local people died as a direct consequence of the hunt for contraband. The locals believe that there are still many bottles of **Loch Shiel** whisky hidden away in the village. In his book *The Sounds Between*, Roscoe Howells tells another story handed down by the older boatmen of St David's. Apparently several casks of strong drink were washed ashore on Ramsey Island where they were found by the men working on the farm. They drank well, and then hid the remaining casks. However, they were so drunk at the time that they failed afterwards to rediscover the casks. That, at any rate, was the story which they told to the enforcement officers, whose repeated searches proved fruitless!

It is natural that those Pembrokeshire folk who live by the sea should have an instinct for looking for wreckage. It is also natural that those communities inhabiting the western tips of the county's several peninsulas should have

A Norwegian barque wrecked on the rocks beneath the Old Fort in Fishguard Bay, November 1893. (Studio Jon)

developed this instinct most strongly, for the areas around the islands of Ramsey and Skomer have always been extremely dangerous to shipping. Ramsey Sound, Jack Sound and Broad Sound (between Skokholm and Skomer) have been the scenes of many shipwrecks, and the people of St David's, Solva and Marloes have been involved in many epic rescues. However, even into the present century newspaper comment about local priorities has not always been kind: "This coast, we believe, has in the ancient times past, enjoyed, or rather been credited with a rather dubious reputation as to whether life saving or property salving comes first in the correct order of things ......" In 1908 the Austrian steamer **Szent Istvan** went ashore on Ramsey Island in dense fog. It was carrying general cargo worth £200,000, and much of this was washed ashore in St Bride's Bay after the ship went down. The newspaper report says 'Parts of the shores of St Bride's Bay were literally strewn with wreckage. From St David's to Little Haven the people were busily engaged on Sunday in salving it ...... At Solva the 'wreckers' - if that term is permissible - included deacons, and respectable tradesmen, publicans and sinners, cobblers and hooligans, all bent on the same errand." Naturally enough the deacons and other good people of Solva were deeply offended by this report, for they all knew that the real wrecking activities of the community were long since over.

There is another delightful tale of a Marloes parson who had one of his church services disturbed by a messenger with news of a newly wrecked vessel beneath the nearby cliffs. The service could obviously not continue under such distressing and promising circumstances; so after imploring his congregation to show moderation in all things, the parson appealed to them to give him a head's start en route to the site of the wreck. He had, he explained, lost something of his youthful turn of speed with the passing of the years.

One of the most infamous episodes in the history of Pembrokeshire shipwrecks concerns the loss of the American three-masted sailing vessel named **Phoebe and Peggy** in 1773. She was smashed to pieces on the rocks near the entrance to Solva Harbour during a fearsome storm, and sixty people lost their lives, including several would-be rescuers. Afterwards, as corpses were washed up onto the beaches, many of them were stripped of their valuables; one dead lady had her fingers cut off by a pair of local ruffians intent on recovering her rings, and her ear-rings were ripped from her ears. Some local people were so incensed by the behaviour of the "corpse robbers" that a simple ballad was composed and published in the county newspaper. It contained the following words: "they stripped the ladies of their jewels.... They left them there like stinking fishes."

While the gathering up of wreckage was a perfectly normal part of Pembrokeshire life in the days of sail, shipwrecks were frequently accompanied by heroic rescues. There were no proper lifeboats stationed on the coast until 1824, and before that date rescues were largely a matter of chance, dependent upon the sharp eyes of local people and circumstances in which vessels for distress could be approached by small open boats or by line from the cliffs. During the nineteenth century lifeboat stations were established at Fishguard, Tenby, Angle and St David's, and these four stations still exist. Other short-lived stations were also established at Little Haven, Newport and Solva. Until 1909 all of the lifeboats were powered by oars and sail. Some of them had to be launched through the surf from cumbersome horse-drawn wagons, and one can only admire the skill, courage and physical prowess of the lifeboatmen who risked life and limb with every launch and every rescue. Their efforts were complemented by the companies of volunteers who operated the "life-saving apparatus" of mortars, rockets, lines and breeches buoys to haul people to safety from sheer cliffs or rocks inaccessible to the lifeboats.

Coxwain David Hicks, who served for 23 years on the St David's lifeboat "Augusta".

There are hundreds of stirring tales of rescues involving the Pembrokeshire lifeboats. The St David's lifeboat **Augusta** rescued nine sailors from the wreck of the **Mystic Tie** in 1877. In 1920 Coxwain John Howells of the Fishguard lifeboat **Charterhouse** was awarded the gold medal of the RNLI for a heroic rescue of seven seamen from the sinking **Hermina** near Needle Rock. In an operation which has become a part of Pembrokeshire folklore, the Angle lifeboat **Elizabeth Elson** rescued 28 people from the wreck of the **Molesey** on Midland Isle in 1929. Between 1930 and 1955 the Tenby lifeboat **John R Webb** rescued 53 people, including eight crew members seized from the jaws of death in hurricane conditions in 1938 as the **Fermanagh** foundered near Woolhouse Rocks.

Possibly the most controversial of the local lifeboat rescues involved the St David's lifeboat **Gem**, in October 1910. The lifeboat put to sea in response to a distress call from the ketch **Democrat**, which was in danger of being swept in a gale onto the Bitches reef. The lifeboat took off the crew just after darkness fell, but conditions were so severe that it was itself swept onto the reef in a "boiling mad" sea. The coxwain and two other lifeboatmen were swept away and drowned, but 15 others managed to scramble onto a rock. Nothing was known of their fate until 9 am next morning, when someone saw a signal from the rock. It was then realised that the **Gem** was lost. The storm was still raging, but a young fisherman named Sidney Mortimer (at that time only 18 years old), together with two other local men, launched a rowing boat from Porthclais. In constant danger of being swamped, they managed to reach the rock where the shipwrecked men were stranded, but had to wait for the tide to drop before being able to take them off four hours later. They managed to land ten of them on Ramsey Island, and were going back for the last five when another local boat arrived to help out. Later, Sidney Mortimer was awarded the RNLI silver medal and was showered with other honours, but the highest tribute paid to him was that he was appointed coxwain of the St David's lifeboat, to become the youngest-ever lifeboat coxwain in the British Isles. Sadly, he proved not to be a very effective coxwain, and in the small community of St David's there was a simmering resentment for many years that young Sidney had received all the honours (and made the most of his instant fame) while others who had played just as large a part in the rescue were largely forgotten. Such is life in small communities.

One of the most famous rescues in Pembrokeshire sea-faring history occurred in the year 1793, when at the height of a terrible storm Mrs Margaret Williams of Treleddyn, near St David's, was scanning the seas with her telescope. She sighted a group of shipwrecked mariners clinging to one of the rocks of the Bishops and Clerks, offshore from Whitesands Bay. Single-handedly she immediately launched a small open boat and rowed five miles through fearsome seas to the rock, where she rescued seven Swedish sailors who were close to death. She carried them back safely to the beach at Porthselau, took them home and looked after them until they had all recovered from their ordeal. Inevitably, the redoubtable lady is now known locally as "Pembrokeshire's Grace Darling", and there is a plaque commemorating her heroism in the small Swedish fishing village which was home to the shipwrecked sailors.

Smuggling and Piracy

During the seventeenth and eighteenth centuries smuggling was officially frowned upon, but it was aided and abetted by local municipal officials, JPs and customs men alike. During this sea-trading era, thousands of profitable voyages to and from Pembrokeshire were made as deliberate smuggling enterprises. Many remote coves and creeks were used, sometimes by "free enterprise" smugglers who simply appeared out of the blue, sold their exotic duty-free goods to local people and then disappeared again. One of the local men thoroughly involved in illicit activities was Sir John Perrott of Carew Castle, who was undoubtedly responsible for the disposal of many smuggled and pirated cargoes through the port of Haverfordwest. At Pembroke in 1570 he was involved in the recovery of a ship and its cargo of salt, which had been pirated on the high seas from a Dutch captain by a gang of pirates. Sir John and his friends quietly disposed of both ship and salt, and made sure that the matter never came to court. In 1609 the notorious pirate Thomas Salkeld, the self-styled King of Lundy, sailed into Milford Haven, robbed the people of Dale and burned their houses down, and then stole two fully-laden sailing vessels. A document dated 1611 records that "great quantities of wine" were brought by French merchants into Pembrokeshire ports and discharged "without paying any impost". Quite respectable ships' masters, who normally operated legally, used to carry the occasional illicit cargo just to provide a little extra income and a little extra excitement.

Piracy, although less prevalent in Stuart than in Tudor times, was still by no means a thing of the past. In the year 1633 a pirate vessel captained by a Breton anchored in Ramsey Sound, and twenty-seven of the crew, armed with swords, half-pikes, muskets and pistols, raided the island and made off with assorted cheeses, lambs and sheep. This caused a great stir locally, since a number of local men were thought to have been cooperating with the pirates. During the Civil War and later wars (such as the Napoleonic Wars), piracy was common in St George's Channel and the Bristol Channel, and French vessels were often involved. During the American War of Independence the famous John Paul Jones paid several rapid visits to Pembrokeshire. On one occasion his vessel **Black Prince** entered Fishguard Bay and he demanded a ransom for a merchant vessel which he had seized. There is some doubt as to whether the ransom was paid, but Jones fired two broadsides onto Lower Fishguard and succeeded in damaging a few chimney pots and injuring Richard Fenton's sister Mary. In the south of the county Jones Bay on Caldey Island is reputed to be the place where Jones went ashore for water. According to legend, the ghostly sounds of digging can sometimes be heard on the beach, which leads local people to conclude that the American pirate's buried treasure is there somewhere, just waiting to be discovered.

Pembrokeshire's own favourite pirate was Bartholomew Roberts, born in the hamlet of Little Newcastle in 1682. In 1719 he turned pirate, earning the name "Black Barty". He operated for the most part on the western fringes of the Atlantic Ocean, terrorising the West Indies and the New England colonies. Now and then he also appeared off the coast of Africa. His most famous capture was the Portuguese **Segrada Familia**, a huge warship which contained treasure worth £21 million -- the entire fortune of the King of Portugal. The king was not amused. Barty was a master of sea warfare, using his little Welsh collier **Royal Revenge** to outmanoeuvre every vessel he encountered. But he eventually became over-confident, transferring to a larger and more cumbersome captured French vessel and also needing two smaller vessels to transport his vast and accumulating treasure. In 1722 a task force under Commander Ogle engaged Barty's ships in a naval action, and the flamboyant pirate (who always dressed in fine scarlet garments) was killed by a single sniper's bullet. It was Barty's choice to live "a short life and a merry one", and during his three years of piracy he captured more than 400 ships on the high seas, earning the title of "the terror of the Spanish main". Because of his scarlet clothes, his good humour and his elegant lifestyle, he was referred to by his French adversaries as "le joli rouge"; his lasting memorial was the scull and crossbones emblem on his flag, which he invented and which came to be known as The Jolly Roger.

Smuggling and piracy continued around the Pembrokeshire coast long after the demise of Black Barty. In 1799 the ubiquitous Lord Cawdor of Stackpole Court was severely beaten up by the crew of a smuggling vessel when he tried to confiscate a cargo of Spanish wine being landed on Freshwater East beach. In the early decades of the nineteenth century a gang of Cornish smugglers settled in the Amroth - Marros area and carried on a successful trade in contraband wine and spirits. They used caves and secret cellars to hide their casks and bottles, and the smuggling ring was never broken up by the excise officers. An eighteenth-century ancestor of Major Francis Jones, who was engaged in the coastal trade, carried legal cargoes of grain and illegal (and probably more profitable) cargoes of salt. An old inhabitant of Abereiddi relates that his great-grandfather was the leader of a smuggling gang until he was eventually caught red-handed with a consignment of smuggled tobacco. For his sins he was put away in Portsmouth Jail for a while. In Solva a number of houses have secret cupboards and shafts which may well have been used for concealing smuggled goods.

We should remember that smuggling has always been, and will always be, a fact of life so long as there is a demand for illegal goods and so long as luxury goods are heavily taxed. Cheap wine from French hypermarkets still finds its way by illegal sales into the homes of Pembrokeshire people, and the Seal Bay incident near Newport in 1983 reminds us that cannabis and other drugs are still being brought ashore on dark nights in some of the creeks and coves of our rocky coast.

Lime Burning

George Owen's classic description of lime burning (reproduced on page 60) reminds us that for a period of over 400 years two vital commodities were shipped in great quantities around the Pembrokeshire coast -- namely limestone fragments and anthracite. The anthracite came from the little mines in the three sections of the Pembrokeshire Coalfield (see Chapter 10), and the limestone came mostly from the limestone quarries of Milford Haven and the South Pembrokeshire coast.

The typical Pembrokeshire lime kiln was a circular stone structure up to 5m high, with a flat loading platform adjacent to its top. Access to this loading platform was

The loading tunnel used by horses and carts for loading burnt lime in the huge lime kiln at Kiln Park. Tenby.

provided by a ramp, and horses and carts could also approach the arch or arches at the base of the kiln. Each kiln had a deep pit in its centre which could be packed from the top with alternate layers of broken limestone and culm (a mixture of anthracite dust and clay). The "kiln eyes" at the sides, set in their arched recesses, provided the draught for the burning of the limestone at temperatures up to 1000 degrees C. In some kilns the "eyes" were also used for emptying the kiln when burning was complete; in more elaborate structures there were additional "draw holes" for this purpose, with iron trap-doors. In some of the larger kilns it was possible to draw off burnt lime from the base while the upper layers of the limestone/culm mixture were still alight; such kilns were therefore used continuously, year in and year out. The smaller and cruder kilns (such as those at Abereiddi and Abercastle) were probably used only intermittently. Some of the later kilns were square; good examples can be seen on Skomer Island, at Stackpole Quay, and at Caerbwdi.

The greatest demand for lime came from the north of the county, where farmers were aware that frequent dressing with lime could counteract soil acidity. The quicklime from the kilns was sold by the cart-load. On the farm it was left in heaps until it rained, at which point it broke down in a chemical reaction into a white powder called hydrated or slaked lime. This was the magical substance spread onto the fields by farmers. There was also a considerable demand for lime in the urban areas, where it was used (before the days of Portland cement) in lime mortar for building purposes, and also for making whitewash for walls and roofs.

The hundreds of kilns built in the eighteenth and nineteenth centuries were almost all on the coast, where they could be supplied at regular intervals with their raw materials by small sailing vessels and (within the Milford Haven waterway) by barges. The quicklime, which was the product of the lime kilns, was hardly ever moved by sea, since it became highly dangerous on contact with water. So the lime was sold and used as close to the kiln as possible. Many vessels were used exclusively for the lime burning trade, since their cargoes were bulky and dirty. Sometimes they could come and go freely, but in the majority of the Pembrokeshire harbours and ports their movements were controlled by the tides; for example the clusters of kilns at Haverfordwest, Solva and Porthclais could only be approached when the tide was high,

and the same was true of the kilns at Abereiddi, Newport, Nolton and many other seafaring centres. In most localities the ships dumped their cargoes on the beach, and horses and carts were used for transferring the stone and coal to the loading platforms of the nearby kilns. Old photographs show that cargoes were also dumped on the river bed at Haverfordwest. Some kilns were located in the most unexpected of places, for example at Caerbwdi, on the muddy shore of the Pembroke River at Lambeeth, at St Bride's, on the banks of the Teifi up-river from Cardigan, and at Shiphill on the Nevern Estuary.

Many of these little kilns, now almost lost in tangles of trees and brambles and in a parlous state of repair after a century or more of neglect, are quiet reminders

A trading vessel below the New Bridge, Haverfordwest, around 1910. Note the piles of limestone intended for the Cartlett kilns.

of the way in which the focal points of economic life shift from century to century. Around the kilns there was always a buzz of activity. They required constant attention, and the lime-burner and his family almost always lived in a nearby cottage, up-wind of the kiln if possible. Tramps and other homeless people were attracted by the warmth of the kilns, especially during the winter; they would sleep on the kiln top, and some died because of exposure to the poisonous fumes. Cart tracks radiated like the spokes of a wheel from the kilns out into the surrounding countryside. During the lime carting season there would be a constant procession of horses and carts collecting quicklime; there would be frequent visits from vessels delivering limestone and anthracite, with episodes of hectic activity at low tide when unloading was under way; and some of the kilns) for example Shiphill near Newport) had adjacent ship-building yards, now mostly lost without trace.

Local author Peter Davies has reminded us, in his little book *The Lime Kilns of Dewisland,* just how important these features are as a part of our local heritage. While many have disappeared, there are good historical records of the main lime-burning centres in particular. For example, we know that in 1908 there were still eight kilns working in Solva, eleven in Haverfordwest, and seventeen in Tenby, including the magnificent complex at Kiln Park reputedly designed by John Nash and supplied direct from its own limestone quarry. The last "draw kilns" operated in Haverfordwest in 1930 and in Tenby as late as 1948. A few culm and limestone barges were still operating around Milford Haven at the onset of the Second World War. However, the lime burning business was eventually killed off because of the ease with which farmers could buy cheap mass-produced lime by the sack or in bulk, delivered by rail to the nearest station or by motor lorry to the farmyard.

The Pembrokeshire Lighthouses

The difficulties of navigating on the Pembrokeshire coast have led to the construction of a number of lighthouses on rocky headlands and islands. The earliest may have been on St Ann's Head, at the mouth of Milford Haven, back in Tudor times; it was probably nothing more than a raised platform with a bonfire on top. The present lighthouse is probably the fourth to occupy the site. There are other lighthouses at Strumble Head, on Caldey Island and on Skokholm Island, and a lightship is stationed off the coast near St Govan's Head.

The most valuable lighthouses of all are those which guard the Bishops and Clerks, off Ramsey Island, and the Smalls, far out beyond the gannet island of Grassholm. The Bishops and Clerks were dreaded by ships' masters in the days of sail, and their evil reputation elicited this poetic and much-quoted statement from George Owen:

"The Bishop and these his Clerks preach deadly doctrine to their winter audience, such poor seafaring men as are forced thither by tempest. Only in one thing they are to be commended, they keep residence better than the rest of the canons of that see are wont to do."

The South Bishop Light was built in 1839, but it was preceded by some sixty years by the famous structure built on the Smalls rock by Henry Whiteside. The Smalls lighthouse was the brainchild of one John Phillips, a Cardiganshire man who was a docks manager in Liverpool. He knew from his friends who were merchants and mariners just how lethal the rock was, and determined to do something about it. Having scraped together sufficient funds for the construction work, he engaged Henry Whiteside as his engineer. Whiteside evolved a cunning plan by which the lighthouse could be built on a submerged rock and yet provide minimal obstruction to the passage of fierce currents and violent storm-waves; it was to be an octagonal house of timber mounted on nine legs, three of which were to be of cast iron and six of wood. This was a revolutionary design, and it was greeted with scepticism by most of the sea-faring community. Nevertheless, Whiteside set to work on the construction project, using Solva as his base. The great timber pillars and all the other materials were shipped the twenty-two miles to the desolate hidden rocks of the Smalls and, in spite of bad weather during the first season of construction, the light was lit for the first time on 1 September 1776.

Henry Whiteside of Solva, the builder of the first Smalls Lighthouse and one of the key figures in Pembrokeshire maritime history.

The vibrations and movement of Whiteside's strange structure during gales caused the lighthouse-keepers to suffer from sea-sickness, so in January 1777 the designer determined to stay there himself with a blacksmith so as to affect repairs and improvements. The weather closed in, and they were stranded on the Smalls during a period of appalling storms. Conditions became almost unbearable, and at last, with all of their fresh water gone and no fire to warm them, they decided to call for help. They wrote out three similarly worded messages, put them inside wooden casks, and threw them into the sea. By incredible good luck, one of the casks was washed up after only a few days near the home of Thomas Williams of Treleddyn. He was acting agent for John Phillips, and it was he who, a few years later, was to raise the alarm at the time of the Last Invasion of Britain. He was also the husband of the intrepid Mrs Williams whose heroism was recounted on page 105. Being a man of action, Mr Williams had the stranded lighthouse builders rescued in no time at all.

After further modifications the original Smalls lighthouse stood for eighty years. Fees were levied on all passing ships, and in its day it was the most profitable lighthouse in the world. Then in 1861 it was replaced by a more modern stone structure. Again the community of Solva was involved in the construction work, providing homes for the workmen and experiencing much activity associated with the import of Cornish granite, the dressing of the stones, and the transport of the shaped blocks by steam tugs and barges out to the Smalls.

The original Smalls Light was the scene of one of the most famous episodes in the history of British lighthouses. The tale is a somewhat gruesome one which made a great impact upon public opinion and upon the management of lighthouses nationwide. In the year 1801 two men (who were not on the best of terms) were keeping the lighthouse when one of them, named Thomas Griffiths, died during a violent storm. His companion Thomas Howell was afraid lest he should be suspected of foul play, so he decided not to cast the corpse into the sea. Instead he made a crude box or coffin from some of the interior fittings of the house, and placed the body in it. Then he lashed it outside to the lantern rail, high above the waves and quite visible to passing ships. Although various seafarers saw this strange object from a distance, none of them stopped, for the light was working and there was no obvious cause for concern. However, as the weeks passed the corpse began to decompose and the coffin, constantly battered by gale-force winds, began to fall apart. According to legend, a bony arm flopped over the side of the box, and fleshless fingers, moved by the wind, tapped against the window of the lonely house where Thomas Howell lived out his nightmare. When at last poor Howell was relieved at the end of his four-month tour of duty he was half demented, and spent the rest of his life in a lunatic asylum. Since that time Trinity House has insisted that all lighthouses should be manned by three keepers working together.

Hard Times for the Little Ships

The nineteenth century was a time of accelerating change in Pembrokeshire as elsewhere, and if we can point to one event which signalled the end of the sea-trading era it was the coming of the railway to Haverfordwest in 1854. From this year onwards bulky goods could be transported rapidly and cheaply overland. As we have seen in Chapter 7, the decade 1854 - 1864 saw the opening of many new railway stations, particularly in south Pembrokeshire. Others were opened in the north in the later decades of the century, and with the passing of the years the Pembrokeshire sea trade suffered a slow, lingering death.

By 1900 there were few local vessels carrying coastwise cargoes. In addition to

An old painting of Solva Harbour in the eighteenth century. Note the lime kilns and beached trading vessels.

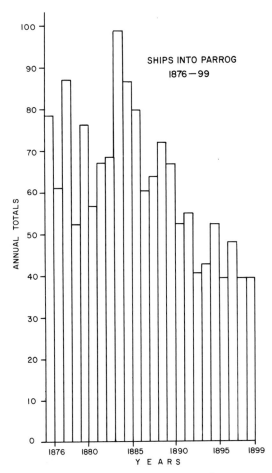

SHIPS INTO PARROG
1876 — 99

ANNUAL TOTALS

Y E A R S

A graph of shipping movements in Parrog, Newport, in the last quarter of the nineteenth century. Note the gradual decline.

the effect of the railways, the road network was now much improved, so that the last of the shipowners and merchants were forced by competition to concentrate on the few largest and most efficient ports (eg Haverfordwest, Fishguard and Milford). Some general cargo trade also survived in the little ports which were remote from the rail termini, such as Dale, Solva, Newport and Porthclais. As we shall see in Chapter 11, Pembrokeshire's industrial activities were crucial in keeping some ports open. For example, Saundersfoot harbour exported coal from Bonville's Court Colliery until about

1930, and the Hook Quay and some other Daugleddau quays continued to ship out anthracite even after the building of the Hook Colliery railway in 1929. As indicated above, limestone and anthracite continued to be delivered to Solva and Newport up until the time of the First World War, and occasional visits were made by small steamships and by ketches such as the famous **Garlandstone** (launched in 1909) during the 1920s and 1930s. Elsewhere steamships were used for the transport of special cargoes, including the export of roadstone and bricks from Porthgain and the import of coke to the St David's gas-works at the head of the little harbour of Porthclais.

After the Second World War most of the quays, jetties and harbour walls fell into disrepair. The old sea-wall across the entrance of Porthclais Harbour became ruinous. On the Parrog in Newport a sea trading tradition that had lasted for 700 years faded away as the estuary was allowed to silt up, isolating the old slate-built quays and warehouses from the open sea. Silt and sand piled up in the harbours of Tenby and Saundersfoot, and at the mouth of the Teifi estuary the sandbar was allowed to extend so far to the west that access to the trading quays of St Dogmaels and Cardigan became impossible for large vessels except on spring tides. However, as we shall see in Chapter 15, trading vessels were soon to be replaced by leisure craft as the local tourist industry developed during the 1950s. Since then, water-based leisure activities have become more important year by year. Small sailing dinghies, motor-boats, cabin cruisers, inflatables and canoes in their thousands are now used by the many holidaymakers (and locals) who love messing about in boats and who love the Pembrokeshire coast. They are keeping the seafaring traditions of Pembrokeshire alive, and they continue to ensure the economic survival of the small communities that sprang up centuries ago in the days of the wooden trading ships.

Chapter Ten

Milford Haven and its "New Towns"

In earlier chapters we have referred on several occasions to the magnificent waterway of Milford Haven. Undoubtedly it is one of the finest natural harbours in the world. It is a long sheltered **ria** (flooded river valley) more than a kilometre wide all the way to Pembroke Dock. In its lower parts it is mostly more than ten metres deep, and there is an even deeper central channel. On both shores there are broad embayments such as Dale Roads and Angle Bay. About 15 km inland the character of the waterway changes dramatically near Neyland and Burton. Upstream from here, the Daugleddau is a beautiful tidal estuary with many small inlets and branches to remind one that the whole waterway is one large river-system cut millions of years ago, and later drowned as the sea flooded in. At Picton Point the Daugleddau branches into two, the Western Cleddau and Easter Cleddau still being tidal as far inland as Haverfordwest and Canaston Bridge respectively. In spite of the great mudbanks to be seen in the Daugleddau at low tide, silting is no problem in Milford Haven. There is a tidal range of up to twenty-five feet but tidal currents are not too strong. The local climate is relatively mild, and compared with almost all other ports in the UK there is remarkably little fog.

All manner of men have praised the qualities of the waterway. Shakespeare wrote: "...how far it is to this same blessed Milford; and, by the way, tell me how Wales was made so happy as t'inherit such a haven." Daniel Defoe, on his famous tour, described Milford Haven as one of the greatest and best inlets of water in Britain. And he added "Mr Camden says it contains 16 creeks, 5 great bays and 13 good roads for shipping, all distinguished as such by their names; and some say a thousand sail of ship may ride in it and not the topmast of one be seen from the other." Clearly Mr Defoe enjoyed a spot of poetic license now and then. Most famous of all is the pronouncement of Lord Nelson, who said in 1803 that Milford Haven was the only seaport for commerce on the west coast of Britain, and that it rivalled Trincomalee in Ceylon as the greatest harbour he had even seen.

While the Vikings and the Normans seem to have appreciated both the strategic and economic possibilities of the Milford Haven waterway, it was never properly developed as a port until the nineteenth century. There had been abortive plans during earlier centuries, and indeed Thomas Cromwell had stressed the need for fortification and survey in 1539. In addition Henry VIII had, in the later sixteenth century, embarked on an ambitious plan to fortify both shores. Two blockhouses were built on the north and south sides of the Haven entrance, but they seem never to have been effectively maintained or used for the defence of the waterway. As we have seen in Chapter 7, the effective defence of Milford Haven came much later, in Victorian times, when there was an urgent requirement for the defence of the Royal Naval Dockyard.

The New Town of Milford

The first of the major maritime developments within the Haven was linked with the growth of Milford. The town was founded in 1793 and grew rapidly as a result of the energy of Charles Greville. Among the earliest inhabitants were a group of Quaker whalers from Nantucket, who continued their whaling activities for only a few years before turning to an easier life of manufacturing and trading. Unfortunately the Navy abandoned the dockyard at Milford in 1814 following a dispute over land purchase. But the small fishing industry was healthy enough, and the town progressed quickly. The Irish steam packet service was based here until 1836, but following its removal to Pembroke Dock there was a period of stagnation, and the population even declined. After many delays Milford docks were completed in 1888, almost a century after the founding of the town. A journalist in the Financial News commented "Milford Haven has been the port of the future for so long that it is surely time that the future should merge itself with the present."

But still the development of the town was slow. After 1888 there were dreams of a great shipbuilding industry and of the town becoming a transatlantic passenger terminus, but these dreams never materialized. The real growth of Milford came largely by accident, arising out of the rapid improvements in the design of fishing vessels and out of the discovery of rich fishing-grounds in the western approaches to the British Isles. Between 1900 and 1914 the proximity of Milford to these fishing-grounds, the excellence of Milford Haven as a port and the size of Milford docks themselves led to remarkable growth in the fishing industry. By 1904 there were 66 trawlers and 150 smacks based at the docks, which were also used by many vessels from other British ports. At the onset of the Great War about 2,000 local people were employed in the Milford fishing industry, and

Part of the fishing fleet in Milford Docks around the year 1905.

The rise and fall of the Milford fishing industry. Annual catches, 1890 -- 1980.

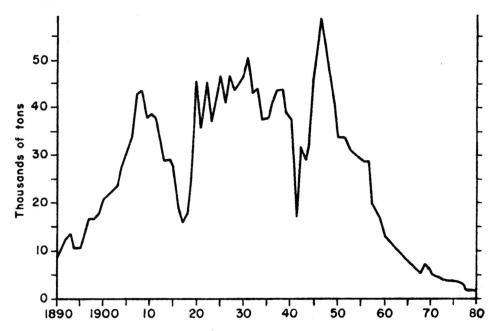

Milford was in the top league of fishing ports. However, the boom could not last and the fortunes of the industry fluctuated violently after World War I as a result of national economic factors and over-fishing in the western fishing-grounds. World War II allowed the fishing-grounds to recover somewhat, and a record catch of 59,286 tons was obtained by the Milford Fleet in 1946. But then a slow decline started and gradually catches have become smaller and smaller and the number of trawlers has fallen drastically.

In 1972 there were only twelve trawlers registered at the port, with only 3,160 tons of fish landed during the year. At that time, the fishing port provided jobs for about 100 trawlermen and 300 ancillary workers. Since then, the crisis in the fishing industry has become even more severe. Reduced catches and rising operating costs placed the trawler owners in great difficulties, and in the period 1972 to 1995

there were a number of attempts to resuscitate the industry, including the provision of fish-handling facilities for foreign trawlers using the western fishing grounds. But the new tactics met with only limited success, and the imposition of EC fishing quotas made life even more difficult for the local trawlermen. In 1991 the last of the old Milford trawler companies went into liquidation. There are still a few trawlers using the Docks, but some of them are registered in Spain, Belgium and France, and the occasional small landings of fish are now related to the tactics of fishing according to current EC regulations. Some catches are "trans-shipped" straight into heavy lorries and taken away by road. The organized chaos of the docks basin and the fish market, once so important a part of Milford life, has all but disappeared - probably for ever. The basic problem is not of Milford's making; there are now simply not enough fish left in the traditional fishing grounds to sustain a local industry of any size.

The Milford Docks Company had a chequered history, losing money consistently during the last 30 years of its life in spite of various injections of capital and changes in the Board of Directors. Now, however, the company has been purchased by the Milford Haven Port Authority, which has much more capital at its disposal from shipping revenues and other sources. The Authority is transforming the docks, and is trying to increase general cargo handling and ship repair work to compensate for the decline of the fishing industry. Ambitious plans have been made -- and partly implemented -- for the use of part of the dockland for housing, recreational and commercial development, and a 200-berth marina has been established. The hosting of the Tall Ships Race in 1991 provided a welcome spur for increased investment in buildings and ship-handling facilities.

Milford continues to have its problems, even though there has been a great diversification of economic activity since 1900. The Royal Naval Armaments Depot at Newton Noyes (opened in 1934) provided employment for 300 people, but with the nationwide reductions in defence expenditure arising from the end of the Cold War, the Depot closed in 1991. An old-established ship-breaking yard at the entrance of the muddy creek of Castle Pill closed in the late 1960s, and a replacement industry based on the import and export of scrap metals was not a great success, partly because of the disturbance experienced by nearby residential areas. Increasingly the town depends upon light manufacturing, and the Thornton Industrial Estate now has a wide range of industrial and business units providing employment for over 600 people. The oil industry made an enormous impact on the town, bringing with it an influx of construction workers during each of the refinery building projects and many new jobs both in the refineries and in the various services which the oil industry requires.

As a town, Milford still retains much evidence of its planned and graceful origins. Sir William Hamilton (husband of Lord Nelson's famous Emma Hamilton) was the owner of Milford, and it was his money which financed the port developments and the building of the town. But his nephew Charles Greville was the planner and builder. He adopted a gridiron layout, with three principal streets running parallel with one another and intersected by side streets. Hamilton terrace, closest to the shore, was given the most stylish houses. Behind that Charles Street was designed as the main shopping thoroughfare, while Robert Street, the third and highest terrace, was given the least pretentious housing. The main public buildings are at the east end of Hamilton Terrace: the Town Hall, the public library and St Katherine's Church dating from 1801-1808. Other links with the past can be seen in the Hakin Observatory, the Friends' Meeting House in the town centre and the old row of cottages on Cellar Hill above the tidal creek of Castle Pill.

Most of the newer developments have taken place to the east and north of the original town centre, and this can be seen quite clearly in both the irregular street patterns and post-1850 style of much of the housing. The old villages of Hubberston, Hakin and Steynton have now been incorporated into Milford, and they have many of the newer housing estates of the post-war era. Both private and council housing developments have occurred on a substantial scale.

Neyland

Further up the Haven but still on its northern shore, the little town of Neyland also started life as a deliberately planned settlement. It was conceived during the railway era of the mid-nineteenth century by the illustrious Isambard Kingdom Brunel.

He chose the site (previously a small fishing-port) as the terminus for the South Wales railway, to connect with the Atlantic passenger service and the Irish packet service. The railway line was completed to the port of "New Milford" (as the town was christened) in 1856 and the huge Great Western Hotel was built on the water-front. Now the future seemed secure, and local people felt that great times lay ahead. Sure enough, the town enjoyed a brief period of prosperity, with much house-building, a rapidly rising population, and even some shipbuilding. A wagon-works was established at the railway terminus on the broad flat coastal terrace beneath the eastern edge of the town. This provided much local employment. The fishing industry boomed, and a refrigeration factory was built to provide ice for the rapid rail transport of the fish catch towards the towns of the South Wales coalfield.

But the good times did not last. Comparatively little shipping used the port. Atlantic vessels were few and far between, and in 1906 even the Irish service was transferred to Fishguard. There was competition, too, from the other towns of Milford Haven which had greater natural potential for growth. On the opposite shore of the Haven, Pembroke Dock acquired its railway link in 1864 and was rapidly developed as a naval dockyard after that date, and by 1863 Milford had its own railway line as well. These developments meant that Neyland's advantages were much reduced, particularly since the Admiralty blocked any schemes for further development so as not to congest the upper reaches of the Haven. The little town declined gradually, losing its fishing industry and its ice factory, losing its shipbuilding and later its wagon-works. Although the rail depot kept some wagon-repairing facilities until the post-war era, these disappeared with the rail service in 1955. In 1971 the track was lifted. Now the

little town finds itself increasingly isolated. In 1974 the car ferry service between Neyland and Hobbs Point was still running but since the completion of the Cleddau Bridge in 1975 all through traffic has by-passed the town.

Nevertheless, Neyland survives happily enough as a small residential and service centre. Its technical college closed with the opening of the new Pembrokeshire College in Haverfordwest in 1990, but ample compensation has been provided through the developments on the Brunel Quay site, which was once the GWR railway terminus. This sheltered and extensive area on the western shore of Westfield Pill has been developed with the help of the local authority as a well-equipped and successful marina, with hundreds of mooring places for pleasure craft, housing areas, small factory units, and also amenity areas for recreational use. Although the development at Brunel Quay is perhaps too self-contained for the liking of many local traders, the economic spin-offs in increased job opportunities and increased visitor spending are considerable.

Pembroke Dock and its Dockyard

Pembroke Dock thrived on the early failures of the other two new towns of Milford Haven, and it is the only town in the county ever to have acquired a real industrial image. Its early growth occurred after 1814, when Paterchurch was selected as the site for the new naval dockyard. The site was sheltered and spacious, and there was deep water close inshore. There was a long tradition of local shipbuilding and a pool of skilled labour on both sides of the Haven. Moreover, the waterway was remote enough from the troubles of the European mainland to serve -- at that time -- as a strategically safe base for many major technological developments in naval shipbuilding, many of which were classified as "top secret."

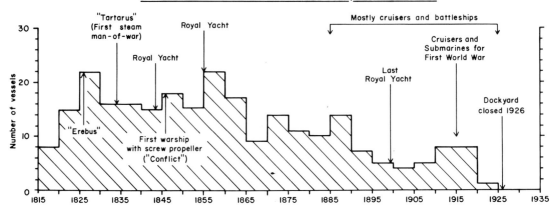

SHIPS BUILT AT ROYAL NAVAL DOCKYARD, PEMBROKE DOCK

A graphic illustration of the key events in the history of the Royal Naval Dockyard.

For this was indeed an exciting time; there were experiments with steam propulsion, with paddles and with screw propellers, and with iron cladding. Warships were increasing rapidly in size. Once established, the dockyard was the scene of many innovations in shipbuilding, and it is not often realized that for most of the century Pembroke Dock was the most advanced shipbuilding yard in the world. The year 1834 saw the launching of **Tartarus**, the first steam man-of-war; in 1846 **Conflict** was launched, being the first warship fitted with a screw propeller; and in 1847 **Lion** was launched, being then the largest warship in the Royal Navy. Five years later there followed **The Duke of Wellington**, the largest three-decker ever built. Five royal yachts were built and there was a long line of naval barques, brigantines, cruisers, gunboats and battleships. By 1875 the Chief Constructor of the American Navy was able to report that "Pembroke Dockyard is the finest shipbuilding yard in the world". In all, the dockyard saw the construction of more than 250 naval vessels, and at its height in the later years of the nineteenth century it employed over 3,000 men. Many employees travelled daily to the dockyard by rowing-boat from other parts of the Haven. Some came from as far afield as Llangwm.

In the early years of the present century Pembroke Dock was still one of the main industrial centres of West Wales, and during World War I the dockyard worked at full pace, specializing in the building of small, swift cruisers. But its remoteness was beginning to count as a disadvantage, and in the hard inter-war years the Admiralty began to think of it as something of an expendable luxury. In 1926 it was abruptly closed, and the town was thrown into despair. The whole community suffered a great deal of hardship, and the bitter memories of this time have still not entirely disappeared. Hundreds of families left the

Pembroke Dock, the Dockyard and the outer part of the waterway. Note the "grid-iron" layout. There have been a number of changes to the Dockyard waterfront since this photo was taken. (Studio Jon)

area, and the unemployment rate approached 25 per cent. Since 1926 there have been various attempts to improve the employment situation and to improve the town's image of poverty and depression.

During World War II the town was made the main Atlantic Sunderland flying-boat base, and part of the dockyard was again used as a naval base for ship-repairing. Innumerable Atlantic convoys in the dark years of the war were assembled here, in the sheltered waters of the Haven, and much minelaying, minesweeping and escort work was co-ordinated from the dockyard HQ. It has been estimated that during the course of the war some 17,000 cargo vessels sailed from the Haven. The town became an important fuel storage depot, and there was a sizeable garrison.

But these wartime activities were a mixed blessing, for the town attracted enemy bombing attacks and suffered greatly from air raids. Although its sheer distance from the Continent provided some protection from enemy bombers at the beginning of the war, Pembroke Dock enjoyed no immunity from aircraft with a longer range. There are still bitter memories of the great destruction and loss of life in the town, particularly during the twelve months between July 1940 and June 1941. The main enemy targets were the oil storage tanks at Llanreath, the Llanion Barracks, the dockyard, and the military airfield a short distance away at Milton (Carew Cheriton).

During the summer of 1940 the attacks built up in intensity, but the event which brought the plight of Pembroke Dock to national attention was the "Great Tanks Fire" of 19 August 1940. A single enemy bomber scored a direct hit on one of the oil storage tanks. An immense fire raged for eighteen days, destroying eleven tanks and 132,000 tons of fuel oil. Six hundred firemen from twenty-two fire brigades helped to fight the blaze, and there were five fatalities and 1,148 other casualties. Mr Arthur Morris, Pembroke's Fire Chief, who was among the first on the scene of the fire, did not go to bed for seventeen days; afterwards there was great local indignation that his heroic efforts received no real recognition from officialdom.

The most severe air raids of the whole war occurred on 11-12 May and 11 June 1941. The first of these was an intense attack with high-explosive bombs, while the second was referred to locally as "the fire blitz", being largely an incendiary attack. The death toll on the night of 11-12 May was at least thirty-six, and nearly 2,000 houses were damaged. Pembroke Dock was never very well defended, and it was inevitable that after the tragedy of that night a flood of refugees left the town. W L Richards, in his book on Pembrokeshire's air raids, described the scene as follows:

"Down over the hill from Pembroke Dock they came in an endless   stream, in cars, lorries and overloaded buses, on motorcycles, bicycles, and horse-drawn carts and wagons. Hundreds came on foot, weary mothers with infants in arms and little boys and girls hardly of school age running behind, wonderment written plain on their faces; old men on sticks, young men with grim expressions, subdued boys and frightened girls. Dusk fell and still they came ....

There were those who, with no friends or relatives outside the town and no money to pay for a roof over their heads, had to face the night in Pembroke Dock or flee to the open country. It is a fact that many people slept in the open in Bush woods and the surrounding fields and hedges for nights after May 12th.

Pembroke Dock was a dark, deserted, dismal town that night ... And so it was the next night and for many nights after until gradually with the general

One of the ill-fated factories built on the outskirts of Pembroke Dock after the War.

slackening of the air attacks, people began to return to their shattered homes."

The unfortunate town, which had suffered cruelly after the closure of the dockyard in 1926, had borne the brunt of the enemy assault on Pembrokeshire. Haverfordwest, Milford, Neyland and Tenby escaped largely unscathed.

Since the end of the war the Navy has maintained a small presence at Pembroke Dock, but the dockyard itself has been used largely by small private shipbuilding and repairing concerns. The town continued to be used as a base for the Sunderland flying-boats of RAF Coastal Command until 1958, and many people have fond recollections of the cumbersome white aircraft in the skies above Pembrokeshire. Although the flying-boat base was the largest in the world there is now little evidence of this. The last Sunderland was taken (in pieces) from Pembroke Dock to the

RAF Museum at Hendon in 1971, where it is now on permanent display. The oil tanks at Llanreath and Llanion have all been dismantled; and the old rotting hulk of the **Warrior**, the first of the ironsides and for so long a feature of the Pembroke Ferry waterside, has been removed to Portsmouth, where it has been proudly restored and opened to the public.

Now Pembroke Dock is largely rebuilt, still preserving its original grid-iron plan and still bearing many traces of its military history such as the Defensible Barracks and the naval depot to the west of the Dockyard. But the town cannot look to the past for its prosperity. It has no tourist attractions to compare with the medieval towns of Pembroke, Haverfordwest and Tenby, and its prosperity must be based on industry and services. A number of "advance factories" were build with government help on the outskirts of the the town in the 1950s, including one which made the famous Davies roller-skates, and another which provided employment for 300 people and manufactured nearly all the fixings for the UK car industry. However, remoteness from the centres of raw material supply and customer demand was always a problem with the Pembroke Dock factories, and few of them were successful on a long-term basis. Other large industrial enterprises, some employing hundreds of local workers, have failed. Sadly, hundreds of thousands of square feet of post-war industrial premises now lie empty and semi-derelict in the town, causing considerable local anger.

Through its suffering Pembroke Dock has acquired resilience and hope, and it has grown used to a seesaw existence of booms and depressions. Like the other town of Milford Haven, its fortunes have always been linked with the sea. In the 1970s all eyes were turned to the sea again as the Celtic Sea oil search got under way, providing business opportunities for a number of local engineering and service companies and opening up parts of the Dockyard waterfront for storage, repair work and oil rig supply operations. Many people were disappointed when the oil exploration work wound down.

But another boost to the local economy came with the decision in 1986 by the B&I Line to open up a ferry service from "Pembroke" (actually Pembroke Dock) to Rosslare, using a new purpose-built RO-RO terminal; and in 1990 there came a brave decision by the Govan Davies Group to excavate a new deep-water basin at "The Port of Pembroke" on the edge of the Dockyard, providing access for merchant vessels at all states of the tide. The new facility was provided with 130,000 sq ft of warehousing and cool storage space suitable for the importation or transshipment of fruit and vegetables. At first this enterprise proved a great success, but in 1995 the operating company was in the hands of the receivers.

Pembroke Dock's emotional and economic roller-coaster continues. By the early 1990s the town had an increasing air of prosperity about it, with new shopping developments, new factory units, new road developments and new community facilities. The rise and rise of Irish passenger and freight traffic has exceeded all expectations, and there is talk of a new "double deck" loading facility at the B&I terminal which will be capable of handling a new super-ferry. The WDA is still investing heavily in new industrial estates around the town, including one on a greenfields site adjacent to the Pembroke Dock end of the Cleddau Bridge. This has caused some local fury, since the WDA seems to be doing very little to fill the other empty factories in the town. The local council is also involved in the trendy capital investment of taxpayers' money nearby. By way of a swansong, South Pembrokeshire District Council is involved in a major "waterfront" development in Cosheston Pill, with the aid of WDA and EC funding. The old die-hards complain that the town streets are neglected while millions of pounds are spent on high-tech brightly-painted "business parks" and marinas for yuppies, in places which would have been better left as green and peaceful havens for wildlife.

Chapter Eleven

Coal, Stone, Slate and Iron
Pembrokeshire's Industrial Revolution

Long before the building of the new towns on Milford Haven, there were small industries scattered about Pembrokeshire. Few people realize how rich the county's industrial past has been, but just like the more densely populated parts of Britain this remote corner of Wales was affected by the Industrial Revolution. Pembrokeshire's own coalfield, specialising in high-quality anthracite, had an exciting history of successes and disasters. The county had its own metal mines and metal-working industries, and at Stepaside there was a combined coal-mining and iron-working industry similar in many respects to the larger concerns which changed for ever the way of life of the South Wales coalfield. As we have seen, Pembroke Dock, between 1814 and 1926, was one of the world's most famous naval dockyards. In the previous chapter we saw how many of its innovations revolutionized shipbuilding in the heady days when steam replaced sail and iron replaced wood.

In addition to these relatively large industries the county has, from the Middle Ages to the present, supported many smaller enterprises. Slates, building stone and roadstone have been produced in hundreds of quarries in the countryside. Most of these are forgotten and overgrown; some, like Rosebush, Porthgain and West Williamston, remain impressive to this day. As indicated in Chapter 9, all around the coast there are lime-kilns to remind us of the past practice of burning lime to improve the land. In the

towns there have been tanneries and rope-works. Corn mills and woollen mills were once widespread, and brick-works and paper mills were thriving local industries. And on the smallest scale village craftsmen have for centuries been making farm implements, coracles, furniture and a host of other useful or decorative items which found their way into local homes.

Most of the traces of these industries have been lost over the years, but there is still much to see, and this chapter attempts to describe some of the industries based on the county's mineral resources of coal, stone, slate, iron and other metalliferous ores.

The Coal Industry

The Pembrokeshire coal industry has a fascinating history. The landscape still bears some of the scars of coal extraction, although most of them are now healed. Traces of the spoil-heaps, railway tracks and pit-head buildings can be found by anyone who knows where to look, but these are not clearly marked on the Ordnance Survey maps and many visitors are unaware of their existence. The small coalfield is the western part of the South Wales Coalfield, being made up of thin and disturbed seams of very hard anthracite. Although the coal has been difficult to work, there is a history of mining going back to the fourteenth century at least.

A coal barge tied up near Old Bridge, Haverfordwest, in the 1950's.

Prior to 1500 coalpits seem to have been concentrated on the western part of the coalfield, especially west of Roch and in the Little Haven area, but by 1600 there were more pits inland of Saundersfoot Bay and around the confluence of the Eastern Cleddau and Western Cleddau. It seems from the writings of George Owen that on the Pembrokeshire coalfield the value of coal for domestic heating purposes was realized earlier than elsewhere in Wales, and during the seventeenth century production for the home market rose sharply. By 1700 Pembrokeshire anthracite was also in great demand further afield, and was renowned for its low ash content and excellent heating properties. It became the chief item of shipment from the Pembrokeshire ports, and for two centuries it was also the basis of most of the industrial activities of the county.

Production on the Pembrokeshire coalfield reached its peak in the later years of the eighteenth century, when annual totals of well over 150,000 tons were achieved. For the next fifty years or so the Pembrokeshire collieries remained prosperous, and in the time of Queen Victoria local anthracite was so highly thought of that she refused to allow any other fuel in the boilers of her royal yachts. However, in the face of increased competition from the major British coalfields, output fell gradually through the latter half of the nineteenth century. Among the factors which caused this decline were the lack of capital investment in mining plant by the colliery owners, the working out of the uppermost seams, the increasing difficulty of deep working in the shattered and faulted lower seams, and the impossibility of loading coal direct to large vessels in the tidal reaches of the Daugleddau.

By the 1890s Pembrokeshire had become a high-cost region at a time when competition was intensifying, and at a time of national depression. As many of the smaller mines closed larger and more efficient units appeared in more favourable localities; but as costs rose inexorably they, too, were forced to close.

Another reason for the closure of the small mines was increasing public concern about the appalling conditions faced by coal miners. In his *Description of Pembrokeshire* George Owen described the working conditions in the pits and "slants" of Elizabethan times, with constant rock falls, waterlogged working areas, low-roofed tunnels negotiated by child "bearers", and "sudden damps.... that oftentimes cause the workmen to swoon." Things had not improved all that much three hundred years later; indeed, in some respects matters had deteriorated, for the Victorian mine owners were constantly seeking to drive down costs and increase profits, with worker's concerns figuring hardly at all in their calculations. The social and political awakening of the working class, described in Chapter 8, led to constant disputes, increasing demands for better wages, better coalface conditions, and better health care. Sometimes these disputes drove mine owners to despair, and led them to abandon their small and primitive collieries.

The section of the coalfield which was centred on the confluence of the Western and Eastern Cleddau rivers depended greatly upon the export of coal from small quays and jetties. One of the earliest areas which shipped out coal and culm in barges and little sailing vessels was the Landshipping area. Before 1844 there were five working collieries here, and Landshipping village was a thriving mining community. There were quays at Landshipping Ferry and Picton Point which were connected by a ferry service. The main quay was at Landshipping itself, and from here over 10,000 tons of coal and culm were exported annually at the beginning of the nineteenth century. The Garden Pit colliery, very close to the quay,

was quite famous locally; but in 1844 it hit the national headlines. The working tunnels were very close to the bed of the tidal river. On St Valentine's Day, at the height of a spring tide, water from the river broke into the workings, and more than forty men and boys were drowned. The locals believed that the figure was closer to seventy or eighty, since no records were kept of under-age child labourers. According to legend, the disaster was foreseen by a dumb miner who noticed water seeping down through the roof of the mine tunnels the day before, but the management refused to pay any attention to his gesticulated warning signals. After the disaster, a mysterious curse was placed on the mine. It never reopened, and the community never recovered. Many families emigrated, and by 1867 all the other collieries in the area had also closed. Further south, the collieries around Yerberston, Cresselly and Jeffreyston were running down, and after 1850 little coal was exported from Cresswell Quay. Surprisingly, the quay is still in a good state of repair.

On the other side of the river the Hook district was much more successful, and over the years shallow workings, drifts and deep mines were dug. For about a century, from the mid-1800s until 1948, Hook was a real mining community, and there were many mining families in Freystrop as well. There were at least sixteen substantial collieries in the area, besides a number of smaller ones which only worked for a few years before being abandoned. Most of the collieries around Hook were closed by 1910, and until 1930 production figures fluctuated around 10,000 tons per annum. Several small quays in the area, such as Black Hill Quay, Little Milford Quay, Hook Quay, Lower Hook Quay and Sprinkle Quay, were used for exporting coal. Of these, we can still see the remains of Little Milford Quay, and Hook Quay is a prominent industrial relic. About 1850 cargo vessels became too large for the smaller quays. More and more barges came into use for carrying the coal to Llangwm Pool and Lawrenny, where it was transshipped. But this was an expensive and time-consuming operation, and Hook Colliery could not have survived were it not for the construction of the Hook Colliery Railway in 1929 to join the GWR at Johnston. At last the Hook Colliery no longer had to depend upon the small coal barges using Hook Quay, and could export coal promptly direct to the major markets. In 1932 a screening plant was built, giving Hook Colliery a great selling advantage over its local competitors, and later £10,000 was spent on a plant for patent fuel. A further stroke of luck was the closure of the Bonville's Court Colliery near Saundersfoot, enabling Hook Colliery to capture its markets. Production rose sharply to a peak of 42,000 tons in 1934, falling to 15,000 - 25,000 tons per annum during the war years; but rising costs, the NCB takeover in 1947, and a severe flood in the Hook West Drift led to the ending of all mining activities in 1948.

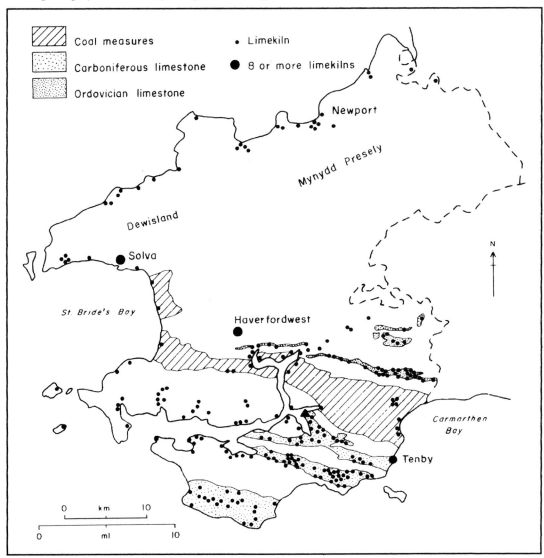

Coal and Limestone in Pembrokeshire.

By far the most important colliery district in the county was that around Kilgetty and Saundersfoot. Before 1900 there were several quite prosperous collieries at work, including Bonville's Court Colliery, Grove Colliery and Kilgetty Colliery (both at Stepaside), Begelly Colliery and Moreton Colliery. At first the coal was transported by horse and cart and by bullock wagon to the beaches at Wiseman's Bridge and Saundersfoot, where it was loaded on to sailing vessels at low tide. During the eighteenth century there were sometimes thirty vessels or more being loaded at the same time on Coppet Hall beach, served by over 100 carts. Everything changed after 1829 when the fine harbour at Saundersfoot was built and the various mineral railway lines came into use. One line ran inland to Begelly and Thomas Chapel, and it was used for taking the miners to work as well as for the export of coal. The other branch ran northwards towards Wiseman's Bridge and on to the Stepaside area, where it served several local collieries and the local iron industry. The line ran along the coast and needed several short tunnels, which are still in a good state of repair.

Coal could now be exported quickly and efficiently, and by the middle of the century the industry prospered. Several new collieries were opened up, and by 1864 over 30,000 tons of coal were being exported from Saundersfoot Harbour each year. New industries, such as the fire-brick works at Wiseman's Bridge, appeared on the scene. But as the best seams were worked out and as high transport and drainage costs began to affect the collieries, they closed one after another. By 1900 Bonville's Court was the only large working colliery in the area. It remained open until 1930, employing some 300 men and producing over 30,000 tons of coal in most years. Several other collieries opened during the twentieth century, including Reynalton Colliery (1914-21), Broom Colliery (1934-9), and Loveston

Colliery (1932-7). At Loveston there was a flood disaster in 1936 in which seven miners died. Until recently one could see the remains of Kilgetty Colliery at Stepaside. This was the last of the collieries in the Stepaside area and it was worked from 1935 to 1939. With the closing of Broom and Kilgetty collieries at the beginning of World War II the long coal-mining traditions of the Saundersfoot area, dating back 500 years or more, came to an end.

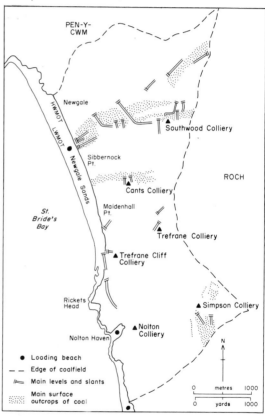

Map of the Nolton and Newgale Coalfield, showing the main workings and loading beaches.

On the St Bride's Bay coast, where there were sandy beaches close to the coal-mining districts, it was difficult to build proper quays. Instead, the coal was always exported in small vessels which were beached on the sand at high tide, loaded amid hectic activity from horse-drawn carts at low tide, and then floated off again on the next tide. The safest loading beaches were at Nolton Haven and Little Haven, but Newgale, Druidston and Broad Haven were also used occasionally. The only real loading-quay seems to have been built at Nolton Haven. Here, at the northern corner of the beach, there is an embankment where the coal was stored and then either loaded direct on to beached vessels or on to horse-drawn carts. There are still signs of the old tramway running down past the Counting House, from which the coal exports were controlled. The Nolton and Newgale coalfield had six main collieries and many "levels" and "slants". Some of the buildings of the Trefrane Cliff Colliery remain, and there are also a few traces of Southwood Colliery. In addition, several levels can be seen in the Coal Measures in the cliffs between Nolton and Little Haven. The collieries were not successful enough to compete with those further east, and by 1900 only Trefrane Cliff Colliery had survived. Even this was closed by 1905, having originally exported coal via Haverfordwest and then via Nolton Haven after haulage in trolleys pulled by traction engines. There were plans to re-open the Nolton and Newgale coalfield after 1915, using a railway line to Milford to export the coal. But these plans came to nothing.

So ended the most important of Pembrokeshire's industrial adventures. After a long history of exploitation, this small coalfield was forced to end operations through a combination of environmental and locational factors. During the present century the physical problems of mine drainage and the working of shattered and discontinuous seams raised production costs, and it is a tribute to the quality of Pembrokeshire anthracite that mining was still deemed worthwhile in 1948. However, the locational disadvantages of the county had become increasingly apparent in the slow adoption of new mining techniques, the reluctance of the colliery owners to invest in exploration and new workings, and the rising costs of bulk coal transport by sea and rail. After centuries of national renown prior to 1800, the coalfield suffered increasingly from competition, for its larger rivals were located much closer to the major markets. Perhaps, in the long run, this was no bad thing for the economy of Pembrokeshire.

Slate Quarrying

The varied geological character of Pembrokeshire has ensured a plentiful supply of a number of different types of stone for domestic use and export. For example, slate has been quarried for several centuries, particularly in the north of the county where the most suitable varieties are found. The local slates vary from silver-grey and black to blue, green and red. Slate was widely used for roofing purposes, but slate slabs were also used for flooring and house-building, for tombstones and feeding-troughs, and for sills and lintels. In all, there are traces of at least 69 slate quarries in the north of the county. Many of them were very small, operating for just a few years and producing slate for use on local farms and cottages. These small enterprises had virtually no mechanisation, and depended on crude explosives, hand tools, and horses and carts.

But at least thirty of the quarries were true commercial enterprises involving substantial investment and trading activities. One such was the quarry at Tyrch, whence came the slate for the County Hall in Carmarthen. The quarry at one time employed over 100 workers, and it was working until 1939. There were other large quarries at Glogue, Rosebush, Cilgerran and Fforest (both on the south bank of the River Teifi), Llandeilo, Summerton and Sealyham. Slate from the Gilfach (Llangolman) quarry roofed part of the Palace of Westminster.

The method of working in Pembrokeshire's "commercial" slate quarries was always the same. There were no slate mines or caverns, and all of the working was done on open galleries or "steps" cut into the hillside. The working face above each step was brought down in sections by blasting with black powder; traces of the long drill-holes into which the powder was packed can still be seen today in many quarries. The steps were worked in sequence, since each step had to be wide enough for the laying of temporary narrow-guage railway lines. Small bogies or trucks hauled by pulley systems carried the slabs to working platforms on the flanks of the pit. In the bigger quarries, the initial dressing of the slabs was done in crude shelters high on the hillside before they were sent down "inclines" to the dressing-sheds below. In the smaller quarries, slabs were fully dressed or split into roofing slates as close to the place of origin as possible. The raising and lowering of the trucks on the inclines was done by means of pulleys, winches and cable drums driven by static steam engines. There is some doubt about the use of "blondins" in the Pembrokeshire slate quarries. These were precarious overhead cables with pulleys which were used for carrying slate slabs (and sometimes fully laden trucks) down and across working pits. They were used widely in the North Wales slate quarries a century ago, but the working pits there were many times larger than those of Pembrokeshire.

At Rosebush and some of the other large quarries, the quarry owners probably installed "water balance" systems on inclines which were wide enough to carry parallel tracks. Fully laden trucks which needed to descend to the dressing sheds were connected by pulley to full water wagons at the base of the parallel track. As the water was released from the water wagons they would ascend, balanced by the descending trucks of slate. Around 1880 there was a strange windmill at Rosebush which was probably used for pumping the water needed by the water wagons and steam engines in the quarry.

One of the principles of slate quarrying is that the slate slabs and slate waste from the working face should never be lifted, but preferably moved sideways or directly downhill with the minimum possible effort. This principle was almost always adhered to, and one consequence was that when a quarry was worked below the natural slope of the hillside to create a deep pit, a narrow cutting would be made for the transport of the slate. The deeper pits were connected to the outside world by tunnels; for example, the newest pit at Rosebush has two steps in it, and two tunnels. It is not often appreciated that up to ninety percent of the material removed from a slate quarry is slate waste, and the efficient handling of this waste is, and always has been, crucial for the commercial success of the quarrying enterprise. The most impressive features in old slate quarries are not the working faces but the massive waste heaps containing thousands of tonnes of broken slate debris. Every working terrace has its associated slate heaps on its flanks; these were built out, bit by bit, by extensions of the narrow-guage railway tracks as more and more material was dumped from the waste trucks. Sometimes a waste heap can be seen to lie on top of another waste heap; for visitors who enjoy detective work, this is a good way to establish the relative ages of working pits and even working faces.

Of particular interest in Pembrokeshire are the tiny "sea quarries" located on the open coast, for the most part where there was some shelter from the prevailing south-westerly winds, and where slate and shale slabs were taken out by generations of "rock-men" using very primitive techniques. Such quarries were easier to exploit than those inland, and the

An old "sea quarry" near Hescwm on the north Pembrokeshire coast.

slate or shale waste could be disposed of by simply dumping it in the sea. Examples of such quarries (often no more than terraces or steps in the cliff face) can be seen at Pwllderi, Hescwm, Pwll Llong near Trefin, and on the cliffs at Cat Rock, west of the Parrog at Newport. Sometimes the slabs were hauled up to the clifftop, but it was always easier to take advantage of gravity and take them out by sea from the foot of the cliff. In some places there are traces of old "docks" at the foot of the cliffs were shallow-draught barges tied up and took cargoes on board. In the later 1800s many loads of slate were exported from the "blue lagoon" quarry at Abereiddi and from Parrog (Newport) in small sailing vessels.

The best-known of the inland slate quarries were in and around Mynydd Presely. Probably the most famous of all are located at Rosebush, near the southern edge of the Pantmaenog Forest. Here, in the Bellstone Quarry, working can be traced back several centuries; but the later Rosebush Quarry owed its short-lived prosperity to the North Pembroke and Fishguard Railway line, as described in Chapter 8. The quarries, which are easily accessible through the hamlet of Rosebush, can be counted among the county's best-known secrets. There are five main pits, in one of which there is a deep dark pool. The main pit (at the eastern end of the complex) is very beautiful, with its dark slate staircase of gigantic steps, each one up to 10m high. The galleries and the vertical rock faces are now becoming well covered with grasses, lichens, mosses, ferns and heather. Here and there fresh rock falls remind one that the pit is not yet quite dead. Black tunnel entrances show where slate slabs and waste were carried through from the pit, or where work was driven in behind the face. There are inclines and ruined buildings in abundance high on the hillside, and down below are the ruins of an old

Construction of the new harbour wall at Porthgain, around the year 1902.

locomotive shed and another building where slate slabs were dressed with the aid of machinery driven by a water turbine. There is a ruined viaduct, used for carrying slate waste across the railway line. The cast iron pipe, used to carry water for the turbine, the village water supply and the Rosebush fountains, is still visible. The main pit is like a hanging garden, and on its floor is a paradise of lush ferns, heather, bilberry, moss and rushes. Specks of cotton grass thrive on the water which trickles down from invisible springs. In July there are foxgloves, and plump bilberries for the picking. The sounds in the air are of sheep and skylarks and distant barking dogs and the alien sounds of traffic on the main road below. The massive ugly spoil heaps of shattered and discarded slate slabs contrast starkly with the lushness of the new green plants. Rosebush may be an industrial relic, but it has its own peculiar beauty.

Other Stone Quarries

Hard rock quarries are scattered throughout Pembrokeshire, since in the early days each community met its own demand for building materials, railway hard core, and roadstone. The best roadstone in the county came from igneous rocks (for example dolerite, andesite and rhyolite) which were quarried and then crushed down to various sizes. Typical quarries are those at Trefgarn, Penbiri, Middle Mill and Bolton Hill, and there are older quarries at Brawdy and Gignog.

Possibly the best known of all the north Pembrokeshire quarries was at Porthgain. Here Porthgain Village Industries Ltd operated a thriving quarrying and brick-making industry between 1878 and 1914. There were two main quarry pits, one producing slate and shale, and the other roadstone from andesite. Following the

Steam vessels loading their cargoes in Porthgain Harbour, around 1910.

rebuilding of the harbour in 1902-4 the little port echoed with the sounds of the stone crushers, and in some years there were more than 100 shipments of stone and bricks to ports as far afield as south-east England. After World War I, however, high costs made it difficult to operate the company efficiently and it was forced to stop working at Porthgain in 1931.

The stone quarries were on the cliffs to the west of Porthgain, and between them and the harbour one can still see several quarry buildings and the route of an old railway track. The stone was crushed and graded and then stored in hoppers on the west side of the harbour for loading direct into sailing ships and steam cargo vessels. The remains of these hoppers are still prominent features of the local landscape. The old brickworks building (now repaired) is a focal point in the settlement, and on the quayside is the entrance to the long tunnel through which shale for the brickworks was carried by trucks on a narrow-guage railway. Despite its air of dereliction Porthgain has its own peculiar charm, and it is certainly

one of the most important of Pembrokeshire's industrial monuments. Thankfully, plans for the "development" of Porthgain were met by strong local protests, and the harbour and quarry buildings are now protected by the National Park Authority.

Many other quarries in the county were worked for building stone. In the north the beautiful purple sandstones for St David's Cathedral were quarried from the cliffs above Caerfai Bay. There were many small quarries in the centre and north of the county where shale was extracted for building purposes. It was mixed with clay (and sometimes straw) to make "clom", which was for centuries the cheapest building material available for poor people.

The hard grey and white limestones exposed in the south of the county have always been of great importance as building materials. As we have seen in Chapter 8, crushed limestone was also used, along with coal or culm, for conversion into lime. Most of the limestone was quarried from the outcrops on the coasts of South Pembrokeshire, although there were some big inland quarries, for example at Ludchurch and Blaencilgoed. As with the shale and slate "sea quarries", the coastal limestone quarries were located where there was some shelter from the south-westerlies, and where cargo vessels could be beached and loaded at low tide. One of the most isolated quarries in Pembrokeshire was located on St Margaret's Isle, south of Penally, where the outline of the island has been transformed by the removal of thousands of tons of rock and where the quarrymen lived in a row of primitive cottages.

While there is now an interest in preserving the best of the lime-kilns in the county (as at Solva and Tenby), little interest has been shown in the old quarries themselves. In the Trefgarn Gorge one of the largest of the old stone quarries has been so effectively landscaped that most visitors passing through on the A40 road do not even recognise it for what it is. Yet only 30 years ago it was a place of constant noise and billowing clouds of white dust. On the open coast there are old quarries at Stackpole, Lydstep and on Caldey Island, where crushing plants and stone hoppers were installed or where vessels were loaded directly from the quarry workings. But in the Daugleddau district more elaborate procedures became necessary as the quarries were worked back from the shore, and at several localities (as at Garron Pill and just south of Haverfordwest) little docks were cut into the limestone so that barges could have access to the flooded quarry interiors at high tide, to be loaded and then floated out later. The quarries at Garron Pill were cut in about 1814, and the stone used for building the Pembroke Dockyard quays.

The most magnificent complex of all is at West Williamston, where there is a maze of old "docks" and quarry workings, now largely overgrown. The site is well off the beaten track and is no tourist attraction,

but like Rosebush and Porthgain it has its own peculiar atmosphere. Perhaps this derives from the very lushness of the vegetation, with smooth grassy banks where stone was once quarried, a wild tangle of blackberry around the old crushing and grading machinery, and reed beds, trees and bushes fighting to keep the tide away from the old docks.

Metal-working

Another group of mineral resources in Pembrokeshire is made up of metallic ores. Not many people realize that such ores have been mined in the county on a small scale for many centuries. For example, copper ore may have been mined on the cliffs overlooking Ramsey Sound and on the south coast of the St David's peninsula from pre-Roman times, and traces of the old workings can still be seen. Copper was once mined near Dale, and manganese ore near Fishguard and at Ambleston. More recently several attempts were made to extract silver-lead ores, particularly during the later part of the Industrial Revolution. The most easily worked ore deposits were in the north-east of the county, and at Llanfyrnach there was a silver-lead mine which was at one time locally quite famous. It was first worked in 1764, but produced no more than 400 tons per year (and in some years no ore at all) before the discovery of a new lode in 1876. At the time of its peak production, from 1880-85, it was producing up to 1600 tons of ore per year.

A small mine which gained a certain local notoriety was the little copper mine at Porth Taflod, near Treginnis on Ramsey Sound. Five men worked under very primitive conditions in the mine. Copper ore and waste, and the miners, were carried in a simple basket which was raised and lowered in a 10m shaft by a hand-operated winch and pulley. On 2nd May 1883 John Reynolds of Solva was being carried up in the basket prior to blasting when, as a result of horseplay by his colleagues, he was tipped out of the basket and fell to the bottom of the shaft, where he broke his neck. He survived for a couple of days, but the winchmen were arrested and charged with manslaughter. At the trial they were acquitted, but the incident made a profound local impact and highlighted the crude equipment and lack of safety procedures in the mine.   Working ceased forthwith, and the mine never reopened. The entrance of the shaft, and traces of the pithead buildings, can still be seen adjacent to the Coastal Footpath.

There was a fine example of an early metal-working industry near Llechryd, beside the River Teifi. Here, because of plentiful water and charcoal, the Coedmore forge was established, perhaps as early as the seventeenth century. The forge was a thriving concern in the early 1700s, depending on imported pig iron and limestone (carried up-river in horse-drawn and man-hauled barges) in addition to its own local resources. The plant, its watercourse, and its

workers' cottages were all located on the north side of the River Teifi, but now few traces remain. The forge closed before 1750. It was followed by the Penygored Tinplate Works, opened in about 1765 and sited on the other side of the river near Castell Malgwyn. There was great investment in plant for the works and on a watercourse and several bridges. Two bridges -- the Hammett Bridge and the Castell Malgwyn Bridge -- and the remains of the watercourse and some works buildings can still be seen. As in the days of the Coedmore forge, materials were imported on horse-drawn barges by river from Cardigan, and at one time 300 men were employed at the works. But the enterprise was too remote to succeed, and, having defied the laws of industrial location for long enough, it was forced to close in 1806.

Most of the other metal-working industries in the county were small smithies and iron forges making tools, domestic and agricultural equipment, and wrought iron railings. There was probably a little forge at Blackpool Mill during the sixteenth century,

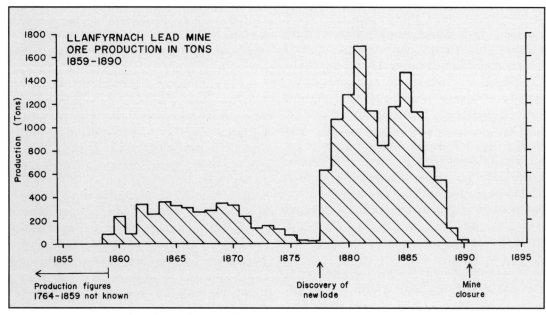

Diagram showing the short but exciting history of the Llanfyrnach mine.

but the main furnace and forge were built between 1620 and 1630. In its heyday it used limestone shipped up-river and local timber for charcoal. The Barlow family of Slebech sold much wood to the Carmarthen ironmasters who owned the forge. An industrial token dated 1792 shows what the interior of the Blackpool forge must have looked like. It pictures the furnace where the pig-iron was reheated before being worked, and a man holding a piece of iron on the anvil where it is being subjected to blows from the massive water-powered hammer. Elsewhere in the county the foundries at Neyland and Woodside (Wiseman's Bridge) were well known. Perhaps the best known of all was the Marychurch works at Haverfordwest which earned great renown for the quality of its agricultural machinery during the later 1800s. It earned even greater renown for the spectacular boiler explosion which showered the lower town with debris and which brought its working life to an end in 1910. Other foundries, as at Milford and Pembroke Dockyard, specialized in castings for the local shipbuilding industry.

In the valley below Stepaside there was once a large iron-working industry. The works was opened in 1849 by the Pembrokeshire Iron and Coal Company. Anthracite mined at Grove Colliery, on the hillside above, was used as fuel in the smelting process. Iron ore and limestone for the furnaces were also found locally. The remains of the colliery can still be seen. Near Coppet Hall the "levels" of the old iron ore mines are still visible in the cliff face. Stepaside Iron Works itself is now in a ruinous state, but we can still see something of its architecture. The old casting shed is the most impressive building, and nearby are old workshops, now becoming very dilapidated. At the foot of the hillside are the remains of two blast-furnaces. At the time of its greatest success, in the 1860s, the works also had an enormous blowing engine and a line of lime-kilns. Up-valley from the

works is a fine Telford causeway with a road arch and a tramway arch. On the valley floor there are traces of an old canal and of the mineral railway lines used for importing raw materials and for exporting pig-iron. Most of the shipments used Saundersfoot Harbour, which was reached by an extension of the railway through Wiseman's Bridge and Coppet Hall. In some years over 4,000 tons of pig-iron were exported, in addition to large quantities sold locally, but production ceased in 1877. After that date only the workshop was kept open to provide a service for the local coal industry. Recently an attempt has been made to re-create some of the industrial features of Stepaside as it was in its heyday. The "Stepaside Heritage Project" has already rescued some old machinery, and there are now permanent displays and a custom-built information centre on the site.

Other Works and Factories

Another industrial activity which was widespread in the county was brick-making from local raw materials. There were about a dozen brickworks in the county. There was one at West Angle which used clay from a brick-pit immediately behind the beach. The bricks were originally made by Staffordshire workmen, and the works had its own small tramway. The red brick buildings still stand near the beach cafe. There was a brickworks at North Johnston until 1935 and others at Penally, Haverfordwest gasworks and Llanddewi Velfrey. Apart from the firebrick works at Wiseman's Bridge there were others linked with the coal industry. The brickworks at Templeton made silica firebricks between 1885 and 1924. After World War I the works employed thirty people, and many thousands of bricks were dispatched by rail each week. There are clear traces of the brick industry at Porthgain, where we can still see the shell of the brickworks and the brick-pit which was connected to the harbour by a tunnel. The Goodwick brickworks closed down only in 1969. It met much of the local demand for building bricks, using shale from a large open quarry behind the works. Another interesting site is at Flimston, where, until about 1880, the old clay-pits produced "pipeclay" which was exported from a crude landing-stage on the cliffs for the making of silica bricks and earthenware.

Several other types of factories existed in various parts of the county. Many of the small woollen mills and furze mills were located in remote areas deep in the countryside, where they depended on farm products and supplied agricultural communities with some of their needs. Furze mills were quite common, producing chopped gorse for animal feed. Little sawmills were widespread, often run by one man and using water-power to drive the saws. However, they declined as local timber resources became scarce. Some of the towns had larger sawmills. The remains of one of these, together with the leat used to supply its water-power, can be seen in Haverfordwest below Crow Hill.

The county town had a number of other water-powered industries along the river, including five paper-mills. The most important of these was built at Prendergast in 1766, originally as a cotton-mill. This gave employment to 150 persons, and was reputed to be the largest industrial concern in the county at that time. A number of cottages were built in Prendergast to house the workers, many of whom were brought from Lancashire. By 1791 the mill had been converted to the manufacture of rough paper, and in the nineteenth century a water turbine was installed to supplement the power obtained from several water-wheels. Rags were collected from far and wide for use in the mill, and they were made into a coarse kind of packing paper. Eventually the import of cheap foreign paper killed the mill's trade, and it was closed down and some of its machinery sold as scrap. Now, although the site is in a ruinous state the leat, the remains of the vertical turbine, and some of the architectural features of the mill can still be discerned.

Another famous Haverfordwest industry was Llewellin's Churnworks, which started life in about 1790 as a timber-importing business. The factory exported butter-churns of prize winning design throughout the world in the 1800s and early 1900s. Many coastal villages had industries making barrels, nets and fish-boxes, and at Milford Docks some of these crafts survived until quite recently. At Neyland and Milford there were ice factories. At Whalecombe, not far from Cosheston, a chemical factory produced naphtha for explosives, and other products for the linen industry. The factory, in a beautiful setting on the banks of the Daugleddau, is still in good repair.

Thankfully Pembrokeshire was spared the worst effects of industrialization because it was too remote from the major markets of England, and because its mineral resources were by no means abundant. Hence the gradual decline of the coal industry and other industrial activities was not accompanied by large-scale depression, for industry had always been rural; colliery owners and other industrialists were often landed gentry who also maintained their agricultural interests. Many of the miners, quarry workers and metalworkers kept their own smallholdings. There were no large-scale displacements of population, since no large urban work-forces were required by the ironmasters and coalmasters of the day. Thus the era which transformed the face of the South Wales valleys and brought their exploited working populations close to revolution did relatively little to alter either the face of Pembrokeshire or the way of life of its people.

Chapter Twelve

Town and Country Today

Most of the man-made features of the Pembrokeshire landscape have been created by groups of people with widely differing interests. In earlier chapters we have seen how our ancestors modified the face of the land to meet their own simple needs. We have seen how, later on, townsmen and countrymen and industrialists and farmers continued this process into the present century. The process of landscape change goes on, at an ever-increasing rate, as our technology allows us to achieve more and more in a shorter and shorter time.

The communities which are altering the landscape most effectively in Pembrokeshire today are those of the towns, for as the population of the county has grown to about 109,000 the towns have spread outwards, consuming areas of farmland and sending suburban tentacles along the main roads. At the same time, the pattern of life on farms and villages has changed. Many people, especially in the Welshry, have left the land, and many of the old northern parishes now have ageing populations. As more and more people have become car owners so rural bus services have declined. Life is becoming ever more "efficient", and in all parts of Pembrokeshire (including the National Park) there is now a policy to concentrate rural people in existing villages. The pattern of development is often prescribed in "local plans". Some villages have grown at a spectacular rate since 1960, for example Broad Haven, Steynton, and Monkton, where the developments have been related largely to the need for overspill or commuter housing for the towns of Milford,

Haverfordwest and Pembroke. This process has been helped by the modern planning philosophy of restricting town centres to commercial use only.

The farming recession of the early nineties has had a serious effect on the farm economy, with hundreds of farms on the market or in serious financial trouble. Most farms will survive, of course, but the cumulative effects of milk quotas, reduced sheep headage payments, declining meat consumption in the population at large, and high interest rates have forced competent farmers off the land and into other professions. Some have adapted by diversifying into holiday letting or into other tourist enterprises such as farm parks, farm museums, rare breed survival centres, and so forth. Some have survived by amalgamating small family farms into larger and more specialized units. Some have moved away from food production and into "energy crops" or industrial crops like linseed or oilseed rape. And some have decided that a return to the old mixed farm economy of the 1950s is the best tactic at a time of increasing concern about over-intensive farming methods. At the far end of the spectrum there are a number of organic farm enterprises based upon the production of high-value vegetables, free-range eggs, and other organic foods.

Beyond the village boundaries, in areas which the planners refer to as "open countryside", the traditional farming landscape, and the traditional farming economy, are undergoing a period of dramatic

*Coast and country: two images of modern
Pembrokeshire. Above: Cenarth Falls.
Below: Lydstep Haven.*

An "ecological" country cottage with grass roof and aerogenerator, near Newport.

change. Farming will continue to be the mainstay of the Pembrokeshire economy, with farms and farm buildings more and more prominent as they increase in size. The thousands of country cottages dotted about in the landscape will also survive. However, few new cottages will be added to their number since planners dislike new rural buildings and since the provision of services to rural locations is now a very expensive luxury.

In the countryside and in the villages cottages and terraced houses were, in the 1970s, being sold at an increasing rate to "immigrants", many of whom kept them as holiday homes or as retirement nests. This caused great local resentment but there was no easy way to halt the trend. The seller always wants the best possible price for his property, and more often than not this is paid by a "foreigner"; young married couples have little chance of competing with the

businessman looking towards peaceful retirement in the country. Some hamlets and villages evolved into summer settlements, busy during the summer season when cottage owners were in residence, and virtually dead during the winter. This problem was of course most severe in the National Park.

However, the trend towards absentee ownership went into reverse in the late 1970s and early 1980s as inflation slowed down and as the "cottage arson" campaign of North Wales began to affect Pembrokeshire also. Consequently many cottages and farms were sold to the settlers of the Green Wave, some of them living alternative life-styles, some attracted by the ideals of self-sufficiency, and others simply escaping from the urban rat-race. Many of the settlers had young families, and brought with them new ideas and a refreshing (if often naive) enthusiasm for rural life. Other settlers were in middle age, bringing with them entrepreneurial skills and capital to invest in new buildings and new businesses. This settlement wave transformed the character of many hamlets and open countryside areas, and inevitably led to stresses and strains in the community; but population levels rose in many isolated parishes, business activity increased, and children's laughter was heard again in places which had been in quiet decline for fifty years or more.

Pembrokeshire life, whether lived in town or country, cannot try to remain aloof from change. Pembrokeshire has changed, with the rise of tourism, the coming of the oil industry to the shores of Milford Haven, and increased affluence on all sides. The community has to adjust itself to these changes, even though the adjustment is at times painful. The following paragraphs are an attempt to summarize some of the means by which present-day Pembrokeshire is trying to adjust itself to changing circumstances.

Modern Haverfordwest

The old county town of Haverfordwest has remained largely unaffected by the booms and depressions experienced by the Milford Haven towns during the past 150 years. The advantages of its central position in Pembrokeshire were already apparent in the Middle Ages, and George Owen was in no doubt about its status as one of the chief market towns of Wales during Elizabethan times. During the seventeenth century it became a great social centre for the landed gentry, many of whom built fine town houses in High Street and Hill Street. Later growth was linked with its administrative and service functions as county town, and there has been irregular expansion of the built-up area along all of the major radial roads. The arrival of the railway in 1854 produced a prompt decline of sea trading and a century of economic stagnation, but nevertheless the

population almost doubled to a total of about 8,000. Today the town is still an important market centre with a current population of about 11.000 and a wide range of services. There is a Unigate cheese factory at the satellite settlement of Merlin's Bridge, and a trading estate at Withybush. There are large areas of housing for the families of the army regiment stationed at Brawdy. The prosperity of the town at the present day is of course helped by the industrialization of Milford Haven. There were real fears that the reorganization of local government and social services in 1974 would lead to the removal of many of the town's administrative and service functions. Several government offices were indeed removed to Carmarthen, which at first benefitted from a range of major town centre shopping developments; but after a decade of uncertainty Haverfordwest is beginning to recover. And some compensation has been provided in the form of the new Pembrokeshire College, bringing educational facilities at a variety of levels in an impressive and increasingly well-equipped modern building.

A much more serious talking-point in the town is the impact of recent commercial development, particularly in the town centre. The riverside area between the two bridges was the subject of expensive research in the 1970s and 1980s, resulting in a series of abortive development proposals. However, the completion of new roads in the town, and increasing concern about the commercial growth of Carmarthen, proved to be catalysts for change, and a custom-built Riverside Market was followed in 1990 by a third road crossing of the Western Cleddau, a large-scale development involving shop units of various sizes, a new multi-storey car-park, and amenity areas on the river banks. Bridge Street, one of the two main shopping streets of the town, has been partly pedestrianized, and the fabric of the medieval town has been changed with the introduction of new shop facades and with the departure of many town centre residents to new housing estates on the outskirts. Although some of the large shop units in the Riverside Development are still empty, the commercial focus of the town has now shifted downhill from Market Street, Dew Street and High Street, and this has of course created great resentment among some of the upper town's oldest trading families. Further pressures on small businesses have been exercised by the large chain stores recently established on "town periphery" sites served by their own car parks. The Tesco superstore in Portfield was the first, and there are now other large retail sites adjacent to the Withybush Hospital and on the old Bridge Meadow.

The Little Town of Narberth

Narberth is one of the oldest towns of west Wales, and it certainly dates back to the days of Welsh saints and princes, several hundred years before the arrival of the Normans. As "Arberth" it features in several of the tales of *The Mabinogion*, with a royal court and a strange castle mound said to provide magical access to the Otherworld. Later on the Normans turned it into a defended castle town which had great strategic importance because it controlled the lowland route between Little England and the other conquered territories of South Wales. The castle, built in stone in 1246, is in ruins and is not open to the public. Since Norman times the town has been a service centre for a large area of eastern Pembrokeshire. and for many years up to 1973 it was the administrative centre for Narberth Rural District, with its own council offices.

Between the Second World War and the mid-1980's Narberth remained a quiet and sleepy country town, with very little in the way of economic development. However, in recent years it has begun to take a greater interest in its own future, starting with the creation of the Taf and Cleddau Rural Initiative. In 1992 the Initiative was expanded to become the South Pembrokeshire Partnership for Action with Rural Communities (SPARC), and this body has now succeeded in attracting millions of pounds worth of inward investment (including much EC money) which has borne fruit in increased job opportunities, new businesses, better community facilities, and tidier buildings and streets. The town is working hard to increase its tourist income, and the community has realised that the church, the Town Hall and other fine buildings are assets which need to be preserved and even marketed to holidaymakers. There is a new Landsker Visitor Centre and TIC, and a new town museum (called the Wilson Museum), which have added greatly to local attractions.

Interestingly enough, Narberth has decided to capitalise on its position close to the Pembrokeshire Landsker, and large-scale funding has been obtained for the promotion of tourism throughout the local area, which has been designated "The Landsker Borderlands". An impressive range of local publications now entices the visitor to Narberth, and with the opening of a wide range of walking routes the town is deliberately seeking to appeal to walkers and naturalists who may not hitherto have fully appreciated the tranquil beauty of inland Pembrokeshire.

Road and Rail

At the present day, the pattern of communications in Pembrokeshire is changing in some respects, but in its main outlines there is little new. As indicated in Chapters 7 and 8, the surprisingly dense network of roads in the county goes back to Tudor and Stuart times at least, although the main trunk

A beautiful stretch of the north Pembrokeshire coast, near Abereiddi. Here the rocks are very soft and are easily eroded.

roads are of course the products of the last century or so. Also, if we look at a road map of the county we can see how Haverfordwest is clearly the central point, attracting roads from all directions. This again is an old-established feature. Another point which must be borne in mind is the influence of the Milford Haven waterway, effectively cutting the south of the county in two and explaining why road and rail services have had to be duplicated for places only a mile or so apart as the crow flies. But the Cleddau Bridge, which opened to traffic in 1975, has had a powerful psychological and commercial effect upon the links between the towns and country districts of Pembrokeshire, and it is worth investigating these links in a little more detail.

The density of the road pattern is perhaps due to Pembrokeshire's remoteness and its "peninsulated" coastal outline. Consequently, there was little ordinary through traffic as in the inland counties of England, and no development of main communicating roads. Life in the numerous small settlements was largely self-contained, each farm producing or obtaining by exchange from neighbouring farms or at one of the many local fairs all or nearly all the necessities of daily life. For commodities which could not be produced locally and for the export of surplus goods, water transport was generally available. Many of the little roads in the south of the county must have originated during the centuries of medieval settlement, but if we look at the O S map we can see that the road pattern of the Welshry is no less dense. The Welshry does, however, have a less organized system of tracks and small roads; this is because of the area's "patterned dispersion" of small farms, with few townships or villages which have acted as growth points. Obvious exceptions are St David's, Mathry and Croesgoch in the west, and Puncheston and Little Newcastle in the east; in the latter two cases the lords of the manor may have been responsible for some at least of the earliest local roads.

Pembrokeshire's many maritime traditions, examined in detail in Chapter 9, have had a great effect upon roads, particularly near the northern and western coasts and in the innermost parts of Milford Haven. For example, the poor road links of such settlements as Trefin, Llanwnda, Nolton, Marloes and Llangwm show that these villages grew up as independent and isolated communities using the sea for contact with the outside world. No less than thirty-six small ports or hard beaches on the open coast and on the Milford Haven waterway have been used for coastal trading, each one acting as a local centre for traffic from the immediate vicinity.

Haverfordwest has always been the natural focus of an agricultural community. The passage of statesmen, diplomats, clerics

and pilgrims to and from the city of St David's must have helped Haverfordwest to grow as a routeway town, but the tracks and roads converging upon Haverfordwest carried little except local traffic until the beginning of the nineteenth century when, as we have seen, the town became the most important western collecting centre on the principality's network of drovers' roads. Later on, the growth of Milford and Fishguard as ports led to the building of better through-roads to maintain contact with the outside world, and it was these roads (the trunk roads of the present day) which more than anything else helped Haverfordwest to become the main distribution centre for the county.

As we have seen in Chapter 8, the railway network was largely complete by the end of the nineteenth century, although some extensions (for example the line to Hook Colliery) were built as late as 1929. Within the last fifty years or so several

Ancient communications. The stepping stones of the old "pilgrim's way" across the Nevern Estuary near Newport.

other changes have occurred in response to the needs of the day. Branch lines were run at the beginning of the last war from Letterston junction to the armaments depot at Trecwn, and also from Milford to the armaments depot at Newton Noyes. In 1965

The "Cleddau King" -- the primitive vehicle ferry which operated between Neyland and Hobbs Point before 1975.

the service to Letterston was discontinued, and we have seen how Neyland also lost its rail link and its depot and workshop. On the other hand new tracks have been laid in recent decades from the Milford-Johnston line to the Esso Refinery (now closed), to the Gulf Refinery at Waterston, and to the Elf Refinery near Hubberston. Without a doubt the presence of four rail termini in the county in the 1950s led to unnecessary duplication at a time when freely available road transport was already a fact of life. The present rail service, much reduced, is based upon the two main termini at Milford and Fishguard, which could supply enough freight and passenger traffic to justify their existence; but the future of the Pembroke Dock branch is still very much in doubt, in spite of the well established B&I ferry service now operating between the "Port of Pembroke" and Rosslare in South-east Ireland. Also, there is great local concern, in the absence of a national transport policy, about the prospects for the west coast rail services under the new privatised railway regime.

The long, branching waterway of Milford Haven and the Daugleddau has always presented a social and economic barrier between the south and south-east of the county and that part centred on Haverfordwest. The road link from Pembroke to Haverfordwest via Canaston Bridge is over twenty miles long. Although the Burton-Pembroke ferry and the Picton ferry once shortened this journey considerably for foot passengers, both have been closed now for many years. The same is true of the other ferries which served the various waterside communities. Examples were the Cosheston-Lawrenny ferry, the Landshipping-Llangwm ferry, the Lawrenny-Picton Point ferry. The only ferry service operating at the beginning of 1975 was the vehicle ferry with a daily schedule of about thirty crossings each way between the precarious Hobbs Point slipway and the pontoon jetty at Neyland. It was a vital part of the county's road network, but no matter what fond memories local people may have of it, it was no adequate alternative to a road or a rail bridge between the north and south shores of the Haven.

There have been innumerable plans for a Haven crossing. In 1921 Sir Frederick Meyrick put forward an ambitious scheme for a barrage from Hobbs Point to Neyland, to be crossed by road and railway and to be equipped with turbine generators and locks to allow shipping to pass upstream to Haverfordwest. In 1945 the county council commissioned a report which suggested a high-level suspension bridge across the Haven between Pembroke Ferry and Barnlake, with a supplementary bridge crossing of Westfield Pill. This, like several other schemes, came to nothing, and it was eventually decided to improve the Neyland-Hobbs Point service with a new ferry boat.

In 1956 the Esso Petroleum Company was examining the possibility of a refinery on Milford Haven, but it required assurance of a water supply of 5 million gallons per day (mgd) by 1970. This led to renewed discussion of a barrage scheme, and the local authorities enthusiastically supported a firm proposal. A private bill was introduced in the 1958-9 parliamentary session for a rubble masonry dam across the Daugleddau from Jenkins Point to Williamston Mountain to carry a road, double-track railway, and footpaths. The potential water yield was calculated at 56 mgd, and the cost £2.5 million. The advantages of the scheme were many, but amid great local disappointment a Commons Select Committee turned down the proposal, on the published grounds that the barrage would provide an amount of water far in excess of demand. The real reason for the decision may have been that a nuclear power-station was at that time being considered for Carew Cheriton, not far away from the proposed barrage site.

Since 1959 the great developments on the shores of the Haven have shown just how short-sighted the government decision really was, and alternative schemes have cost the taxpayer in excess of £20 million. The Pembrokeshire Water Board had to construct a pumping station on the Eastern Cleddau to meet the rising demand for industrial water, and was further involved in a £5 million reservoir scheme at Llysyfran for the provision of up to 19 mgd to meet foreseeable demand. In addition, the government has had to accept the need for a road link between the two shores of the Haven.

Work on the Milford Haven High Level Bridge started in 1968, largely as an act of faith by Pembrokeshire County Council. The estimated cost was £3 million, and the bridge was to be a box girder structure more or less on the site originally proposed in 1945. Things proceeded well at first. However, tragedy struck with the collapse of a section of the bridge in June 1970. Work on the project stopped, and the Government embarked upon an investigation of box girder

The Cleddau Bridge following its tragic collapse in 1970.

structures which held up the builders for a year. The Cleddau Bridge (as it is now called) did not open to traffic until 1975. By this time the cost had quadrupled, to almost £12 million, and the local authority had no option but to take responsibility for the debt and to impose heavy toll charges. In spite of numerous appeals to the government over the past twenty years, there has been a blanket refusal to help in paying off the debt. Little wonder that the people of Pembrokeshire, when faced with this long saga of indecision, expense and misadventure, are cynical about government transport priorities.

The various roadworks connected with the bridge have made a great impact upon communications in the county. The roads on the north shore of the Haven are much improved, and the trunk road between Haverfordwest and Milford has been reconstructed to dual carriageway standard in places. There have been other improvements on the A40 trunk road between Whitland and Haverfordwest, and between the county town and Fishguard. These have been necessary because of increased private and commercial traffic, and because of the great volume of heavy traffic carrying loads to and from the Milford Haven refinery sites. Around the refineries themselves access roads have also been widened and straightened. The new southern by-pass of Haverfordwest (Freeman's Way) carries through traffic to Milford, Neyland and the Elf and Gulf refineries; and a major road scheme in the lower part of the town has greatly improved the flow of traffic on the A40 trunk road. The new eastern by-pass, running from near the railway station to Withybush, has succeeded in keeping the increasing volume of heavy container traffic out of the town on its way to and from the Irish freight terminal at Fishguard Harbour. In 1995 a new by-pass was built to take St David's traffic away from the City Road bottleneck.

The result of all these road improvements is largely, but not entirely, beneficial. Many shopkeepers feel that as more traffic by-passes the town, they have lost a great deal of passing trade. There is now much more rapid access from all parts of Pembrokeshire to London and South-East England, and vice versa, and this fact has been of great importance for the local tourist industry (see Chapter 15). Also, whereas local businesses were held back by the "remoteness factor" in the 1950s and 1960s, changing technologies and the new accessibility of the county have enabled the new generation of local businesses to compete on more or less equal terms with businesses located elsewhere in the UK. Changes in information technology involving the use of personal computers, modems and the InterNet have been crucial in this respect. Moreover, local businesses can boast certain competitive advantages - low business rates, low wage costs, and a clean and attractive working environment. But as far as local residents are concerned, the new roads (and especially the Cleddau Bridge) have in a sense given Pembrokeshire a stronger regional identity in 1995 than it had in 1974.

Farming Today

Agriculture is still the most important local industry in terms of employment and general economic importance. The "standard output" of farming in the county is about 17 % of the total agricultural output of Wales. In the early 1970's there were 3,300 farm holdings, but over the last 25 years this figure has declined considerably. About 3,000 persons now find employment on farms either on a regular, part-time or seasonal basis. This compares with around 6,000 in the late 1940s, but we should not forget that many other people are now employed in activities connected with agriculture - for example, in sales and deliveries of farm supplies, milk collection, dairy work, and land drainage. Together with farmers' and workers' wives and families, the total work-force dependent upon agriculture in Pembrokeshire must be about 15,000. Although tourism and related services probably provide more jobs in total, many of these are seasonal and very poorly-paid; and earnings from agricultural sales are probably still greater than earnings from tourism.

The success of farming depends upon many different factors. Weather and climate are perhaps of the greatest importance, and it is not surprising that farmers become preoccupied with sunshine and cloud, wind and rain, frost and snow. On the whole the local climate is favourable to agriculture. Its main characteristics are its equable and maritime nature; its mild winters and its cool, changeable summers; its abundant and well-distributed rainfall; and its exposure, particularly to winds from the south-west. At St Ann's Head temperatures fall below freezing point only on three or four exceptional occasions each year, and for ten months of the year the average monthly temperature is about 5.6 degrees C; this means that ordinary crops and grasses can continue to grow throughout most of the year, and that livestock can generally be kept in the open even during the winter months. Many hedgerow plants are in flower in Pembrokeshire by 27 April in most years, as early as the Scilly Isles and the south coast of Cornwall. On the coast annual rainfall totals may be no more than 80 cm, and sunshine totals 1,700 hours; however, rainfall increases sharply inland, and the average annual rainfall for Mynydd Presely is more than 200 cm. Thus the climate gradually becomes less favourable as one moves from west to east across the county. Perhaps the biggest problem of all is the wind. Trees carved by the westerly gales into grotesque distorted forms are very much a part of the Pembrokeshire scene, and the outer coasts are bleak and occasionally treeless, not just because of the wind but also because of the effects of salt spray. This spray kills natural vegetation and crops, and a stormy spring and summer can present a real danger to the livelihoods of farmers whose fields line the cliff tops. In most years more than thirty gales are recorded at the coast, and in a stormy winter gale-force gusts may be recorded on average every other day.

Another important factor in Pembrokeshire farming is the nature of the soil. Sometimes the nature of the soil is determined largely by the character of deposits left during the Ice Age; till and fluvio-glacial sands and gravels are particularly common in the northern part of the county and around the shores of St Bride's Bay. Where sands and gravels or sandy till occur they give the soil a stony, open texture and high fertility; such soils in Dewisland were believed to retain heat, and were much valued for cereal production. On the other hand soils which occur on sticky clay till are generally thin and rather acid as a result of heavy leaching, and fertility is much reduced in the moorland commons around St David's and also in the Fishguard-Dinas area where pockets of Irish Sea till are found. Other types of soils which are not particularly closely related to bedrock

geology are the lowland peats and the alluvial and sand-dune soils in some river valleys and coastal embayments respectively. In the uplands (above 150 m) "gley soils" are much more common, with wide expanses of hill peats in the higher areas and many occurrences of "mountain soils". Some of these soils occur very close to sea-level in Pembrokeshire as a result of the county's oceanic location, its exposure and its heavy rainfall.

Most often the soils of the county can be related quite closely to the underlying bedrock type. Over much of the north of the county the rocks of the Lower Palaeozoic outcrops have produced medium to heavy silty loams of brown or greyish-brown colour containing many shale or "rab" fragments. In the south of the county the best soils are encountered on the outcrops of Carboniferous Limestone and Old Red Sandstone; soils which have formed on the former are fine deep ferruginous loams, and on the latter deep red loams with much sand and silt. Both soils are among the most fertile in Wales. The Coal Measures and Millstone Grit outcrops in the centre of the county give rise to thin, shaly, grey-brown soils of low or moderate fertility.

As a result of all the various combinations of relief, climate and soils, a wide variety of environmental conditions faces the Pembrokeshire farmer at the present day. Naturally enough, the potential of the land varies greatly from place to place, and the pattern of farming is made even more complicated, when we look at it in detail, because of local farming expertise, or local traditions, or local shortages of capital. The environment is suited above all to various types of grassland, mostly with rushes in the north and with ryegrass in the centre and south of the county. In the uplands the environment favours heather moorland and fell, with some areas of special mountain grassland.

There are several distinct farming regions in the county, each specializing in slightly different combinations of farming activities.

Around the eastern, northern and western margins of the Presely Hills there is mixed farming, with the rearing of cattle and sheep alongside arable agriculture. Farms are generally of medium or small size. To the east of the uplands dairying is rather more important than the growing of arable crops, whereas barley and wheat are grown in greater abundance on the St David's peninsula, mostly as animal feedstuffs. In the south-west of the county, bounded by a line running approximately from Newgale via Trefgarn to Saundersfoot, arable farming is an essential part of the way of life, with stock raising or dairying to a lesser degree. Here the greatest effects of the oceanic warming of climate are felt, for the Milford Haven-Daugleddau waterway allows sea water to penetrate far inland. In addition, this area has a lot of fertile land, so that cereals (particularly barley and wheat) and potatoes and other root vegetables are popular among farmers. The eastern dairying region, occupying an arc of land from the southern foothills of Mynydd Presely as far west as Haverfordwest and thence eastwards along the lowland towards Whitland, experiences rainfall totals in excess of 100 cm. Consequently, there is a true pastoral way of life, in which dairy herds are more common than stock herds and where barley is the major cereal crop. Finally, up in the mountains, including the detached moorlands of Mynydd Carningli, Mynydd Cilciffeth and Mynydd Castlebythe, sheep rearing is the main occupation, although cattle are often kept on the lower slopes. Where cultivation is possible, grass crops and barley are again most important.

If we examine some of the trends in Pembrokeshire farming since the last war we see that oats has become less popular as a crop while the combined wheat and barley area has increased to 16,000 ha. Mixed corn production has declined, having been popular for a while because of subsidy payments. Trends in dairy farming show that while the number of milk producers has fallen since 1947 to about 1,000, the dairy herd of the county has stabilised at around 70,000 animals. Since 1983 milk sales have been controlled by the infamous quota system which caused such distress when it was introduced.

While Pembrokeshire farming has become much more efficient over the last thirty years, it has not become much more specialized. Agriculture in the county remains variable in character, with the greatest part of the arable acreage each year devoted to grass crops of various types and to cereals for animal feed. There are still over 70,000 sheep in the county, and in the upland areas they form the basis of the farming economy. Pig farming has declined dramatically in recent years, partly because there is no local registered abattoir. However, it must be remembered in the case of livestock that, as with arable farming, government subsidies, health scares, food fashions and EC policies can all have a great influence.

The major specialized crop in Pembrokeshire is early potatoes. Before 1937 early potatoes were not grown on a large scale in the county, but after experimental planting had proved successful around the Pembrokeshire coast, over 1,600 ha were devoted to early potatoes in 1944. For about 30 years after the War acreages were maintained at a level of approximately 2,800 ha per annum, according to demand and price fluctuations. Peak production was in 1963, when there were almost 3,600 ha of early potatoes, as against 600 ha of maincrop potatoes. The early crop is still much the more important. Nevertheless, increasing specialization is evident on the coastal farms; out of the 780 growers participating in the early potato trade in 1962, only 370 remained in 1971. And now, in 1995, the rising cost of early potato production has forced even more growers to concentrate on less risky ventures. Today the early potato area is down to about 1,500 ha, and it will reduce further in size in the future.

Early potato growing and marketing follows a set pattern. Planting begins on most farms in January, with plastic sheeting now widely used to minimise the risk of frost damage. Given a good spring, the crop is well advanced by late April. Lifting is generally started in mid-May. Casual labour is employed, with teams of "spud bashers" moving from farm to farm. During the lifting season (which usually lasts for about six weeks) merchants from many parts of Britain visit Pembrokeshire and negotiate purchases individually with growers. Some growers consistently sell to the same merchants while others deal on a day-to-day basis. Growers may start lifting at a yield of only 3 tons per acre, for the price at this time may be as high as £500 per tonne. After a fortnight the price per tonne is more than halved, and it falls to an average of about £95 on the thirtieth day. On the other hand yields may be as high as 15 tons per acre at the end of the lifting season and growers acquire great skill in planning their lifting programme each year in order to obtain the maximum benefit. In particular, they have to try and assess the market impact of early potato imports from Spain, Cyprus and Jersey. Local marketing is greatly helped by the locally-owned Puffin Produce Ltd, set up originally to promote early potato sales but now also involved in the marketing of other vegetables. Nowadays the greater part of the early potato crop is exported by road, and the potato lorries are a common sight on the A40 trunk road during May and June. Most of these lorries are destined for the South Wales and Midlands markets, although some travel much further afield.

Other cash crops are not of great importance at the present day, although wartime production of flax rose to a level of 1284 ha in 1944, and there were 682 ha of sugar beet in 1942. In 1995 about 600 ha of oilseed rape was grown in the county, together with about 400 ha of flax and 400 ha of maize. Market gardening and indoor flower growing have generally been looked on as hazardous enterprises, even though the coastal environment is as favourable as that of Cornwall or the Scilly Isles. That having been said, there are a number of long-established market gardening enterprises in the county, based upon sales of tomatoes, lettuces, cut flowers and other high-value products grown under glass or in poly tunnels. Some of the nurserymen and horticulturalists have become more financially secure by moving into the "garden centre" business and catering for the rising urban demand for bedding plants, shrubs, seeds, fertilisers and a host of gardening supplies. There are one or two farmers who run their own farm shops and "pick your own" enterprises, but the local urban population is not really large enough to sustain this type of enterprise.

In the 1970s a number of enterprising farmers entered the bulb-growing business, for they found that the disease-free Pembrokeshire bulb fields had a marked advantage over the traditional bulb-growing areas such as Lincolnshire. One grower entered the export market with considerable success using the freezing plant and large refrigerators at one of the turkey farms to store cut daffodils and other flowers for winter and early spring sale in London and elsewhere just at the time of year when flowers were very scarce. There is still considerable potential for this type of activity, for farm plant and buildings can be used during part of the year for turkey breeding and during the rest of the year for potato, bulb and cut flower storage and even cattle fattening. Turkey breeding is less popular in Pembrokeshire than it used to be but, nevertheless, about 30,000 birds are reared each year on large turkey farms for the Christmas market. Cauliflower and broccoli growing is a vulnerable but potentially profitable business, but has declined since 1974 when over 150,000 crates of cauliflowers were sent to the main vegetable markets. At present there are about thirty commercial and specialised growers in the county, but more farmers are being attracted into early vegetables as a sideline. The marketing of vegetables has been greatly helped by the expansion of Puffin Producers Ltd.

Military Establishments

Military establishments of one sort or another have been very much a part of the Pembrokeshire scene ever since the prehistoric period. The promontory and hill forts of the Iron Age were followed by stockaded earthworks and then by more sophisticated motte and bailey castles. After the Conquest the mighty stone fortresses of the Normans appeared in strategic locations. Later there came the forts planted on the shores of Milford Haven during the Napoleonic era, and garrisons such as the Defensible Barracks (1843) and the Llanion Barracks in Pembroke Dock. Finally there were the other structures dating particularly from World War II - airfields, gun emplacements, concrete coastal defences, lookout posts and radar stations. Twenty years ago many of these latter features still remained as derelict and dangerous ruins, particularly along the coastline where they spoiled the beauty of several sections of the Coastal Footpath. Now, however, most have been demolished and removed. Others are cherished as important parts of our military heritage.

There were no less than twelve military airfields in the county; the best known were around the coast, for example at St David's, Talbenny, Angle and Dale. The earliest "air stations" were at Sageston and Goodwick, and they were used during the First World War. The later airfields were used, for example, for coastal reconnaissance, convoy escort and anti-submarine work, and the aircraft based in Pembrokeshire included Mosquitoes, Hurricanes and Wellingtons. Some of the squadrons based in Pembrokeshire were detailed to the protection of the naval convoys using Milford Haven. This work was particularly important in the early years of the War, and after 1942 the Sunderlands based at Pembroke Dock played an increasingly important role with their sorties far out into the Atlantic. At the end of the War many of the Pembrokeshire-based squadrons were moved or disbanded, and most of the airfields were taken out of operational use. But traces of the airfields and airstrips still remain, most obviously in the form of derelict buildings. Runways are notoriously difficult to remove; so most of them remain as crumbling expanses of concrete and tarmac, used only by farm vehicles and increasingly colonized by encroaching weeds.

Other installations included a string of "Chain Home" radar installations and camps including Kete, near St Ann's Head, a balloon base near Milford, a large radar station and camp at RAF Folly, near Nolton, anti-aircraft installations at Tenby and Dale, a substantial RAF radar-radio installation at Angle, bombing decoys at Trecwn and Cosheston, and lookout stations and searchlight batteries near Strumble Head, St Ishmael's and Broad Haven. There are 431 known military sites in Pembrokeshire dating from the nineteenth and twentieth centuries. The "last generation" of these buildings, made for the most part of red brick and concrete (rather than stone) are now almost 60 years old, and a recent study suggests, quite reasonably, that at least some of them should be kept as valuable components of our historic heritage.

Nevertheless, many of the least attractive buildings have been removed from these wartime sites in the last few years.

As recently as 1990 the Army, the Air Force and the Navy were still present in force. Their establishments and their activities aroused strong feelings, particularly because they made a great impact upon the peace and quiet (not to mention the freedom of access) of several sections of the National Park. But they provided employment and brought a great deal of money to the main towns, and Pembrokeshire people were, on balance, prepared to put up with them.

The Ministry of Defence currently holds over 2,600 ha (about 5 per cent) of the National Park, 24 per cent of the Pembrokeshire "heritage coast", and eleven miles of the long-distance Coastal Footpath. At Castlemartin, in the south Pembrokeshire section of the National Park, the Ministry of Defence tank range occupies some 2.300 ha of what used to be good farm land. In the middle of it stands the ghost settlement of Flimston, with only its chapel maintained in a good state of repair. The firing range, criss-crossed by tank tracks and in places littered with great piles of scrap metal, prevents summer access to what is probably the most magnificent stretch of limestone coast in the whole of Britain, and firing shatters the peace of much of south Pembrokeshire. Some of the modern buildings erected on the range, in a wild and open landscape, are massive and ugly. On the other hand the range provides some local jobs, and there is grazing for some 12,000 livestock (mostly sheep) from the Presely Hills during the winter months.

In the north-east corner of St Bride's Bay, on the fringes of the National Park, HMS Goldcrest was established at Brawdy as an RNAS training base for naval jet pilots. Later it was transferred to the RAF, and a number of schemes were put in hand to lengthen the old Second World War runways and to improve hangars and other facilities. The base became a key training establishment for fighter pilots, and Hunter and Hawk jets were seen (and heard!) flying low over the Pembrokeshire landscape every working day. The base provided employment for hundreds of local people, and supported many small service businesses in the north of the county. The base was also used by the Sea King helicopters of the RAF Search and Rescue Unit, and Pembrokeshire people grew very attached to the cumbersome and noisy yellow monsters, especially around the coast where they were constantly involved in rescues from the cliffs and from the coastal waters. They were frequently also pressed into service for long-distance rescues or medical emergencies on board ships in the South-Western Approaches.

Less welcome in the days of the Cold War was the US Naval "Facility" at Brawdy, referred to in 1971 as an "Oceanographic Research Station" but commonly assumed to be used for high-tech monitoring of Soviet submarine movements in the Celtic Sea and eastern Atlantic. In 1972, in conditions of great secrecy, a mysterious cable was planted underground from the "facility" to Penycwm, whence it travelled westwards on the floor of St Bride's Bay. Large numbers of local people, some of them members of CND, saw the base as a symbol of American military colonialism; the Pembrokeshire planning authorities had no say at all in the decision to build it, and everybody knew that it was one of the prime Soviet nuclear targets in western Britain. Not surprisingly, it attracted its fair share of demonstrations and marches in the heady 1980's when CND acted out its role as the conscience of the nation.

Between 1950 and 1993, with constant low flying over the St David's peninsula, the surrounding area was much less peaceful than it had been in the immediate post-war years. Villages such as Llandeloy suffered a great deal of noise as a result of jets landing and taking off directly over them, and after complaints from residents soundproofing of many homes was undertaken at government expense.

Since the last war the number of Ministry of Defence establishments in the county has been greatly reduced, but some (in particular Brawdy) remain as valuable employers. Most of the wartime airfields and other bases were closed soon after the war, but HMS Harrier at Kete remained open until 1960. Some years ago the AA gunnery school at Manorbier released most of its 276 acres on a valuable coastal site in the National Park for use by the community. Of greater local significance was the release of ninety-eight ex-ministry houses nearby. In 1990 the most important of the remaining military sites were at Newton Noyes, just east of Milford, and at Trecwn, in the deep Nant-y-bugail valley in the western foothills of the Presely range. Both of these were Admiralty depots concerned with the manufacture and storage of armaments, and between them they provided employment for more than 1,300 local people. With the cut-back in defence expenditure during the mid-1970s there were real fears that the Newton Noyes and Trecwn establishments, like the small naval base at Pembroke Dock, would be closed as economy measures. In the event they remained open until 1994; but at last closure was forced by the defence rationalisation following the collapse of the Communist Empire and the payment of the "peace dividend."

In 1993 RAF Brawdy was closed by the MoD, sending shock-waves through the whole of Pembrokeshire. A determined and sustained battle to save it, coordinated by the "Western Telegraph" newspaper and with the full backing of the local MPs, was ultimately unsuccessful, as was a campaign

to retain the Sea King S&R service at the base. The beneficiary of the closures was RAF Chiverton in Wiltshire, and there were strong local suspicions that politics, rather than defence or operational considerations, lay behind the closure decision. However, in 1994 a further vociferous campaign was mounted with the object of convincing the Defence Minister that the economic impact of total closure would lead to vastly increased unemployment and would all but cripple the Pembrokeshire economy. It was also argued that the Brawdy base, having had many millions of pounds invested in it in recent years, would represent a scandalous loss to the tax-payer should it close completely. Happily, the Minister saw some merit in the arguments placed before him, and as a result the base was passed over to the Army, initially for use by the Royal Welch Fusiliers. Although the runways are no longer in use, the base facilities have been modified for Army use. In 1996 the base becomes the HQ of the 14 Signal Regiment, involving 800 Army personnel.. Of equal importance is the occupation of the base housing estates in Haverfordwest by hundreds of young families. Like all service families, their roots in the community are shallow, but they bring life and laughter to the streets, children into the local schools, and cash into the pockets of local shop-keepers.

With the passing of Trecwn and Newton Noyes, the only military establishments remaining in Pembrokeshire in the final years of the century are at Brawdy, Castlemartin, Penally, Manorbier and Pembroke Dock. In addition, some employment is provided in the north at RAE Aberporth, devoted to the testing of rocket propulsion and guidance systems, and at Pendine, where propulsion testing also takes place on a small base now operated largely by private contractors to the MoD.

Chapter Thirteen

The English, the Welsh and the Landsker

Everyone in Pembrokeshire knows that the county is divided into two regions of approximately equal size. Those regions are, according to Professor Emrys Bowen, "sharply distinct from one another in language, race type, place-names, traditions, ecclesiastical architecture and general culture". In the south is the Englishry, created by the Normans and still referred to as "Little England beyond Wales". In the north is the Welshry, a region which has evolved over many centuries of Welsh settlement as a stronghold of Welshness. And between these two halves runs a vaguely defined frontier known, in recent times at least, as the Landsker. The Englishry, the Welshry and the Landsker have been referred to earlier, particularly in Chapter 5, but it is of interest to examine the regions and their people in a little more detail, for Pembrokeshire's split personality is something which intrigues natives and tourists alike.

The Englishry

The south of the county is, for many people, a land of castles and nucleated villages, of small green fields and high wooded hedgerows, of winding, sunken, flower-fringed lanes, of English place-names and English speech. Some of the features of the landscape and culture of the area have already been explained in Chapter 5, where it was noted that towns, village distributions and individual village layouts, field

patterns and many other features can be directly attributed to the Norman genius for organization. This organization of a new type of society created a new type of landscape.

By trying to map some of the features of this landscape one can appreciate just how fundamentally the Englishry differs from the Welshry. Margaret F Davies has shown quite impressively, for example, how place-names and church types can be mapped in order to emphasize the character of the Englishry and to show its approximate northern border. The place-name evidence is difficult to interpret because there is so much doubt about what the earliest forms of present village names really were; but church types are easier to define. Margaret Davies recognized an "Anglo-Norman" church type as characteristic of the Englishry. This type has a high, battlemented tower which is often quite out of proportion with the rest of the church. In many villages the church served not only as a place of worship but also as a place of sanctuary in case of attack by Welsh raiding parties; the tower would have been used often as a watch-tower and perhaps as a beacon, even as late as the Civil War. Architecturally there need not be anything particularly "Anglo-Norman" about these churches, but they are quite different from their simple counterparts in the Welshry because they were built to serve prosperous village communities. In addition, the various medieval manorial lords looked upon

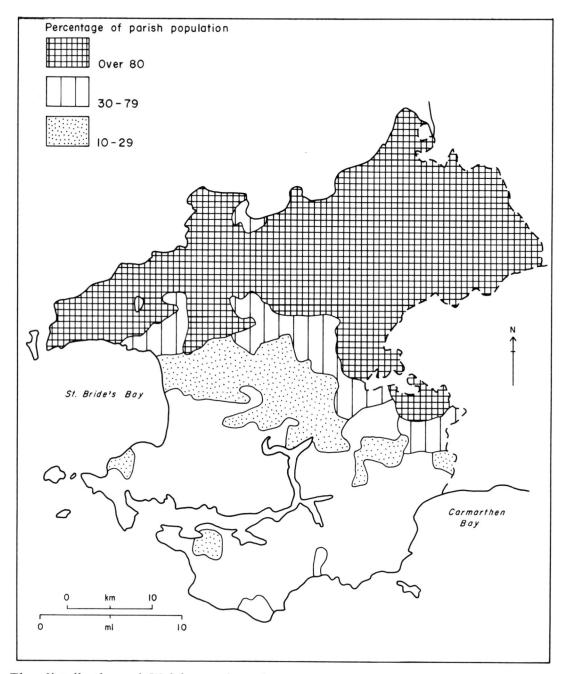

Percentage of parish population

Over 80

30 - 79

10 - 29

St. Bride's Bay

Carmarthen Bay

N

The distribution of Welsh speakers in Pembrokeshire in 1931, showing that over 80% of people in the north at that time spoke the language. In contrast, under 10% in the south spoke the language.

church building as a means of demonstrating their prestige. There was no such tradition in the Welshry, and the churches there were built for the most part by dispersed farming communities which had few resources available for the construction of lavish places of worship.

Language is now, as in George Owen's day, the most obvious measure of the Englishness of south Pembrokeshire. Pembrokeshire English has evolved over a long period of time in an isolated enclave, cut off from direct contact with England by the Welsh-speaking areas of Cardiganshire to the north-east and Carmarthenshire to the south-east. Nowadays, of course, a standardized English prevails, but until quite recently south Pembrokeshire people spoke a strong regional dialect which included a great number of words not used in the other English-speaking parts of Wales. Some of these words are still in use today, and the regional accent is, thankfully, still strong enough to allow a south Pembrokeshire man to reveal his origins whenever he opens his mouth.

In his *Guide to the Place Names and Dialects of Pembrokeshire*, Valentine Harris argues that many of the words of the Pembrokeshire dialect are pre-Chaucerian, and that they are related to the vocabulary of the Danelaw in eastern England. Dr Bertie Charles has shown that many more words have resemblances with words used in the Welsh Borders and the West Country, while others appear to have come from County Wexford. Again, there is a strong Flemish element, as suggested by Douglas James in his list of words and phrases used in old Haverfordwest. In his comprehensive *English Dialect of South Pembrokeshire*, Dr Charles shows that many words of Welsh origin have infiltrated into south Pembrokeshire, although a great many are so changed as to be almost unrecognizeable. Welsh influence is also felt in intonation and

in the construction of sentences. Typical is the Pembrokeshire habit of using "trousers" and "scissors" in the singular instead of the plural. Also, phrases like "I'll be having a half pound of cheese with you" and "There's tidy you are looking today" can be heard both north and south of the Landsker, although they are clearly derived from Welsh patterns of speech.

Some of the old South Pembrokeshire words still in use are as follows:

cutty small, minute
pyatt magpie
aclush all in pieces
beauty beautiful (as an adjective)
nowjust a moment ago
to pile to throw
caffled entangled
pill a pool or creek
to clanch to beat or thrash
rab broken stone or shale
to mitch to play truant from school
couple a few, several
siggy-wiggy a blue tit
drang a narrow passage
to take to bring
dull foolish, silly
tamping exceedingly angry
lake a brook or stream
tidy good, first-rate
to lam to beat or thrash
trash cuttings from a hedge
maid a young girl
tump a small haycock
skew a high-backed settle
kift clumsy, awkward
wroth angry
lonker rope for hobbling animals
grunkle dell or small valley
eligug guillemot
main very much, greatly
naked without a coat
tish nonsense
trolly oatmeal dumpling
penny-sow wood-louse
nisple sea-urchin

dollin a pint jug
cranted of stunted growth
bodder deaf
austy an old woman

The old towns of the Englishry, because they grew as self-contained communities over the past few centuries, developed strong corporate personalities. Douglas James considered that this may have been due to the overall lack of emigration or immigration, so that the histories of most families were common knowledge. There was "an intimate knowledge of the diverse idiosyncrasies of most of the townfolk, and hence the application of many a nickname". Some nicknames were handed down through three or four generations. Among the best of them are the following, most of which are self-explanatory:

Will Population	Horizontal Harry
Davy Seven Waistcoats	
Life and Death	Davy Daft
The Missing Link	Vest and Drawers
Cold Feet	Satan
Full Moon	Quarter of Lamb
Drips	Dai Loco
Billie Lumpy	Hell Cat
Beattie Blackdrawers	
Hairy Mary	Johnnie Wee Wee
Billie Flappers	Quick Dick
Tootsie	Butter Jaws
Unconscious	Cold Pudding
Georgie Lovely	Marvel
Hamlet's Ghost	Klondyke
Georgie Fourpence	Thankyou Ta

Concerning the physical and other characteristics of the people of south Pembrokeshire, it is difficult and perhaps dangerous to generalize. Much has been made of the fact that south Pembrokeshire people have blood-group characteristics which are rather different from those of north Pembrokeshire folk. The high frequency of blood-group A in the Englishry is probably due to the import of Scandinavian blood via Normandy, and certainly there do seem to be more tall, fair-haired people of Nordic type in the south than in the north. But south Pembrokeshire people are very mixed racially, for the present population is the result of intermarriage taking place between Normans, English, Welsh, Flemings, Irish and many other groups over the last thousand years. Typical family names of south Pembrokeshire are Philpin, Reynish, Gambold, Bateman, Gibby, Warlow and Skyrme; but there are many typically Welsh surnames as well. It should not be forgotten that the original Welsh population of Little England was never entirely replaced by immigrants. Very many Welsh surnames have survived, and parts of the Englishry appear never to have been settled with foreigners. One such area was the Amroth-Narberth-Canaston Bridge area, which at the beginning of the fourteenth century was still largely populated by Welsh people. Elsewhere, too, as we have seen in Chapter 5, the church lands around Llawhaden and Lamphey retained many Welsh inhabitants, although by the Middle Ages these populations were speaking English rather than Welsh.

Comparing the people of south Pembrokeshire with the Welsh, R M Lockley described them as "undoubtedly more open-hearted, smiling, easy-going, even indolent. They like music but sing badly. They talk excessively..........They drink much, are amiable when drunk. They are fond of children and animals. Illegitimate children are numerous and not regarded with disfavour." Others have described the people as conservative in politics, orthodox in religion (meaning that they prefer not to go to church at all), unemotional, adaptable, resentful of outside interference, and hyper-sensitive of criticism. But however they can be described, south Pembrokeshire folk

A typical Englishry church tower at Llawhaden, in an area that was once a Norman Bishop's Lordship.

cannot be described as English; they are proud of their Welshness, and they will tell you that they are as fanatical in their support of the Welsh Rugby XV as the people of the Welshry. But they will insist that their Welshness is different from that of other Welshmen...

The Welshry

The Welshry of the guide-books is a land of Celtic mystery, of wide windswept vistas of rocks and moors and stunted trees. Its people live on farms or in small hamlets which sometimes nestle in deep wooded valleys. As noted earlier, simple churches predominate; often these are not in villages at all, but stand in isolation on the sites of old monastic cells. Similarly, many of the nonconformist chapels dating from the religious revivals were built in remote sites, as if their builders were determined to continue the lonely traditions of the ascetic Welsh saints. There are few castles. Farms are smaller than in the south, and more widely dispersed. In some areas the field pattern has remained unchanged since the days of Celtic tribal society, and often field boundaries are stone walls or low treeless hedges. Place-names are for the most part Welsh. Using landscape features alone, it is still possible for the practised eye to distinguish between Welshry and Englishry.

To some extent the Welshness of north Pembrokeshire has declined, particularly during the present century as agricultural practices, systems of land-holding and the overall way of life have all

Page 157

evolved towards the English model. But the Welsh language is still strong, and many features of Welsh life retain their importance. Menna Gallie, in an amusing and perceptive study of *Little England's Other Half*, wrote "Perhaps it is because they still feel themselves to be a last, threatened remnant of Celtic culture in Pembrokeshire that the people of the Welshry sometimes seem aggressively Welsh, as if motivated by some ancient challenge, some urge to defiance."

An architypal scene from the Welshry: coracle fishing on the Teifi near Cilgerran. (Robert Evans)

Pembrokeshire Welsh, like Pembrokeshire English, has developed somewhat differently from the mother tongue. Dr Bertie Charles has studied the local dialect, and he has traced its evolution along its own peculiar lines in vocabulary and pronunciation. Today it is a dialect apart and often far removed from standard or literary Welsh. There is also a considerable English element in its vocabulary. He believes that English words have been finding their way into the language for many centuries - probably an inevitable consequence of a long period of intercommunication between the two halves of the county. Many of the English words in the Pembrokeshire Welsh dialect have become almost unrecognizable, for their original spellings and pronunciations have been adapted to Welsh and have evolved along with the rest of the language. Menna Gallie said that Pembrokeshire Welsh has "its own macabre beauty", and it has been the medium of many works of prose and poetry. North Pembrokeshire still produces far more literary men to the acre than south Pembrokeshire does to the square mile, and among the well-known poets born here are T E Nicholas, Dewi Emrys, J Brynach Davies, James Nicholas and Edgar Phillips, otherwise known as the Archdruid Trefin.

Concerning the personality of the Welsh people of north Pembrokeshire, opinions vary. Writing in 1957, R M Lockley compared them with south Pembrokeshire people as "more cautious, introspective (not to say inhibited), dour and reserved...They have outwardly a stricter religious code, attend principally chapels, and do no work on Sundays. They drink less intoxicating liquor. They are better singers. They live simply and efficiently on land where an Englishman might starve." Others refer to their nationalist politics, their rich folk-lore, their open and generous hospitality, their love of food and drink. In outward appearance, it has been said that they are mostly dark-haired, stocky folk having much closer racial affinities with the Celtic people of north and central Wales than with their neighbours in Little England.

Surnames in the Welshry are as familiar as they are limited in number. Rees (Rhys) and Evans (Ifans) are of real Welsh origin, while surnames such as Thomas, Jones,

Davies, Williams and Morris are alien Christian names which became Welsh surnames only in modern times. In those areas colonized by the Normans surnames such as Martell, Miles and Reynish belong to families which are now thoroughly Welsh; and there are a number of old English surnames, too, such as Cooper, Turner, Miller and White. But generally the Welsh-speaking community has had to put up with its scarcity of surnames in the usual manner, by providing extra specifications. Hence:

Jones the ghost   Two-foot Jones
Jones the loaf   Jones the Kremlin
Jones that won the war   Jones Great Western
Jones pop-bottle   Jones King's Arms

and many more appreciated only by those blessed with the gift of the Welsh language. Even more common are family names embellished by the names of places of abode, as in Emlyn Pontiago, Evans Brynawelon, Morse Good Hope, and Richards Llanfallteg.

The Culture of Folk Tales

In looking into the soul of Pembrokeshire, we can do far worse than examine the culture of the two communities as revealed in folk tales and traditions. Such things may appear frivolous; but in fact folk tales tell us a great deal about past events, social and religious customs, lifestyle and economy. They also teach us about ourselves - our likes and dislikes, our morals, our taboos, and our superstitions. Very many Pembrokeshire tales concentrate on the eccentric, the idiosyncratic, or the unexpected, and so in the telling of them we reinforce the stability of the community in which we live. Without this stability, we as individuals feel insecure, and indeed society itself is under threat.

In Wales, as in Ireland, there is a particularly strong tradition of non-material culture - that is, the culture of words and music, of prose and poetry and song. Story-telling is a part of this culture, and in Wales the art of story-telling was maintained and developed by the bards, those mysterious men who learned the history of their nation, and who taught and entertained their listeners with prodigious feats of memory, with profound insights and with finely-turned phrases. The bardic tradition is kept alive today by the Gorsedd of Bards and by the thousands of people, young and old, who participate in the annual eisteddfodau all over Wales. Mostly the tradition is maintained through the medium of the Welsh language, and many of the oldest stories in Wales (for example, those found in *The Mabinogion*) were told and re-told from generation to generation in Welsh and eventually written down in Welsh. Now those who are not blessed with an understanding of the "language of Heaven" can enjoy these ancient stories in various English translations.

Pembrokeshire is particularly lucky in that its rich storehouse of folk tales comes from several cultures. Over the centuries, each group of immigrants brought its own story-telling traditions, its own folk memories and its own peculiar way of looking at the world; and after the Norman Conquest the English, the Flemings, the Normans and the Irish added extra spice to the rich mix of Welsh tales already circulating in the community. Our multi-racial forefathers were our benefactors, as were those (ranging from Giraldus Cambrensis in the twelfth century to Richard Fenton in 1811 and Rev Meredith Morris in 1899) who had the good sense to write down the best-known tales of their day.

In recent years, work undertaken for *The Pembrokeshire Folk Tale Trilogy* has revealed that there are at least 500 recorded folk tales in the county ranging in age from the 1990's back to the Iron Age. There are many stories of the Celtic saints and of the great heroes of *The Mabinogion* (including King Arthur) who left their mark upon the consciousness of the Welshry in particular. There are stories of heroic deeds, eccentric characters and strange happenings galore. Tales of witchcraft and magic abound, as do stories of fairies, dragons, mermaids, goblins, great black dogs and evil spirits. Among the spooky tales ghosts figure prominently, as one might expect, but there are many stories of phantom funerals, corpse candles, premonitions and strange omens. All of these tales remind us of the worries and suspicions of Pembrokeshire folk in the centuries before the twin blessings of education and science provided explanations for almost everything and at the same time removed the magic and the fantasy from everyday life.

There is no space here to delve deeply into the meanings of typical Pembrokeshire folk tales, or indeed to recount them in any detail. However, two brief tales, one from the Welshry and the other from the Englishry, will perhaps suffice to whet the appetite of the reader.

A Tale from the Gwaun Valley.

This tale (translated from the Welsh) is typical of the "darker" stories which still circulate by word of mouth in North Pembrokeshire. On the northern side of the Cwm Gwaun there is an ancient footpath which has been used for centuries by local people on their way back and forth between the valley and the town of Newport. The footpath climbs up steeply from the farm of Llanerch, on the valley bottom, to the farm of Penrhiw, on the lower slopes of Mynydd Carningli; and on the valley side it runs through a dense woodland of tall dark trees. In the old days people said the woods were haunted, and indeed many lonely walkers saw strange shadows and heard eerie sounds among the massive tree-trunks of oak, ash and beech.

Once upon a time there was a strange old farm worker called Tom Jenkins, who worked at Dolrannog Uchaf, not far from the top end of the woodland path. One dark winters night, following a visit to the farm at Llanerch, he was walking home alone through the woods. There was a cold northerly wind moving the treetops, and there was just enough moonlight for him to make out the path ahead. All of a sudden Tom began to experience a sense of unease, and as he hurried on he became convinced that he was being followed. At last he could resist no longer, and he swung around to see if there was anybody there. His blood froze as he saw a tall figure dressed in a black coat, with black gaiters and boots, a black cloak over his shoulders, and a tall black hat upon his head. The figure stood perfectly still, about twenty yards away, staring at him.

Old Tom thought he must be dreaming, so he swung on his heel and hurried off again up the track between the shadowy tree-trunks. But he felt that he was still being followed, and eventually he turned sharply again to look behind him. And there was the same ominous figure, standing perfectly still, and still twenty yards behind him on the path. Now the old man began to feel very scared indeed, and he started to run up the track, gasping for breath on the steep slippery slope. As he neared the edge of the wood he had to stop for a breather, and he looked behind him for the third time. The tall man in black was still there, staring at him, and still only twenty yards away.

With great relief old Tom reached the edge of the woods and the open farmland beyond, and he stumbled home in the moonlight without daring to look back again. But after this terrible experience he became quite convinced that he had met "The Grim Reaper" in the woods, and that the encounter with the stranger in black could only mean one thing. Within a few days he had taken to his bed. The doctor could not discover what was wrong with him, and a few days later he was dead.

A Tale from Amroth.

This is a charming fairy tale from the Pembrokeshire -- Carmarthenshire border country. Many, many years ago a young man with golden hair and blue eyes hired a cottage not far from Amroth. He was named Crythor, after the old Welsh stringed instrument, the crwth, which he played brilliantly; and whenever a Noson Lawen was being held in the villages round about he would play on his fiddle until the people were too weary to dance any longer.

One summer evening when the merry-making was over he was returning to his cottage among the gentle green hills when he came across a band of fairy folk (Tylwyth Teg) dressed in scarlet and green. They were standing in a wooded glade, and they were quite unafraid as he approached. "Crythor", said one with a mischievous grin, "make music for us so that we can dance". So Crythor, being an amiable sort of fellow, played his fiddle while they leapt and tripped and weaved about him in the moonlight.

At last, as the dawn approached, the little people began to drift away, but before the last fairy disappeared into the shadows she turned to Crythor and said "Remember, my friend, that under the hills not far away there is a cave that goes on for ever. Inside it, your fiddle will turn to gold and you will learn the music of the fair folk."

This was an offer too good to resist, for Crythor had always been poor, and the magical haunting melodies of the Tylwyth Teg were the wonder of country folk everywhere. Just think how famous he would be if he could play fairy music on a golden fiddle! So he started to search for the cave. He asked everyone and hunted everywhere, and kept on searching as summer turned to autumn and as autumn turned to winter. By now the quest for the cave was an obsession. Every time he found a cave he would enter it and call into the darkness "Is anyone there?" Then he would play the tunes he had played to the little people in the fairy dell all those months before. He never received an answer to his question, and nobody ever appeared to dance to his tunes.

Then, one day in the depths of winter when the snow was lying in deep drifts across the lifeless landscape, he set off into the hills again to find his magic cave. He was never seen again. Some folks say he found his cave. Others say he was lost in the snowdrifts. But some of the old people of the district say that if you take the footpath through the hills north of Pendine you can hear strange music echoing in a deep underground cavern, where the ghost of Crythor plays the music of the Tylwyth Teg on a ghostly golden fiddle.

The Landsker Today

In earlier chapters there were descriptions of the changing course of the Landsker from medieval to Elizabethan times. Since George Owen, with perhaps a touch of poetic licence, described the Elizabethan Landsker so vividly, it has undoubtedly ceased to be a strong racial and cultural divide. But the Landsker has continued to separate two distinct communities. In 1888 Edward Laws wrote that there was still little intercourse between the Welsh and the English. He considered that the boundary between the two racial groups was rather stable, but stated "...the racial line is not now-a-days quite so hard as it was in times past". Within the present century it has been assumed that the ancient line of linguistic demarcation has become blurred to the extent that it can no longer be recognized. There is some merit in this view. English-biased education has made more and more impact upon the Welshry, and from an examination of the Welsh language data in the Census Reports we can see how rapid the decline of Welsh has been. It is now possible to compare the information for six census years - 1931, 1951, 1961, 1971, 1981, and 1991.

1931 The greater part of the Welshry contained over 80 per cent of the Welsh speakers. The Englishry contained less than 10 per cent of Welsh speakers, and across the centre of the county there was a narrow belt (one or two parishes deep) where 10-60 per cent of the people could speak Welsh.

1951 The Englishry was still solidly English-speaking, but in the Welshry the number of Welsh speakers was declining rapidly. Much of the St David's peninsula and the area between Trefgarn and Goodwick now contained less than 80 per cent of Welsh speakers, and the "Landsker Zone" with a lower percentage of Welsh speakers was becoming broader.

1961 The area with less than 10 per cent Welsh speakers was growing, and there was a marked reduction of Welsh speakers in the Landsker zone. Whereas in 1951 the upland area was solidly Welsh, now the Welsh-speaking "core" had broken down into separate groups of parishes, showing that the decline of the language was accelerating.

1971 Broadly there was a similar pattern to 1961, but with the status of Welsh still declining in the western part of the Welshry and especially in the Landsker zone.

1981 Between 1971 and 1981, partly because of the aggressive Welsh-language policies of the new Dyfed County Council, many south Pembrokeshire parishes experienced an increase of Welsh speakers of more than 50 per cent. However, numbers remained numerically low. In most north Pembrokeshire parishes the Welsh language continued to decline in importance, to the point where only two small areas (around the Gwaun Valley and Crymych) had more than 80 per cent Welsh speakers.

1991 In south Pembrokeshire, most parishes had between 5 and 20 per cent Welsh speakers. In the north, there were now no parishes with more than 80 per cent Welsh speakers, and in many areas the figure had dropped below 50 per cent.

From evidence such as this, with the rapid anglicisation of the Welshry and the gradual spread of Welsh speaking in the Englishry, it is not surprising that many historians have argued that there has been no sharp division between Welshry and Englishry for many years. The language maps, for example those produced by John Aitchison and Harold Carter in *A Geography of the Welsh Language 1961-1991*, simply seem to show a slow gradation in a broad belt across the centre of the county between the solidly English south and the Welsh-speaking core of the north. In recent years some writers, intent upon proving that Welsh influence has always been strong in the Englishry just as English influence has affected the Welshry, have suggested that there is now no strong racial or linguistic line across the county. Sadly, some authors have sought, for reasons of "political correctness", to deny the unique cultural traditions of the Englishry and the Landsker Zone. Major Francis Jones went so far as to regret the use of the term "Landsker", implying that even if there is some sort of line between Welshry and Englishry it is too insignificant to deserve the blessing of a proper name.

But the Landsker is far from dead. In detailed field surveys undertaken across the Landsker zone in 1961 and 1971 attempts were made to establish the real status of the Welsh language in the centre of the county and also to discover whether there was any sharp divide between the Welshry and the Englishry. In 1971 a party of students undertook the survey and questioned 561 householders in the area. From their results there was little doubt concerning the continuing presence of the Landsker as a linguistic divide. Although most of the people questioned had not heard of the Landsker (indicating that the term itself had passed out of common usage), everyone was aware of the presence of the linguistic divide, and most of the interviewees had no difficulty in locating it with reasonable accuracy within their own neighbourhood.

Overall, the 1971 position of the Landsker was similar to that plotted for 1931 by D T Williams. Its sharpest section was in the west along the parish boundaries of the Trefgarn ridge. The divide was also very sharp along the southern edges of New Moat and Bletherston parishes, coinciding partly with the course of the Afon Syfni; but here the census statistics and language maps failed completely to bring out the sharpness of the divide. In the centre of the county, around Spittal and Walton East parishes, and in the south-eastern lowland area between Pembrokeshire and Carmarthenshire, the divide was more difficult to find; there the mixed language loyalties of the past thirty years provide an indication of the complicated settlement history of the Anglo-Norman period.

Since the completion of the detailed fieldwork in the Landsker Zone more than 25 years ago, the 1981 and 1991 Census data have shown that the slow decline of the Welsh language in north Pembrokeshire is continuing. However, there are some hopeful signs that all is not lost. Since the early 1970s there has been a great rise in attendance at Welsh language classes, and many English immigrants in St David's,

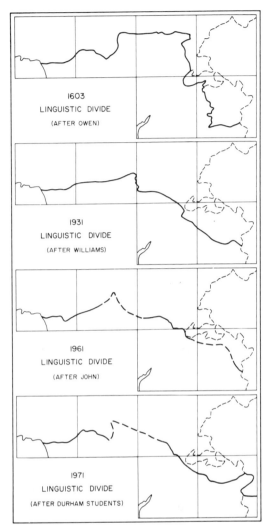

1603
LINGUISTIC DIVIDE
(AFTER OWEN)

1931
LINGUISTIC DIVIDE
(AFTER WILLIAMS)

1961
LINGUISTIC DIVIDE
(AFTER JOHN)

1971
LINGUISTIC DIVIDE
(AFTER DURHAM STUDENTS)

Maps showing how remarkably stable the Landsker has been since the days of George Owen. In the west, for example, it has hardly moved at all since Norman times.

Fishguard, Crymych and Newport are strongly motivated to learn Welsh and to integrate, as far as possible, into the local Welsh-speaking community. The teaching of Welsh in both primary and secondary schools has expanded, and in primary schools throughout the Welshry much teaching of science, history and other subjects is now conducted through the medium of Welsh. Expenditure on Welsh-language

Deep in the Welshry. An aerial photograph of the landscape of St David's Peninsula, seen from above Solva Harbour. (Studio Jon)

books has increased sharply, and the Welsh-language television channel S4C has been transmitting an increasingly wide variety of programmes. So long as Welshness persists in the north the Landsker will continue to exist. Indeed, the recent marketing of "The Landsker Borderlands" in the Narberth - Whitland area has done much to raise awareness of the Landsker both among locals and visitors.

In spite of the slow decline of the Welsh language in the Landsker zone of Pembrokeshire, the linguistic divide is as easy to find as it ever has been during the past thousand years. It may be less easy to **see** than the distinctive landscape features of the Welshry and Englishry, but it is very much a reality in the minds of the local people. The Pembrokeshire Landsker, which has in turn been a fortified national frontier, a social and economic divide, and an invisible linguistic divide, may be a historical relic, but it has remarkable persistence.

Chapter Fourteen

Natural History

We have already looked in some detail at the geology and landscapes of the county, and through the book we have seen something of the archaeological remains and other cultural features which lie within its boundary. We have not yet looked in any detail at the natural history, and the main part of this chapter is devoted to a brief survey of plant and animal life.

Extinction and Adaptation

At the end of the last glacial episode Pembrokeshire was a barren tundra, inhabited by wild beasts including mammoth, reindeer, wolf, cave bear, glutton, giant ox and giant deer. Gradually the bleak treeless expanses were transformed by the warming climate to a scrub woodland dominated by dwarf willow and birch, rowan, hawthorn and juniper. Later (by about 7,000 BC) this evolved to a denser woodland with ash, alder, holly and oak until the whole landscape was covered by a vast primeval forest which thinned only towards the exposed coast and towards the higher parts of Mynydd Presely. In these areas heaths and grasslands were better able to withstand the rigours of climate. Already there was some forest clearance going on, for the Mesolithic tribes knew how to kill trees by burning and ring-barking. In the main river estuaries, there was a type of "wet woodland" characterised by alder, willow, hazel, aspen and oak, with expanses of marshes, pools and gravel banks, and sand dunes close to the coast. Here and there salt marshes inhibited the growth of trees.

There was still a rich and varied animal life, although most of the tundra animals (for example mammoth, reindeer and glutton) were already extinct in Pembrokeshire. Wolves, bears, wild boars and deer were still common in the forests, and there were beavers and otters in the rivers. Bird life was particularly rich, probably with many more species than we have today.

We should remember that the coast of the day was well to the seaward of the present coast since sea-level was still low, but rising, as the great ice sheets of the world melted. The cliffs of today stood high and dry, some of them plastered with loose glacial deposits (for example on the north coast and on the west-facing coast of St Bride's bay), and others standing up as barren rock faces providing refuges for various arctic and alpine plant species. For example, the massive limestone ramparts of Linney Head, St Govan's Head and Stackpole Head must have looked particularly impressive, standing proud of extensive wooded plains and fringed by banks of scree. Little wonder that the limestone caves of these cliffs were popular places of residence for the local Stone Age tribes; from the comfort of their own homes they could scan the distant horizon for herds of wild animals and also for the tell-tale smoke rising from the camp fires of their enemies.

By about 5,000 years ago more of the exotic animal species had become extinct because of changing climate or hunting. Sea level had risen to more or less its present position, and the bulk of present-day plants were already established.

In Neolithic times more forest clearance with axes, accompanied by the herding of domesticated animals and the cultivation of crops, had a marked effect upon Pembrokeshire's natural history. Both plants and animals were introduced from other parts of Britain (and from the continent) and became "naturalised". Since the Neolithic, pastoral activities and the growing of crops on an ever-increasing scale, have led to the reduction, year by inexorable year, of the forest cover and the expansion of "field landscapes", acid grassland, heath, marsh and peat-bog.

Within the present century, the onslaught of mechanisation, and the increasing use of agri-chemicals, have had a dramatic effect upon local ecology. There is probably no entirely natural or "climax" vegetation left in Pembrokeshire; the moorlands look the way they do because of many centuries of "managed" grazing by domesticated animals, and even our most ancient woodlands have been coppiced and harvested by man.

New plants and animals have been introduced on an ever-increasing scale and at an even faster rate, sometimes filling in ecological 'niches" and blending so effectively into the background that we do not recognise them as alien. For example, introduced tree species include beech, sycamore, maple, crab-apple and wild pear, walnut, rhododendron, lilac and horse chestnut. Introduced flowers include wallflower, tansy, evening primrose, Russian comfrey, and some daffodils. Mammal introductions include rabbit, grey squirrel, red deer and mink, and typical birds which have spread as a result of human activity are lapwing, house sparrow, barn owl, Canada goose, feral pigeon and mute swan.

Plant Life

In his book *The Pembrokeshire Coast Path* John Barrett, the pioneer clifftop walker, pointed out the huge variety of coastal habitats available for plant life. There are the cliff faces and clifftops, the storm-beach ridges at the heads of some sandy bays, the salt-marshes and valley floors, the sand dune areas as at Freshwater West and Whitesands, and the damp little valleys cut on clifftop sites by streams before they plunge into the sea. On many of the exposed clifftops plants have to adapt to gale-force winds and the burning of salt spray, but elsewhere there are stretches of coastline where the effect of the wind is negligible and where plants can thrive in warm sunshine. The lee coasts on the eastern side of the Dale peninsula and between Saundersfoot and Monkstone Point are good examples. A similarly wide variation of habitats is found inland, from the exposed bleak hillsides of Mynydd Presely to the marshes and moorlands of the St David's district and the wooded steep slopes of the Gwaun valley and the beautiful Daugleddau. And everywhere the local factors of soil type, drainage conditions and aspect exert their own subtle influences over which plants will or will not thrive.

Because the climate of Pembrokeshire is mild and oceanic, plants can grow almost throughout the year. Spring comes very early, and some plants seem to make their own private decisions about which season is which. One or other of the two local species of gorse is in bloom at almost any time of the year, and even in the first week of January there are liable to be more than fifty flower species in full bloom. During February celandines and snowdrops are often in flower. In March these are joined by dandelions along the hedgerows and pink and yellow primroses around the fringes of the woodland. By the end of March the scurvy -grass is white on the clifftops, and

Pembrokeshire primroses in early Spring, This is the time of year when Pembrokeshire hedgerows are at their most beautiful.

there are bunches of violets for those who know where to look. Now the common gorse is reaching its full glory, and blackthorn is blossoming in the hedges. More and more plants burst into bloom, including the sea campion, sea-pink, ox-eye daisy, and prostrate broom on the exposed cliffs. In the woodlands there are wood anemones, and on marsh valley floors wide patches of yellow marsh marigold catch the eye.

Daffodils are of course a great part of Welsh life, and there is local distress if they are not in bloom by 1 March, St David's Day. Spreads of daffodil are not so common as they were, but there are good springtime displays on the lawns of the old country estates, and occasionally they have spread into woodland from adjacent gardens. The truly wild daffodil is now very mixed up with the cultivated varieties, but Pembrokeshire has its own special species called the Tenby daffodil. This daffodil has the same bright yellow colouring over the whole flower, and it has a somewhat mysterious origin. Because of its unusual beauty and its early flowering qualities (it is usually out by mid- or late February) it became the object of a steady export trade to London. From the fields around Tenby, where it was previously abundant, half a million bulbs were dug up and exported by enthusiastic Victorian entrepreneurs between 1883 and 1885. The daffodil was almost exterminated, but now it has recovered again and it is quite common in old gardens and derelict cottage sites in several districts of Pembrokeshire.

Around Whitsuntide the spring blossoms are joined by bluebells, thrift, red campion and foxgloves. The islands of Skomer, Skokholm and Ramsey are magnificent at this time; on the west coast of Skomer there is a sward of thrift several acres in extent, and further inland there are great sheets of bluebells interspersed with patches of the richly coloured red campion. Elsewhere, where there is more shelter and less competition, there are lesser celandines and primroses. As high summer approaches the colour subsides, and large parts of the island become blanketed with bracken.

The flowers of July and August are no less abundant. On the limestone cliffs of south Pembrokeshire one can see the reddish-purple flowers of greater knapweed, the golden samphire and three different species of sea lavender. On some of the salt-marshes there are purple and blue sea lavender, and sea aster and sea purslane. On the outer cliffs there are pearlworts, sea mayweeds, and many other delicate flowers, and banks of thyme and heather. And in many clifftop areas gentle green springy turf extends right up to the cliff edge. Inland, in the Presely Hills, the vegetation is quite different, with blossoming bog asphodel alongside sphagnum mosses, various rushes, cotton sedge, bilberry, bog myrtle, cranberry, and bog orchid. Further west the moorlands of Dowrog Common, Tretio Common and Trefeiddan Moor have other rather local plant species including a number of orchids and, in the pools of open water, plants such as bogbean, pillwort and water horsetail. These and many other local species are described in the book *Plants of Pembrokeshire.* and there are a number of other DWT publications which can be recommended. One booklet which is of particular value to the amateur botanist is the NPA Subject Guide entitled *Identifying Flowers Common Along the Coast Path.*

There is now not a great deal of natural woodland left in the National Park,

and conifer plantations are being established in large areas of countryside, particularly in the Presely Hills. However, there are still several large areas of durmast oak woodland, as in the Gwaun valley and on the banks of the Daugleddau, and this is natural woodland, creating an ideal habitat for many other plants, insects, birds and animals. Sycamore is also common, together with ash, elder, hawthorn, alder and birch. Higher up, out of the valleys, rowan and birch survive and succeed alongside the introduced conifers where many other deciduous tree species fail. Many of the damp woodlands have a prolific vegetation of mosses and ferns; and around the edges, where the tree canopy breaks up and allows light to penetrate, brambles build up impenetrable thickets.

The plants which live in the sea are somewhat less accessible than those which grow above sea-level, but they are no less interesting. Most of the outer coasts of Pembrokeshire are subject to a large tidal range and to attack by storm-waves through much of the year, so one would expect the growth of large seaweeds to be discouraged. But they are remarkably resilient, and where there is some shelter, several species thrive above and below the mean tide mark. One of them is Porphyra umbilicalis, which is still collected for making laver-bread, one of the great delicacies of Wales. Even on rocky headlands which are exposed to the full strength of storm-waves, larger seaweeds appear in the zone between mean tide-level and low-water mark. Particularly common are the wracks, the best-known of which is the knotted wrack with its thongs up to seven or eight feet long. Larger seaweeds from below low-water mark are seen best when they are uprooted and cast ashore during storms. Among these are saw wrack, thong weed and kelp; the latter, generally fastened to a rock surface by its powerful "holdfast", can grow as much as twelve feet in a single season.

Mammals

Pembrokeshire is not particularly well endowed with the higher forms of life, and there are few mammal species. Without a doubt the Atlantic grey seal is the most interesting of the mammals of the National Park. The seal herds are the largest in the southern part of the British Isles, and of the 2,000-3,000 grey seals around the Welsh coast most are concentrated around Pembrokeshire. The main breeding herds are on Ramsey Island (about 200 pups born annually), and probably there are 100 or so other pups born to smaller herds in caves and on isolated rocky beaches around the mainland coast. The seals enjoy basking in the sun, and even in bad weather they will often haul up on their own favourite beaches at the time of low water or to recover from a large meal. Generally they hunt at the time of high water. The herds around the Pembrokeshire coast are now used to man, and they show little fear; but they are still cautious and rather timid when humans are nearby, and because they are so ungainly on land they seldom stray far from the water's edge except at very low tide.

Most of the seal pups on the Pembrokeshire coast are born in late September or October. They may weigh 15 kg at birth. They are suckled for three to four weeks, putting on from 1 to 2 kg per day while the mother loses 50 kg or more. The mother seldom feeds while suckling. When the pup weighs 40 kg or so, the mother deserts it, leaving it to face the winter gales alone. The bulls mate with the females on their private beaches only ten to fourteen days after the birth of the pups. While many of the adults stay in "home waters", the pups wander widely through the winter months, travelling as far afield as the Bay of Biscay, the English Channel, and the west coast of Ireland. But the centre of their territory is the Celtic Sea and St George's Channel. The seals are fascinating creatures

Grey seal pup on a Pembrokeshire beach in the early autumn (Robert Evans).

when studied intensively, and a more detailed description of their habits is contained in R M Lockley's book *Grey Seal, Common Seal.*

As mentioned above, among the other large mammals of the county, deer were at one time numerous, as indeed were wolves and wild boars. All of these figure in Celtic mythology, but as a result of the medieval love of hunting nearly all the larger mammals were extinct in Pembrokeshire by 1600. In 1834 Baron de Rutzen of Slebech Hall re-introduced wild boar into Slebech Woods so as to indulge his pleasure for the chase; but the experiment was not at all popular with the neighbours, and the animals were all killed within a few years. During the eighteenth and nineteenth centuries the only deer in the county were kept on private estates; there was a herd of fallow deer at Lawrenny, for instance, as late as the 1930s. The Deer Park at Martin's Haven was designed to contain the deer for the Kensington Estate. Recently there have been attempts to rear red deer for slaughter, to satisfy the local demand for venison. A herd was introduced to Ramsey Island in 1979 and has remained there ever since, much to the surprise of visitors who arrive expecting to see little besides seabirds. Other red deer herds now exist at Esgyrn, near Mynachlogddu and elsewhere as a result of more recent commercial enterprises. South American llamas (and even ostriches!) are now occupying little niches in the Pembrokeshire landscape as a result of the desperate drive in the farming community towards diversification.

The next largest land mammals are the fox and the badger, both of which are very common. The county has the reputation of being great badger country, and a few years ago every small wood, copse and spinney had its own colony of badgers in residence. They are harmless, attractive creatures; long may they remain a part of Pembrokeshire wild life, for there are few enough mammal species left. The badger population has suffered to some degree as a result of badger baiting, and there are many farmers who would like to see the badger population reduced because of fears about the link with bovine tuberculosis. Otters may still be common along many of the streams and rivers, but they have been hunted by the local pack of otter-hounds and numbers have decreased. They are sighted occasionally in south Pembrokeshire (for example near Orielton), in the valley of the western Cleddau above Trefgarn and in the valley of the River Alun near St David's. Hares are becoming more common again in one or two areas after a period of comparative rarity, but the once vast rabbit population has still not recovered properly since myxomatosis, and the colonies are at present rather scattered and small. They are, however, abundant on Skomer, Skokholm and Ramsey. The elusive stoat is still quite common in Pembrokeshire, as is its cousin the weasel. The polecat is becoming much more common, and sightings of the animal have increased sharply in recent years. It has begun to breed in the county again, after a long break. The American mink has been breeding wild for twenty years or more, having escaped from some of the early mink farms. Moles and hedgehogs are common, as are a variety of rodents including the field vole, the water vole, the house mouse and the brown rat. The dormouse exists in small numbers, although Pembrokeshire seems to have no harvest mice. The black rat is found especially around the port of Milford Haven. Three of the British shrews are found locally. The red squirrel was once quite common in the woods around Benton, Lawrenny, Hook and Orielton, and also in the north of the county; but now it is so much reduced in numbers that it may even be extinct. In contrast the grey squirrel, a relatively recent arrival, is much more successful. Bats are quite common. Pipistrelle and long-eared bats exist in large numbers in many parts of Pembrokeshire, and some of the caves in the limestone cliffs of the Castlemartin peninsula house sizeable colonies of great and lesser horseshoe bats.

One animal which is a local curiosity is the Skomer vole, believed by some to be a unique subspecies. Certainly it is different from voles elsewhere in having a greater body-weight, a more tawny colouring and a less timid disposition than the mainland species. Perhaps it has evolved from ordinary mainland stock which was taken over (accidentally) to the island by the Iron Age settlers of 2,000 years ago.

Bird Life

The abundant bird life of the Pembrokeshire Coast National Park is of course one of its great glories, and many naturalists consider that Pembrokeshire has a richer sea-bird life than any other county of England and Wales. The various species and their distributions have been well recorded in a number of recent publications, so there is little point in attempting a comprehensive survey here. Instead the following paragraphs draw attention to some of the more interesting localities and some of the more unusual bird species of the county.

The vast seabird colonies of the Pembrokeshire islands can be counted as major tourist attractions, and perhaps it is no bad thing that the main nesting period does not coincide with the holiday months of July and August. The best-known of the islands is Skomer, now a national nature reserve managed by the West Wales Naturalists' Trust. David Saunders calls it "without question one of the finest seabird islands in Europe". There are large colonies of kittiwakes, razorbills and guillemots, and many puffin colonies. Manx shearwaters are numerous on the island, but because these birds are nocturnal they are seldom seen by day visitors. In the interior of the island

there are large colonies of lesser black-backed gulls, and other nesting birds are oystercatchers, lapwings, curlews, short-eared owls and wheatears. There are shags and cormorants, too, and in common with the other coasts of western Britain, Skomer has seen an explosive increase in the number of nesting fulmars in recent years.

Ramsey and Skokholm are also superb bird islands. The latter is not so frequently visited, for it has no facilities for day visitors. However, Ramsey now has more day visitors than Skomer, and is now (with due caution) being opened up for visitors by the RSPB. Again the main nesting sea-birds are kittiwakes, fulmars, shags, guillemots and razorbills. Ramsey has no puffin colony today, although the bird certainly nested there 200 years ago. Probably rats caused the decline and fall of the colony, having been carried accidentally to the island on one of the farmers' boats. Ramsey is also well known as the island stronghold of the chough.

Among the other islands Caldey does not have a rich variety of sea-bird colonies, but it does have a large colony of nesting herring gulls. The adjacent island of St Margaret's which is a bird reserve, has one of the largest cormorant colonies in the British Isles - almost 350 nesting pairs. The most remote of the Pembrokeshire islands is Grassholm, an RSPB reserve with a justly famous gannet colony. The island is only twenty-two acres in extent, and the gannetry occupies only one flank, but there are now about 16,000 pairs in residence. This makes Grassholm the fourth largest gannet colony in the North Atlantic, a surprising fact, for little over a century ago there were only about twenty pairs present. R M Lockley estimated that Grassholm supports about 60,000 gannets in the middle of summer, including the newly hatched chicks and other immature birds. The splendid white birds do their fishing over a wide area, and

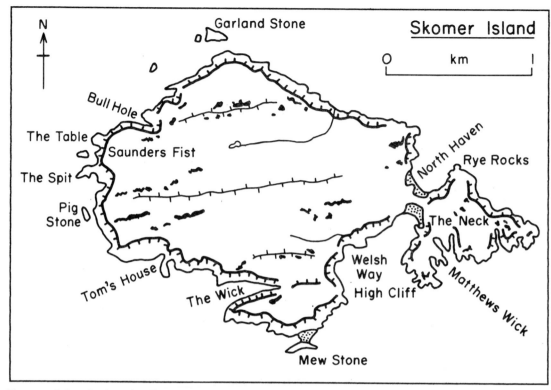

Skomer Island, the "jewel in the crown" of Pembrokeshire natural history. The island is a National Nature Reserve.

particularly within St Bride's Bay. There can be few more beautiful sights than gannets diving close inshore, wheeling and swooping on the bright, clean wind of a Pembrokeshire summer's day.

Among the most interesting of the seabirds mentioned above is the Manx shearwater, which certainly nests on Skomer and Skokholm, and in small numbers on Ramsey also. In its migration it covers vast distances, but in early summer it congregates on the Pembrokeshire islands. During the breeding season one partner sits quietly on its burrow during the day, but at night the areas around the colonies are transformed by tens of thousands of the birds screaming in from all directions in an endless multitude. And then at sunrise, all becomes quiet again. Skomer and Skokholm between them hold the world's largest concentration of shearwaters, probably totalling more than 135,000 pairs.

There are few large sea-bird colonies on the mainland of Pembrokeshire, although razorbills and guillemots nest on the outer cliffs of Dinas "Island" and elsewhere. The same species, and more especially guillemots, nest close inshore on the famous limestone Stack Rocks, close to the Green Bridge of Wales on the south coast. In several other areas, too, fulmars, kittiwakes, and the various types of gull can be found nesting on the mainland cliffs.

The other birds of Pembrokeshire are of great interest, for they give some indication of the wide variety of habitats already mentioned. At present the list of breeding birds totals more than 102, and the

Gannets nesting in their dense (and smelly) colony on the island of Grassholm (Robert Evans).

majority of these are found on the mainland, each one in its own ecological niche. In addition, Pembrokeshire is superbly situated for receiving visitors, and there are some very exotic birds among the 304 species recorded. Among the birds which occur widely in the countryside we can include the heron, the buzzard, the mallard, the kestrel, the skylark, the raven, and the rock dove. Less common, but still definitely resident, are the peregrine falcon, the chough, the mute swan, the collared dove, the barn owl, the shelduck, the kingfisher and the dipper.

We may conclude this chapter with brief mention of some representative sites where different types of birds can be seen. The Gann Flat near Dale attracts many different waders and wildfowl. Typical are little grebe and goldeneye, Slavonian grebe and red-breasted merganser. Also during the autumn and winter there are widgeon, brent geese, greenshank, green sandpiper and little stint. Many of the birds feed on the intertidal mud flats, which have also attracted generations of marine biology students based at the Dale Fort Field Studies centre. Other habitats around The Gann include lag gravels, blown sands, grassy "saltings", and a large lagoon created by the wartime extraction of gravel needed for the construction of the Dale Airfield.

In the Cleddau wildfowl refuge, between Little Milford and Llangwm, there are resident Canada geese, and also wintering

The tawny owl, which occurs for the most part in the woodlands and which is quite common throughout Pembrokeshire. (North Wales Naturalists Trust)

parties of widgeon, teal, goldeneye and red-breasted merganser. Shelduck breed here, and in 1978-79 about 300 of these beautiful birds wintered here. In hard winters such as that of 1962-3 large numbers of white-fronted geese have visited the waterway. Around the shores in winter and spring there are lapwing, golden plover, curlew, redshank and dunlin. This is a most attractive area with its mud banks and swirling tides, and its steep dense deciduous woodlands above the river banks.

In the wooded Gwaun valley there are buzzards and ravens, together with dippers, redstarts, wood warblers, and grey wagtails. And higher still, on Mynydd Presely and the other uplands, one can see redpoll, buzzard, raven, merlin, and ring ouzel. The lesser redpoll is found particularly in the new conifer plantations. During the summer there are meadow-pipits and nesting wheatears, and the air is filled with the cascading songs of resident skylarks. During the winter, when the uplands are sometimes dusted with snow beneath heavy leaden skies, snow buntings can be seen on the highest summits.

Back in the lowlands, a favourite location is the Bosherston lily ponds, created in the late eighteenth century and a good example of an artificially created wildlife habitat. The ponds are now nationally valued as prime examples of calcareous marl lakes, and they are at their best in June when the water lilies are in full bloom. Coots are particularly common around the junction of the three branches of the lakes, and grey herons are frequently seen. More than 20 species of ducks have been recorded on the lakes. Greater spotted woodpeckers nest in some of the adjacent woodlands, and they can be heard from the footpaths of the "lily ponds walk." Kingfishers can also be seen. During the summer months it should not be too difficult for even an amateur ornithologist to identify at least 30 common bird species around the ponds.

Finally, a word about the bird life of the Welsh Wildlife Centre near Cilgerran. Since the Centre came into the ownership of the Dyfed Wildlife Trust a few years ago, the bird life of this fascinating "mix" of saltmarsh, old grazing meadows, reed marsh, alder carr and woodland has been intensively studied, and common birds include moorhen, coot, shelduck, teal, red-breasted merganser, lapwing, dunlin, buzzard, mute swan, and kingfisher. Because of the wide range of habitats here, the check-list of recorded bird species is in excess of 120. The Centre is managed by a small staff based in a highly imaginative custom-built exhibition building which also serves as a restaurant, gift shop and research facility.

Chapter Fifteen

The National Park
For Better or for Worse?

The Pembrokeshire Coast National Park, created in 1952, is at once Pembrokeshire's crowning glory and its greatest headache. It covers 583 sq km, or just over one-third of the area of Pembrokeshire; it has about 320 km of outer coastline followed in part by the Coast Path; it has at least twenty-four well-known sandy beaches and many that are less well-known; and it has at least ten main boating centres and fifteen centres for sea fishing. As shown in Chapter 2, among the immensely varied environments of the Park are many stretches of cliffed coasts with intermittent sandy bays, the offshore islands with their huge seabird populations, the inner and outer reaches of the Haven, and the inland moors and wooded valleys of Mynydd Presely.

As we have seen, the rich tapestry of the Pembrokeshire landscape provides the Park's main asset, for it is something all can enjoy. But the complicated coastline of the county has created a major weakness from the point of view of Park management. Because Pembrokeshire is a peninsula made up of peninsulas and deeply penetrated by the branching Milford Haven Waterway, the National Park is not a contiguous unit, but consists of four detached portions. This has led to very unusual problems of Park administration and planning. Between 1973 and 1996 the NPA has had to deal with three local authorities, namely Dyfed CC and South Pembrokeshire and Preseli Pembrokeshire District Councils. A more difficult and complex administrative scenario can hardly be imagined.

The NPA has its headquarters in Haverfordwest. It currently employs 85 permanent staff and (during the summer season) about 60 temporary workers. It has an annual budget of £3 million, of which 25 % comes from the local authorities and £1.6 million (75%) from direct government grant. The key responsibilities of staff are in the fields of planning, information provision, ranger services, education, ecology and conservation, footpath and bridleway management, farm liaison, access and land management agreements, and car park and picnic site provision.

National Park officers are charged with the duties of resisting inappropriate development of all sorts, encouraging sound farming practices and woodland management, and conserving historic buildings and archaeological sites. They also have responsibilities to encourage small-scale developments which can help to meet local housing and employment needs; but the NPA does not have a clear economic development remit, and this causes considerable local resentment. Only about 1 % of the National Park budget goes to the support of the local community, whereas over 23 % goes on management and administration. The former figure is among the lowest for the twelve National Parks, and the latter figure is among the highest. The "governing body" of the NPA is the National Park Committee, made up of 12 local authority councillors who are delegated to the Committee, and 6 members appointed by the Secretary of State for Wales. No members are directly elected onto the Committee, and this means that the public views it more as a government quango than as a democratically accountable body. This is one of its weaknesses.

The NPA does not market the National Park as a holiday destination, and this task has in the past been the responsibility of the two district councils. As from 1996 the baton is in the hands of the new Pembrokeshire County Council. On the other hand the NPA is responsible for the operation of six Information Centres, which are designed not to attract visitors or indeed to encourage tourism in the National Park, but rather to inform and educate those who have already arrived in the area. Much to the confusion of most visitors, these are not Tourist Information Centres of the usual sort, and they are indeed independent of the Wales Tourist Board network. The NPA also owns or leases a number of centres which are visitor attractions in their own right -- for example the re-constructed Iron Age fortified settlement at Castell Henllys and the old Tidal Mill at Carew. Other properties owned by the Park include the old Countryside Unit at Broad Haven (which contains facilities of use to visiting school parties) and the new Woodland Centre at Cilrhedyn in the Gwaun Valley.

Since the creation of the county of Dyfed the National Park Authority has actually been a department of the County Council. To some degree this has constrained the NPA, since in planning matters, for example, it has had to operate within the confines of the Dyfed Structure Plan. On the other hand this administrative arrangement has provided certain checks and balances which have been broadly supported by local people, and has ensured some degree of consistency in development control with other parts of the county. Now, however, with the passing of Dyfed and the re-

emergence of Pembrokeshire as a unitary authority, the government has taken the opportunity (through the Environment Act of 1995) of giving the NPA a greater degree of autonomy. From May 1996 it will become a "free-standing authority" within the Pembrokeshire CC framework. It will control its own budget and create its own policies. These policies are outlined in the National Park Plan which is currently (1995) going through the public consultation process, together with a somewhat daunting set of documents which address local planning issues in individual communities. The increased powers being given to the NPA have not been universally welcomed, and there are many communities which have protested very strongly against the planning policies which have been proposed by the National Park Committee.

We should never lose sight of the fact that the Park is viewed by the government as a **national** asset, held on behalf of the nation for all to enjoy. This means that on many issues, for example on the protection of the landscape, national needs take priority over the social and economic interests of the people who live within the Park. Thus in implementing national policies "for the common good", the NPA is in grave danger, even if it operates with rare sensitivity, of alienating local people who feel themselves marginalised and even put upon. The problem is exacerbated by the fact that the NPA actually owns very little land; about 86% of the land managed on behalf of the nation is actually owned by Pembrokeshire people who have the same aspirations for living, building, farming and carrying on their businesses as those who live in the other parts of Pembrokeshire. When they are asked to control their businesses in a different way, or build in a different way, from their neighbours over the National Park boundary, the inevitable result is big trouble!

Solva Harbour, one of the honeypot locations in the National Park.

Managing Tourism

Pembrokeshire, with a current resident population of about 110,000, attracts a large summer holiday population. According to one of the strange statistics of the holiday industry, about 13 million "visitor days" are spent in Pembrokeshire each year. This means that about 1.8 million visitors come to the county annually. The tourist industry provides employment for about 20,000 people and an annual income of some £200 million for the county. Many local people have come to depend on the tourist trade, although there are worries that its strong seasonal rhythm contributes to an unstable local economy.

The major attractions are of course in the National Park, and holiday accommodation is widely scattered throughout the coastal belt, but the greatest concentration of tourist beds and holiday amenities lies in the south, around Tenby and Saundersfoot. At present the county provides about 79,000 "bed spaces", with 13% in hotels and guest-houses, about 41% in stationary caravans, 20% in self-catering units, 18% in touring caravan pitches, and 9% on tent sites. From these figures it is clear that caravan holidays have become increasingly popular as holidays in serviced accommodation have become increasingly expensive. Caravan parks are a major amenity problem, in spite of the fact that many sites are beautifully landscaped and immaculately managed. The Tenby-Saundersfoot area, where most sites are concentrated, has been recognized as a "caravan saturation area". Planning policy now dictates that no further caravan sites may be established within sight of the coast. Tents and tent sites are less of a problem, although the advent of the large frame tent transported by car means that some camping sites now make just as large an impact on the environment as touring caravan sites.

In the past the two district councils have competed with each other quite openly for a larger and larger share of the Pembrokeshire "tourist market." This has been in spite of the different holiday traditions and public image of their two areas. South Pembrokeshire has always had a greater appeal on the "mass market" front, with more hotels, more caravan parks and genuine holiday resorts in Tenby and Saundersfoot. Preseli Pembrokeshire, on the other hand, has appealed more to self-catering visitors, and has sold its coastline as Wales's best-kept secret, with wide skies, wonderful cliffs, abundant bird life, and quiet villages. The words "heritage", "wildlife" and "wilderness" have appeared over and again on PPDC leaflets and posters. However, with the return of Pembrokeshire County Council, the tourist staff of the two district councils have worked together during 1995 to coordinate their marketing strategies. This has resulted in a new "Pembrokeshire Holiday Guide" for the 1996 holiday season with an initial print run of 200,000 copies.

Other promotion work is done by the Wales Tourist Board and by the new privatised regional tourism companies which were brought into being by a Conservative government. Tourism South and West Wales provides services to accommodation establishments and attractions, but there is some disquiet among those at the sharp end of the tourist industry about the rising costs of quality assessments, advertising and membership. The interests of small entrepreneurs are protected to some degree by the Pembrokeshire Tourist Federation and by its constituent Tourism Associations which are centred on the Presely Hills, the St Bride's Bay area, the St David's Peninsula and so forth. The Federation provides a forum for debate, and it is particularly valuable in that it involves representatives of the National Park, WTB, the district councils and other bodies concerned with the environment and the local economy.

Nowadays, almost all the holidaymakers who visit Pembrokeshire have their own cars, and this has encouraged many people to explore the county in depth. While the coastal settlements such as Newport, Broad Haven, Freshwater East, Tenby, and Saundersfoot keep holidaymakers busy during good weather, many of them lack wet-weather facilities. Indeed, only Tenby and Saundersfoot can claim to have a wide range of indoor amusements designed to entertain family groups when the weather is bad. In some smaller centres (for example Newport, Solva and Dale) communities have decided to resist the pressures for holiday developments and to promote the merits of "quiet tourism" (based upon activities such as walking, bird-watching and sailing) instead.

The apparently inexorable rise and rise of the August beach-based family holiday slowed down in the early 1980's, and (with the possible exception of Tenby and Saundersfoot) Pembrokeshire's sandy beaches are now much quieter in the peak holiday season than they were fifteen years ago. The reasons for this change are actually quite complex. Virtually every part of the UK is now marketed aggressively as a desirable holiday location, including the South Wales Valleys and the Durham Coalfield; this means that competition for holiday bookings is more severe than ever before. Most holidays are now one week rather than two weeks in length, and the recent recession has had a profound effect on the disposable income of those who come to Pembrokeshire during the peak summer months. Increasing car ownership, and the advent of the cheap foreign package holiday in the sun, has forced a change in holiday marketing strategy, and nowadays tourism chiefs and operators promote out-of-season holidays in an attempt to stretch the tourist season. In recent years the attractions of the county's landscapes have proved to be popular with tourists, and there has been a parallel decrease in the popularity of family holidays based upon the old concept of "sea, sun and sand". It remains to be seen whether the recent scare about the damage to the ozone layer, and the link between sunbathing and skin cancer, will have a further negative effect upon the traditional seaside holiday.

Attractions Old and New

The county has an abundance of "honeypots" or popular day-trip destinations, as one might imagine from the content of the earlier chapters of this book. Natural features such as The Green Bridge of Wales, the Witches Cauldron near Ceibwr, the tors of Lion Rock and Maiden's Castle, the spectacular rock outcrops on Marloes Sands, and the bluestone tors of Presely attract not only geologists but also thousands of walkers and car trippers. The city and cathedral of St David's have long been centres of holiday pilgrimage, as have the castles of Cilgerran, Pembroke, Manorbier and Carew. Haverfordwest has become the main shopping centre for holidaymakers, especially since it now has a number of major superstore developments. Visitors are attracted in increasing numbers to the Llysyfran and Scolton Manor Country Parks, to Trefgarn Gorge and the Gwaun Valley, and in the south to the Bishop's Palace at Lamphey, to the lighthouse on St Ann's Head, and to the secluded peace of Bosherston Pools or Swanlake Bay. The supertankers in Milford Haven still prove an undoubted attraction for small boys and their fathers, and old industrial sites such as Stepaside, Porthgain and Rosebush are much visited.

Pembrokeshire is beginning to realise the potential of its maritime and coastal environment, and boat trips to the Pembrokeshire islands are now very popular. Whereas a few years ago only Caldey featured on the average holidaymaker's agenda, nowadays "round the island" and landing trips are also available to Skomer, Skokholm, Ramsey and Grassholm. As indicated in Chapter 14, all four of these islands are nature reserves, renowned in particular for their bird life. Other boat trips take visitors close to St Margaret's Isle and Cardigan Island, and there are pleasure trips within the Milford Haven waterway and around various stretches of the Pembrokeshire coast. Departure points include Tenby, Saundersfoot, Pembroke Dock, Neyland, Martin's Haven, Solva, and Cardigan. One of the entrepreneurial success stories of recent years involves "Thousand Islands Expeditions", based on the concept of exhilarating trips in high-powered water jet boats around Ramsey Island and through the Bitches tidal race in Ramsey Sound. The same company also takes visitors on landing trips (weather permitting!) to the Smalls, the scene of the lighthouse adventures recounted in Chapter 9. Also capitalising on the public interest in matters maritime are the two sea aquariums (the Marine Life Centre and the Oceanarium) which compete aggressively against each other in St David's.

Traditionally, the wet-weather attractions of Pembrokeshire have been based upon museums, art galleries and craft workshops. The most popular museums are at Tenby, Haverfordwest (the Castle Museum), Milford Docks, and Scolton Manor, although it must be said that the marketing of the local authority museums has, over the years, left a great deal to be desired. Nowadays there are a number of private museums concentrating on specific themes, such as the National Coracle Centre at Cenarth, the Pembrokeshire Motor Museum at Simpsons Cross, the Museum of the Home in Pembroke and Cilgwyn Candles Mini-museum near Newport. The National Trust maintains the Tudor Merchant's House in Tenby as a small museum illustrating the style of life of a typical Tudor merchant and his family, and Penrhos Cottage near Llanycefn is the only thatched cottage left in Pembrokeshire. Blackpool Mill, Carew Mill and Castell Henllys also serve as museums since they each seek to illustrate specific aspects of local history. A recent addition to the museum scene is the refurbished Martello Tower in Pembroke Dock which illustrates aspects of the nineteenth-century defence of the waterway.

Art galleries and craft workshops are thicker on the ground in Pembrokeshire than in any other part of Britain. In a relatively small area there are at least thirty art galleries displaying the work of local professional artists. The best known is probably the Graham Sutherland Gallery at Picton Castle (due to be moved to another Pembrokeshire venue in 1996), and other long-established galleries include Workshop Wales in Fishguard, John Knapp-Fisher's Gallery in Croesgoch, the John Rogers Gallery in St David's, and the Golden Plover Gallery at Warren near Castlemartin. All the local art galleries are listed in the free *Coast to Coast* newspaper. Craft workshops are even more numerous, and with the faithful support of holiday visitors they have kept many ancient Pembrokeshire crafts alive, including blacksmithing, pottery, knitting, leatherworking, weaving, woodworking and candle making. The oldest-established craft businesses are probably the woollen mills at Tregwynt and Middle Mill. Newer crafts (mostly introduced by newcomers to the county) include glass blowing, slate carving, dried flower work, toy-making, papermaking and pyrography. There are three local organizations devoted to the promotion of local crafts and the raising of local craft standards: the Pembrokeshire Craftsmens Circle, established over 20 years ago, organizes periodic selling exhibitions of members' work, Pembrokeshire Craft Markets organizes craft markets and exhibitions in

venues all over the county, and Origin Dyfed is a craft producer's cooperative which promotes high quality crafts and seeks to increase craft sales opportunities. There are a number of free publications available for the holidaymaker which give details of summer craft events and craft workshops open to the public.

Interesting recent additions to the list of holiday attractions are the gardens at Penlan Uchaf (Gwaun Valley) and Bro Meigan near Boncath, and the "good food" manufacturers springing up in rural locations. Llangloffan Dairy has been making cheeses for 19 years now, and Leon Downey's demonstrations of the ancient skill are well-known partly because of his continuing clashes with faceless bureaucrats and the resulting very welcome media exposure! Other famous cheeses are made by Thelma Adams at Caws Cenarth, and many visitors are attracted to Y Felin (a working water-driven corn mill) at St Dogmael's, Pemberton's Chocolates near Llanboidy, Carew Oysters at West Williamston, Cwm Deri Vineyard near Martletwy, Mary's Farmhouse Ice-cream in Crymych, Upton Farm Ice-cream near Cosheston, and a number of other mouth-watering locations.

There has been an almost explosive growth in larger-scale holiday attractions in recent years, particularly in the south-east of the county. Like the galleries and workshops, they provide facilities which are particularly welcome to families when the weather is too wet or windy for beach expeditions. The pioneering enterprise was Oakwood Park, near Canaston Bridge, opened on a wing and a prayer (not to mention very careful market research and capital investment) by the McNamara family in 1987. As a family theme park designed to provide "a funtastic day out", it is the nearest thing in Pembrokeshire to Disneyland, and it has deservedly become one of the top tourist attractions in Wales. In

1995 it was visited by c 350,000 people, many of whom travelled to Pembrokeshire on car day trips or coach excursions with Oakwood specifically in mind. Nearby, the same developers have now opened the Canaston Centre, with the Cyberdrome Crystal Maze and a ten-pin bowling alley. Another recent development is the Great Wedlock Dinosaur Experience near Gumfreston, another family enterprise involving major capital investment. Also in the "south-east quadrant" is the long-established Manor House Wildlife and Leisure Park near St Florence, Folly Farm at Begelly, and the beautifully landscaped Heron's Brook Leisure Park near Narberth. It is no coincidence that all of these major developments are outside the National Park and within easy reach of the Tenby-Saundersfoot "holiday coast". They are also within 15 minutes' drive or so of the improved A40 trunk road near Whitland, and are thus easily accessible to day trippers from Cardiff, the South Wales Valleys and even Bristol.

Further to the west and north in Pembrokeshire the major visitor attractions have to depend very largely upon visits by local people or by holidaymakers based in the county. Examples are the St David's Farm Park, Kaleidoscope interactive discovery centre on Milford Docks, and the Welsh Wildlife Centre near Cardigan. A number of other enterprises in the north and west have failed in recent years, partly on account of their "peripheral" locations, and there is now a grave danger that Pembrokeshire is over-supplied with major holiday attractions. Recent developments include the Stepaside Bird and Animal Park and the nearby Stepaside Craft Village. The market for such attractions cannot be extended indefinitely, and as the new and hopeful developers compete with each other for larger and larger slices of a smaller and smaller cake, there will inevitably be some who will go hungry.

Selling the Environment

Wisely, the local authorities (including the NPA) have adapted to the mobility of modern holidaymakers and to their increasing interest in the environment. Information centres distribute maps, booklets and fact sheets on a wide variety of topics, and many guides for walkers and motorists have been published by local firms in the last few years. In addition, the Park's Information Section has a rolling programme of publications on a wide variety of topics ranging from local history to wildlife. One of the most successful ventures of the last twenty years was the Countryside Unit at Broad Haven, which disseminated information through its bookshop and exhibition centre. Now it is a National Park Information Centre with facilities for laboratory work and nature study. Under John Barrett the NPA also pioneered the immensely popular Coastal Footpath walks devoted to simple field study. These guided walks have evolved over the years into the comprehensive "walks and talks" programmes of today, widely publicised in the NPA's free *Coast to Coast* newspaper.

Every year the staff of the Park's Information Section organize several hundred walks and talks. The walks, either full-day or half-day, and usually covering less than ten miles, are open to all at a nominal charge, and they are led by volunteers or staff members. All leaders are expert in something or other; while some walks are of a very general nature, others may be concerned largely with geology, or botany, or bird life. The walks take place in all parts of the National Park, and at the height of the summer season there may be four or five simultaneous events in places as widely separated as Saundersfoot and Newport, St David's and St Dogmael's. The events are designed for people of all ages, and (except on the few occasions when walks are pre-booked) leaders have no idea how many will turn up; this is at least partly dependent upon the weather. From many years of experience as a walks leader myself, I can record that the number of participants turning up at the start point has varied from over fifty to zero! One of the pleasures of leading groups of people of all ages and backgrounds through a beautiful piece of the National Park is the strong possibility that the party will contain (entirely without warning) a botany professor, or a railway buff, or an expert in the industrial archaeology of slate quarries. Sometimes the leader learns almost as much from a walk as those who are nominally in his charge ......

The talks are similarly varied, usually taking place in National Park Information Centres or other convenient venues. Almost all of the talks are illustrated, and speakers are chosen for their scientific skills, their ability to communicate at different levels, and their detailed local knowledge. Here are a few recent evening talk titles: "Dragons, Giants and the Hounds of Hell", "The Marcher Lords of Pembrokeshire", "Fascinating Fungi'" and "Springtime along the Coast Path." Again there is a nominal charge for those who attend.

The walks and talks programme, which is almost self-sustaining financially, is more highly developed than in any other British National Park, and it is universally appreciated by visitors and locals alike. Through this programme the Park makes its most obvious "face to face" contact with the public, and although the walks leaders and speakers are not asked to "toe the party line" on issues that may arise, the common thread that runs through all the events is **respect for the environment**. Without exception, the speakers are conservationists. Some are "greener" than others, but the opportunity for questions and answers (and even heated discussion) on issues which can be quite controversial, can do nothing but good, spreading the conservation ethic further and further afield with every passing holiday season.

Changing Priorities

The majority of holidaymakers who visit the county come to enjoy (in one way or another) the pleasures of the coast. In spite of the trends outlined above, the traditional seaside holiday is still alive and well at resorts such as Tenby, Saundersfoot, and Lydstep. The enjoyment of safe bathing and sandy beaches, spectacular cliff scenery and largely uncommercialized holiday settlements draws a large number of families to the smaller centres also. Other families are nowadays attracted by the prospect of good sailing at Solva, Little Haven, Dale, Saundersfoot, Lower Fishguard, Newport and elsewhere. The marinas at Neyland and Milford Docks, which were criticised in the early days as "out of character" and doomed to failure, have confounded the critics by capitalising on the great expansion in small-boat ownership.

A recent trend has been the expansion of the "activity holiday" market, and there are now a number of centres offering adventure holidays and a range of sporting activities. These include rock climbing, pony trekking, canoeing, sea angling, surfing (at Freshwater West, Newgale and Whitesands Bay), water-skiing (as at Freshwater East, Burton and Dale), and golf, cycling, gliding and rowing. St David's has become a popular residential centre for activity holidays, and there are other well-run centres at Sealyham and Dale, with courses and equipment hire at many other places including Mathry, Newgale, Pembroke Dock and Newport. Two activities which have become immensely popular in recent years are cliff-face rock climbing (particularly on the limestone cliffs of the Castlemartin

Peninsula) and sub-aqua diving. Because these are specialist and potentially hazardous activities, both are carefully controlled by their own national supervisory bodies, and the majority of participants belong to clubs which provide their own leaders for visits to Pembrokeshire. In spite of past problems involving "rogue" climbing groups inside the Castlemartin RAC Range, and "rogue" divers in the Skomer Marine Reserve, there is now a good working relationship between those who are intent upon exciting sport and those who are charged with the conservation of wildlife.

For visitors who are seriously unfit, or who do not wish to undertake activities which they may consider hazardous, some of the newer holiday attractions in South Pembrokeshire cater for supervised "fun" activities. Examples are Oakwood near Canaston Bridge, the Heatherton Country Sports Park near Tenby, Heron's Brook near Narberth, Whispering Water Valley near Llanddowror, Groveland near Whitland, and Ritec Valley Buggies at Penally. At the other end of the scale there a number of serious sporting events for those who are highly proficient at their chosen sport. These are now great spectator attractions, and large crowds turn out to support such events as the Ras Beca fell race at Crosswell, the White Water kayak competitions in Ramsey Sound, and the races of the Pembrokeshire Longboat League.

Already there is great pressure on holiday resources on the coast and after an excellent 1995 summer season it was calculated that there may be a demand for 100,000 bed spaces at the holiday peak by the end of the century. The Tenby-Saundersfoot area has changed enormously in character over the last decade; it has been likened to a "little Torbay", and there are fears that commercialization is also going to spoil some of the other more attractive coastal areas of north Pembrokeshire.

The Coast Path and Other Walking Routes

For many people the Pembrokeshire Coast Path is the most special and valuable feature in the National Park, for it provides immediate public access to most of the coastline. It allows walkers to visit all the main beaches, all the coastal towns and villages, and all the famous scenic "honeypot" locations. It is about 320 km long, and can be walked by most serious walkers from one end to the other in 10-12 days. But the walk involves a great deal of hard work, for in addition to the sheer distance involved, there are over 9,000 m of climbing, equivalent to an ascent of Mount Everest from sea-level. But there are strategic stopping points along the whole route, and it is now possible to complete the Coast Path walk by using the local chain of YHA youth hostels for accommodation.

The Coast Path was officially opened in 1970 after almost 20 years of surveying, planning, rights of way negotiations, footpath construction, and waymarking. More than 100 footbridges were built, 479 numbered stiles were installed, and thousands of steps had to be cut into steep and muddy slopes. Since then the path has been the scene of constant work by National Park staff. Cliff falls during the winter are common, and parts of the path have to be re-routed every year. Gradually the number of stiles is being reduced as landowners install fences on the landward side of the path itself. And plashing of the route has to be carried out on most sections at least twice a year if the encroaching jungle is to be held at bay.

Sadly, there are still a number of sections which do not conform to the popular image of the Path as a journey through paradise. It is still possible to go astray in the built-up areas of Hakin, Milford, Neyland, Pembroke and Pembroke Dock.

The Tudor Merchant's House in Tenby, now owned by the National Trust.

Over a million people each year now walk parts of the Pembrokeshire Coast Path, and walking is by a long way the most popular form of land-based recreation in the county. Because of this, the NPA has worked closely with the county council, the district authorities, the Countryside Council for Wales and voluntary groups to up-grade and extend the footpath network. Within the National Park alone, there are now over 700 km of rights of way, many of them linked to the Coast Path. Some local organizations, like SPARC in the Landsker Borderlands region and the Carningli Rural Initiative in the Newport - Nevern area, have worked hard to extend their local footpath networks; and in cooperation with the NPA and other agencies they have arranged improved waymarking, maps and publications designed to increase tourist use. The National Park itself is extending, year by year, its impressive list of self-guiding walks booklets, based on various parts of the coastline and often involving sections of the Coast Path. These booklets are aimed at walkers of all abilities, and they always include at least one short circular walk which can be tackled in the course of a leisurely afternoon.

Sections of the path on both the north and south shores of the Waterway leave much to be desired, and the walker proceeds with his eyes set on oil installations, his ears filled with the hum of heavy machinery, and his nostrils assailed by oil fumes. Most frustrating of all is the long, dull inland section of the path as it skirts the Castlemartin Tank Range; through most of the summer season the walker is denied access to the Green Bridge of Wales, Stack Rocks, Linney Head and St Govan's Chapel, undertaking instead a long roadway walk to the accompaniment of loud explosions and gunfire. Such things are a reminder that Pembrokeshire is, for better or worse, a part of the modern Britain in which urban environments, oil refineries, power stations, and defence training all have a part to play in the great scheme of things.

Planning for Tourists

Recognizing the problems involved in planning for the tourist boom, the planning authorities and other local committees have decided that large-scale holiday development should be concentrated at selected centres. Using the criteria of coastal "quality", the need to stick to National Park policy objectives, the "heritage coasts" defined by the Countryside Council for Wales, and the location of National Trust properties and sites of special scientific importance, the planners have designated "remote areas" which should be preserved as far as is practicable in their present natural state. In these areas additional holiday accommodation will, in theory, not be permitted, and certainly badly located developments will be cleared away.

Two major holiday developments have been encouraged by the National Park Committee. The first of these is at Broad Haven, where an already large holiday village is being expanded further, particularly through the provision of private houses and holiday chalets. The second is at Freshwater East, where an "unsightly conglomerate of shacks and bungalows" has for many years been something of an eyesore for some and a cherished haven of peace for others. The bay is already an important south coast holiday centre, providing accommodation for 1,700 people, but the planning authority has put forward a comprehensive plan for its conversion to a holiday village with high-density holiday flats, houses, chalets and caravan sites with car-parks and service centres. Most of the financial risk should be borne by a private company, eventually providing accommodation for about 4,000 holiday residents. However, in a celebrated recent conflict between environmental and development interests, an attempt to build a holiday complex on the sand dunes at the northern end of the beach has resulted in a victory for the environmentalists and a refusal of planning consent.

There have been modern chalet developments at Lawrenny, Timber Hill (Broad Haven), Cenarth and elsewhere. The Neyland Marina has also attracted new housing, with houses and apartments on the site proving particularly attractive to serious sailors. Additional housing developments may be linked with the Milford Docks marina. But it is doubtful that the proposed new developments at Freshwater East will ever be completed, since visitor numbers in Pembrokeshire appear to have reached a plateau, and investment is nowadays hard to come by.

Thus, the Pembrokeshire tourist industry is changing character in a number of ways. The remoteness of the county will probably keep it beyond the range of most day-trippers from England, but improved road links (including further improvements to the M4, a new road bridge in Carmarthen, and new by-passes at Whitland, St Clears and near Stepaside) have resulted in sharply reduced travel times into Pembrokeshire. This means that day-trips to the coastal resorts are perfectly feasible from Cardiff and the South Wales valleys. Cardiff is now less than two hours' drive away.

Tourist chiefs now predict that fewer families will wish to stay in the county during the peak holiday months of July and August, but that there will be more "mid season" and "low season" visits. The holiday trade has become more organized and is in places very commercialized, and careful planning is required to ensure that the National Park remains an amenity. If the development of the remote areas can be carefully controlled, the charm of rural Pembrokeshire may be preserved; if not, the enormous benefit which the county gains from tourism may well turn sour.

On the other hand, improved accessibility has been balanced by the effects of the economic recession, and the period 1985-1995 was difficult for the local holiday industry. However, the signs are that things are improving again, and increased promotional and marketing efforts by the new Pembrokeshire "shadow authority" and a greatly improved information service within the National Park Department should help the process of recovery. Pembrokeshire can cope with increased tourist numbers, but it remains as true as ever that very careful management and planning policies are required if the region's environmental assets are to be protected for the common good.

Planning for the Locals

Finally in this chapter, it is worth reminding ourselves that the NPA has anything but an easy task in satisfying local people that it is working in their best interests. Although most of the 23,000 people who live in the Park generally approve of what it stands for, there is still a widespread antipathy towards the NPA when it comes to planning matters. In part this is because the staff of the NPA have to apply stricter planning standards to housing and commercial developments than do the adjacent local authorities.

But that having been said, many locals would argue that NPA planning decisions are unpredictable and sometimes downright illogical. (Park officers and committee members would disagree, saying that the public does not adequately understand the book of rules that they have to work to!) There is grave disquiet about the fact that the Park does not publish detailed domestic planning guidelines. Decisions by Park officers concerning "acceptable vernacular features" sometimes appear to be made on the hoof; and there is a rich mythology about next-door neighbours being given wildly different advice as to what is or is not acceptable when it comes to roofing materials, window shapes, and wall treatments. There is disquiet about the apparently cavalier attitude of the NPA towards comments made by Community Councils on contentious applications. There is little doubt that many of these problems could have been avoided had there been more effective communications between NPA staff and local communities.

The NPA has been involved in very serious confrontations with a number of Pembrokeshire communities over the last few years. There have been severe public relations crises in Tenby and St David's, but possibly the greatest difficulties have occurred in Newport. In this small and very ancient borough full of strong-minded people there have been difficulties over planning applications, over sand dune management schemes, over the refurbishment of the old port area of Parrog, and particularly over the refusal by the NPA to allow free parking for local people on Traeth Mawr (Big Beach). The locals claimed that this was an established right, and protested that in implementing new car parking charges the NPA was making it impossible for the community to use its own beach (which, unlike most other "community" beaches in Pembrokeshire, can only be reached after a long drive around the estuary). After vociferous protests which included a symbolic "gate smashing" episode in the style of Rebecca and her Hosts, the matter ended up in court. The NPA won, but the community has not forgiven it for what was considered to be a heavy-handed and legalistic approach to a sensitive matter.

Sad to say, matters have not improved at the time of writing. The NPA has upset more of the locals by seeking to influence the wording of a Newport Environmental Survey commissioned from a team of outside consultants, simply because it does not agree with some research findings and recommendations of the authors. Saddest of all, Newport Community Council is now seeking to leave the National Park altogether, on the grounds that the town and community will receive fairer treatment from the new Pembrokeshire County Council. An exit from the Park is hardly a feasible proposition, and the community should perhaps be more grateful for much of the excellent work done by the NPA in and around the town, and for the inward investment which it has attracted for the community. But whether the NPA is viewed as Fairy Godmother or Devil Incarnate, the fact of the matter is that many local people do have serious and unresolved reservations about the role of the NPA in the community.

Chapter Sixteen

Buildings: Castles, Palaces and Churches

Pembrokeshire is widely known as a county of castles, but it is not often realized how greatly its castles varied in design and function. Mostly, however, they were the products of the great colonizing movement by the Normans in the early part of the Middle Ages, and many of the imposing buildings of today date from the fourteenth century or earlier. The same may be said of the magnificent Bishop's Palace at St David's and at Lamphey, which were two of the architectural splendours of Wales. And while the Englishry was being strengthened by massive stone castles and fortified residences and beautified by stone palaces, the increasing skill of the medieval stone-masons and architects was used, too, in ecclesiastical buildings. Fine stone churches were erected in many of the manorial settlements, and priories and abbeys also appeared on the landscape. In the sacred hollow selected by Dewi Sant for his monastery the early cathedral was raised, stage by stage, to its present magnificent proportions. The legacy of this burst of military, ecclesiastical and domestic building is still with us. It fundamentally altered the cultural landscape of Pembrokeshire, and this chapter concentrates upon some of the medieval buildings which remain.

In Chapter 5 we have already seen how castles were essential for the establishment and then the defence of the Englishry. Some of the early earthworks and stockaded forts were built by the Welsh princes, but all the stone castles which were erected in twelfth- and thirteenth-century Pembrokeshire were the work of the Anglo-Norman lords. These castles were built and improved in several stages, and some did not reach their final form until the fifteenth century or even later. We have seen how several of the more important fortresses were used during the Civil War, and how Cromwell started the process of their demolition. Some castles were in a state of advanced decay even in George Owen's time, and the history of each castle can be related to such factors as its strategic importance, the wealth of the community which it protected, and the detailed history of warfare, politics and marriages among the medieval ruling families. The castles can be classified into four main types, as follows:

1. The great strategic fortresses (Pembroke and Haverfordwest).

2. Other major castles (Newport, Cilgerran, Carew, Manorbier, and Tenby).

3. The Landsker castles (Roch, Wiston, Llawhaden, Narberth, Amroth and Laugharne).

4. The lesser strongholds such as Picton Castle and the smaller fortified structures at Dale, Angle, Benton, Upton, Bonville Court and Eastington.

In the sketch map on page 47 the distribution of these castles is shown with

Pembroke Castle, the most popular of all the castles of Pembrokeshire (Squibbs Studio).

respect to the medieval Landsker, the Englishry and the Welshry. Some forts and castles have entirely disappeared, while others can be traced only with difficulty. Some are not open to the public, for they are still used as private residences; and it should be remembered that the lesser strongholds mentioned here were but the most spectacular of a number of fortified residences which dotted the countryside. Some of these are mentioned later in the chapter.

The Strategic Fortresses

First and foremost among the medieval buildings of Pembrokeshire were the great strategic fortresses, upon whose successful defence the fortunes of the whole Englishry depended. Pembroke Castle was the most important of these, sited in the heart of the Englishry and capable of relief from the sea, albeit via the vulnerable Pennar Gut.

It was the first and greatest of the "round keep" castles of Wales, and has many of the classic early medieval features such as inner and outer wards, a strong outer curtain wall with defensive towers, a great gatehouse, and various inner ward buildings such as two halls, a chancery and a chapel. After a long period of neglect the fabric of the castle was partially restored in the 1880s, and more extensive renovation has been undertaken since 1929. Now, quite naturally, the magnificent castle is a popular tourist attraction, partly on account of its architectural qualities and partly because of its Tudor associations; in 1457 Henry Tudor was born in the castle, and here he spent much of his boyhood.

The other great strategic fortress of the Englishry is at Haverfordwest, some way behind the Landsker but close enough to it to act as the main bastion in case of attack from the north and north-east. Like

Pembroke Castle, it was built as part of a planned Norman town, with its strong town walls, its riverside warehouses and quays, and its castellated and spacious parish churches. The castle was different from Pembroke Castle in design, being of the rectangular type. It was built on a fine strategic site, surmounting a steep, rocky bluff above the Western Cleddau river. It has a battlemented curtain wall up to twelve feet thick and a number of strong towers, and it was renowned as one of the strongest castles of Wales. But it was partly dismantled at the end of the Civil War and was sadly neglected thereafter. Today the remaining buildings are parts of the castle keep, surmounted on the northern side by the structure of the County Gaol which was completed about 1820. Recently the buildings have been further extended, and the castle is now the home of the Castle Museum and County Records Office.

Other Major Castles

The other major castles of Pembrokeshire vary greatly in their style of building and in their state of preservation. At one extreme is Newport Castle, built as a stone fortress about the end of the thirteenth century and already in a state of disrepair by the mid-1500s. Little now remains of the original stone castle, but the gatehouse was converted into a residence in 1859 and is still in use today. At the other extreme are the spectacular fortresses of Carew, Manorbier and Cilgerran, all relatively well preserved and open to the public. And in between is Tenby Castle, built like Pembroke and Haverfordwest castles in conjunction with a walled town, but now preserved only in part. William de Valence planned to make Tenby impregnable, and the building of the massive town walls, in several stages, took fully 250 years to complete; but the castle has proved less resistant than the walls, and only a few fragments remain today.

Cilgerran Castle occupies a commanding site above the River Teifi, and it is not surprising that it has long been a tourist attraction. The first castle may have been built here in 1093 by Roger, Earl of Montgomery, but the main buildings of stone and slate were constructed in the thirteenth century. The most splendid features of the castle today are the two great drum-towers which defend the landward side of the inner ward. Although Cilgerran maintained its status as an independent lordship throughout most of the medieval period, it was too far from the main colony of little England for safety, and it was assaulted by the Welsh princes time and again. In complete contrast, Manorbier, on the south coast, was so far removed from the ravages of the Welsh that, as far as we know, it was never besieged. The fabric of the castle has survived well. It was one of the seats of power of the de Barri family, and formed part of the lordship of Pembroke. The stone castle was built, stage by stage, through the twelfth, thirteenth and fourteenth centuries. It has an approximately rectangular inner ward with high curtain walls and corner towers. There is no keep, but a strong gatehouse was one of the later additions to the fabric. Today the picturesque castle is a great favourite with holidaymakers, and understandably so, for as it stands in ivy-covered splendour in its gentle valley one can picture the world of Giraldus Cambrensis eight centuries ago.

Carew Castle was another subsidiary castle of the lordship of Pembroke. It stands on a low limestone outcrop surrounded by meadows and at the head of navigation of the Carew River. It was begun about 1200 to replace a simpler structure, and the west front, built around 1300, shows it to have been a typical medieval fortress. The most striking features are the massive round towers. castellated on top and supported below by spur buttresses which rise to first-floor level. Other features of the castle show it to have been altered greatly during the fifteenth and sixteenth centuries, and it eventually became a fine Tudor residence. Much of the rebuilding was done by Sir Rhys ap Thomas, who supported Henry Tudor on his march through Wales and who reputedly placed Richard's muddy crown on Henry's head after the triumph at Bosworth Field in 1485. After this Carew, somewhat surprisingly for a fortress so solidly established in the centre of the Englishry, became a great centre of Welsh culture, and as we have seen, Sir Rhys gave the last of the great tournaments here in 1507.

Carew Castle passed to Sir John Perrott (who was, according to legend, an illegitimate son of Henry VIII) in the middle of the sixteenth century, and he was responsible for the last major phase of reconstruction. He continued Sir Rhys's work of transforming the dark medieval fortress into a light airy palace, and he was responsible for the rebuilding of the north front with its series of beautiful mullioned windows overlooking the Carew River. But the castle was not to continue for long as a stately mansion-house. After the death of Sir John Perrott in the Tower of London the ownership of Carew changed several times.

One of the tenants around the year 1603 was the terribly wicked Sir Roland Rhys. A famous legend relates that Sir Roland kept a pet ape, probably brought to Britain from Africa in an Elizabethan trading vessel. In a dispute with one of his estate workers Sir Roland set the ape onto the poor man, who was seriously injured in the attack. But Sir Roland got his just desserts on the following night, for the ape turned on its owner and killed him, at the same time disturbing coals from the fire and setting the castle ablaze. The building was repaired and later figured prominently in the Pembrokeshire campaigns of the Civil War. By 1686 it had long ceased to be used as

a family home, and since then it has gradually declined to the status of a magnificent ruin.

Landsker Castles

The Landsker castles are something of a puzzle, because as a group they are very varied in style. Also, as we have seen in Chapter 5, the castles defended a military frontier only for a short period of time; even before 1150 the Anglo-Normans, helped by Flemish immigrants, were colonizing the central parts of the county well to the north of the line of castles. Castles like Roch, Wiston and Narberth were seldom used as part of an overall Norman strategy to define and defend the frontier, for they were themselves somewhat disunited.

Probably the Landsker castles generally functioned, like the larger fortresses further south, as the defensive headquarters of individual baronies. Because they were so close to the periphery of the Englishry they were extremely vulnerable to raids by the Welsh, and it is understandable that they never prospered to any great extent. Wiston, Narberth and Laugharne castles in particular, exposed near the eastern flank of the Englishry, suffered greatly from Welsh attacks. Nevertheless, neither the English kings nor the lords of the Englishry had any doubts about the strategic importance of maintaining the defences of the eastern frontier. For example, after the destruction of Wiston and Narberth castles by the Welsh in 1220, Henry II instructed all knights and free tenants from the lordships to assist William, Earl Marshal, in the immediate reconstruction. This shows that there was some strategic design for the Englishry as a whole. But Narberth and Wiston continued to bear the brunt of Welsh attacks, and today, as a consequence, very little remains of the original stone fortifications.

From the remains of the Landsker castles we can see how widely they varied in style. Laugharne Castle was probably begun in about 1100, but most of the imposing stone fabric visible today was the work of Sir John Perrott, who turned it into a fine mansion during the reign of Henry VIII. Narberth Castle was a simple rectangular castle with drum-towers at each corner. Probably it had no keep, but there was a fortified residential part. It was built about 1246, but it is not on the site of the original castle of Arberth which figures so prominently in Welsh history and legend. After a turbulent history of assault, destruction and rebuilding it came into the hands of the redoubtable Sir Rhys ap Thomas. He renovated it and made it habitable, but after his death in 1524 the castle continued its troubled existence. It was considerably battered during the Civil War, and after 1677 it ceased to be habitable. Now it is but a crumbling ruin, closed to the public and sadly in need of renovation before it is too late.

Wiston Castle was the centre of a lordship granted to one Wizo the Fleming. It was called Daugleddau, and it was the frontier territory settled by Flemings to provide a defence against the Welsh; and they were not too popular with the Normans either. They bore the brunt of many Welsh attacks, and the castle was never developed as a powerful stone fortress because it was too vulnerable and insecure and because the lordship was always short of funds. The early motte and bailey castle of Wizo himself was later modified by his sons, and a shell keep was built in stone on the 13 m high mound. In 1220, as mentioned above, the castle and settlement at Wiston were savagely attacked by the Welsh, and in spite of Henry VIII's exhortations it seems that the keep was never properly repaired or reconstructed. Now, over 750 years later, only the base of the keep walls can be seen as a graphic reminder that even stone fortresses burn and fall.

At the seaward ends of the Landsker lay the castles of Amroth and Roch. Little is known of the Norman Amroth Castle, but there are several earthworks in the vicinity, and there are records of a small stone castle at Earweare, close to the sea shore. There are no remains of this castle today (except perhaps for the restored gateway), for the modern Amroth Castle is a mansion-house dating from the early nineteenth century. Roch Castle is better preserved, standing on its imposing rock outcrop within sight of the sea and dominating the bleak countryside for miles around. The spectacular peel-tower was probably built during the thirteenth century by Adam de la Roche. Local tradition tells that he built the tower in order to defy a prophecy that he would die from the bite of a serpent: but adders thrived on the bracken-covered rocks around the castle, and one was carried into the castle by mistake inside a bundle of firewood. Of course it bit the luckless Adam, upon which he obediently died. The castle was never completed, although there are signs that curtain walls were originally planned to enclose an inner ward. In any case the tower was used and inhabited until about 1700. Among its more illustrious inhabitants were the Walters, the family of Lucy Walter who was mistress to Charles II. For about 200 years the castle was in ruins, but it was restored and extended in 1900-1902 by the Viscount St David, and it has been further improved as a residence since then and is now self-catering units, used for holidays.

Llawhaden Castle, located between Wiston and Narberth on the eastern frontier, can certainly be classified as a Landsker castle; but it differs greatly from the others in that it was a bishop's fortified palace. As we have seen in Chapter 5, the episcopal lordship of Llawhaden retained much of its Welsh character even though governed by Norman bishops of St David's. The Normans were certainly aware of its defensive importance, and it was garrisoned strongly during periods of Welsh insurrection. But once the stone castle was built it seems to have been largely immune from the violence which attended the more lowly fortresses at Wiston and Narberth. This may have been due partly to the castle's great strength, and partly to the reluctance of the Welsh princes to commit violence against the bishop. And an early motte castle was built at Llawhaden in the early twelfth century, followed by a stone tower and curtain wall about a century later. The present impressive fortress took shape during a great rebuilding between 1250 and 1300, and other major additions to the fabric were made in the early fourteenth century. When it was complete the castle was a lavish fortified mansion, fit for the entertainment of bishops and their important guests, and providing accommodation for a large household staff and a large garrison. Until the 1530s it was maintained as a palace on the grand scale, but the infamous Bishop Barlow is said to have commenced the dismantling of the castle so that the sale of the lead roof could provide a dowry for one of his daughters. A sad end indeed for a military structure of such magnificence.

Lesser Strongholds

Most of the lesser strongholds of Pembrokeshire have faded out of history because their original motte and bailey structures were never replaced by more permanent stone buildings. Professor Grimes estimated that there were at least thirty such sites in Pembrokeshire, many of them associated with the church, mill and manor house of the typical manorial settlement. Some of the strongholds remained as lords' residences for several centuries; elsewhere (as at Picton) the manor house was moved away from the castle mound with the advent of more peaceful times, especially in the better protected parts of the Englishry. Some of the strongholds were built on prehistoric

sites, as at Nevern and Walwyn's Castle. Elsewhere the conical flat-topped mounds and their earthworks were built by the Welsh and then taken over and adapted by the Normans with the superior castle-building techniques. Some of these old strongholds are still impressive, even though they support no ruined buildings today. For example, there are the castle mounds at The Rath (Rudbaxton), New Moat, Hayscastle, Camrose, Pointz Castle, Castlemartin and Puncheston. At Nevern the motte and bailey have now been cleared of jungle, and the site is well worth a visit; fragments of masonry can still be found on the summit of the motte.

Perhaps the best known of the early strongholds which developed into fortified residences are the "castles" around the Daugleddau waterway. The best preserved are at Benton, Upton and Picton. Benton was probably built as a subordinate fortress for the protection of the lordship of Rhos; like Roch Castle, it seems to have been a home of the de la Roche family. Little is known of its history, but it seems never to have been particularly large, comprising only a thirteenth-century peel tower and a small irregular courtyard protected by a thick curtain wall. The tower contained no fireplaces, so possibly the original residential part of the castle was at the opposite end of the court. From the end of the Civil War until 1930 the castle was in ruins, but after that it was rebuilt, almost single-handed by Ernest Pegge. Now it is in good repair and is used again as a private residence. Upton Castle, on the other side of the river, is still a very imposing building. Its frontage comprises three drum-towers, and there was a gateway at one end. When it was built, probably in the thirteenth century, there was probably a walled enclosure at the rear but no trace of this now remains and the greater part of the building of today was constructed in the eighteenth century. Upton Castle can never have been a serious fortress in military terms, and it

The ruined gatehouse of Llawhaden Castle, which was once a Bishop's residence.

seems rather to have been a fine example of a medieval fortified house. For many generations it was occupied by the Malefant family and its descendants, and it is still used as a private residence. Parts of the grounds are, however, open to the public during the summer season.

Further up-river, on a commanding site above the confluence of the Western Cleddau and the Eastern Cleddau, is Picton Castle. As noted above, it does not occupy the original motte site, and the oldest part of the castle building of today was probably commenced in about 1302 by Sir John Wogan. The western half of the castle was added about 1800 by Lord Milford, but it retains the style of a Norman fortress with its battlements and projecting bastions. The castle has been continuously occupied since it was built, and since it seems to have been by-passed by the more violent of the conflicts between the Welsh and the Normans even its older section is still in a remarkably good state of repair. The Castle is only rarely open to the public.

Near the outer reaches of Milford Haven are two other fortified residences, at Angle and Dale. The Old Rectory at Angle is similar in some ways to the peel towers at Roch and Benton, although it occupies a much less imposing site. The original "castle" at Angle seems to have been square, protected to the north and west by a moat and on the south side by an inlet of the Haven. Now only the single tower remains, roughly square in plan with a rounded projection housing a corner stair. It was probably three storeys high, and entered at first-floor level across a drawbridge. An interesting feature of the exterior wall is a row of stone corbels which must have supported a wooden walkway near the top of the tower. The house may have been a baron's residence, for there is a dovecote nearby as well as other medieval antiquities. But there is no accurate record of the history of any of these buildings. Across the Haven, Dale Castle was probably built originally by Robert de Vale as his manor house. The south wing may be on the site of the original fortified house, and it has a number of vaulted rooms and battlemented external walls. Most of the building is, however, of nineteenth century date, and the castle is still used as a private residence.

Most of the other old fortified halls of Pembrokeshire have disappeared or are in ruins, but some of them have been preserved at least in part. One which has disappeared is the three-storeyed fortified house at Bonville Court near Saundersfoot. This probably consisted of two towers set corner to corner protecting other buildings behind, but no plans of the building survive, and it was probably abandoned in the 1700s before being destroyed in the Bonville's Court colliery workings in the present century. Another interesting building which was probably fortified is "The Palace" at Cresswell, a rectangular structure with a turret at each corner. It may have been the home of Bishop Barlow in the sixteenth century, but the age of the building itself is in doubt.

Other fine fortified houses (much modified by the hand of time) can still be seen at Eastington near Rhoscrowther, and at Monkton Priory Farm near Pembroke. Eastington, in its heyday, must have been particularly impressive, with its embattled parapet and turret and its fortified wall-walk. In his fascinating little book on *Pembrokeshire Architecture*, Michael Fitzgerald refers to the house as a "tower house" and reminds us of similarities with the much more numerous tower houses of Scotland and Ireland. The Old Rectory at Carew has a corbelled tower of uncertain date, and a fine arched doorway. On Caldey Island there is an old battlemented tower with walls four feet thick and a vaulted basement. This was probably a free-standing fortified residence in medieval times, but subsequently it has been incorporated into the monastic buildings. There were many other fine fortified houses in the county, but their remains have for the most part been built into more recent structures.

The Bishops' Palaces

During the Anglo-Norman period the diocese of St David's was the largest in Wales, and its lands provided the greatest revenues. Not surprisingly, the bishops' palaces of the time were built to reflect the wealth and power of the bishop, and in addition to the fortified palace at Llawhaden other fine residences were built at Trefin, St David's and Lamphey. Of the former nothing survives, but much of the fabric of the St David's and Lamphey palaces remains, and from the ruins we can gain some idea of the building techniques and life-style of the age.

The Bishop's Palace at St David's is justly famous, and some authorities consider it superior architecturally to the adjacent cathedral. The palace was built as a successor to an early motte and bailey castle which served as the bishop's residence until the thirteenth century. The first major building on the site of the present palace took place between 1228 and 1293, but the palace attained its final splendour under Bishop Gower (1327-47). He was an inspired builder, and it was he who was responsible for the great hall with its vaulted basement and the magnificent arcaded parapets. This must have been a fine fortified building, stronger and much more imposing than the early smaller hall which is connected to it at right angles. It had a fine entrance archway and a rose window, and the great east gable was flanked by turrets. Bishop Gower even added purple and yellow stone for parts of the parapet and the gable end. To some, the palace must have appeared as an exercise in exquisite bad taste. The Tower Gatehouse and the high defensive wall surrounding the whole of the cathedral close were also probably improved by Bishop Gower, although they must have existed in something like their present form during the late thirteenth century. With the coming of the Reformation the Bishop's Palace at St David's fell upon evil days, and again it was

Bishop Barlow who hastened the decay of the buildings. It does not seem to have been occupied permanently since the end of the sixteenth century.

The bishop's residence at Lamphey was another fascinating building. It was constructed as part of a pleasant rural retreat for the bishop, nestled in a little valley and surrounded by fishponds, orchards, and vegetable gardens. There was also a windmill and a dovecote, and two watermills. The adjacent park held a herd of about sixty deer. Some of the buildings of the palace date from the early thirteenth century, and a fine, well-appointed camera, or private apartment, was added by Bishop Richard Carew between 1256 and 1280. He obviously employed imported stone-masons for the work, which is of superior quality to that undertaken by Bishop Bek around the end of the century. But again it was the redoubtable Bishop Gower who gave the palace its greatest splendour, adding a new hall and remodelling the courtyard, giving it a battlemented wall and a new gatehouse crowned with his characteristic arcaded parapet. There were various other phases of rebuilding, but after the Reformation the palace passed from the Church to the State, and in Elizabethan times it was a home of the Devereux family, who were later the Earls of Essex. Now it is a ruin, looked after by the Department of the Environment.

Churches Great and Small

Earlier in this book we have seen how Little England acquired characteristic churches typified by high castellated towers during the early medieval period.

Like the castles, fortified residences and bishop's palaces, the churches were the products of an unsettled age, and it is worth mentioning a few typical examples here. Some of the earliest churches, dating from the period of colonization between 1100 and 1400, have been greatly modified since. In particular, there was a great phase of church rebuilding in the later part of the nineteenth century, and on many of the parish churches of today only the castellated towers remind us of their medieval origins. The churches are not particularly distinguished architecturally, and it has been said that Pembrokeshire churches are seldom real works of architecture at all. They have been referred to as "wild and wondrous structures" full of character, and they are in turn charming, grotesque and picturesque. The simplest churches were built on a straightforward rectangular plan with a tower at one end or near a side entrance. Later on a wide transept or aisle was added, and some churches also have lengthened naves or added vestries, all contributing to the usual "patchwork" style.

Typical churches, dating from the thirteenth and fourteenth centuries, with high, tapering towers and castellated parapets, are at Steynton, Johnston, Ludchurch, St Thomas's (Haverfordwest), Begelly and Gumfreston. Other churches, like St Martin's (Haverfordwest) and St Mary's (Tenby) have had spires added on top of their medieval towers, and there is an ancient leaning spire on the church of St Illtyd on Caldey Island. Other churches have squat towers dating from the medieval period, as at Rudbaxton, Nevern, Newport, Llawhaden and Uzmaston. Some churches have their own particular quirks of character. For example, the church at Llawhaden has an old northern tower and a later southern tower; the latter was built during fourteenth-century extensions to the nave and chancel. A sad remnant of a once-proud church occurs on the shore near Slebech. Here are the ruins of a famous church which was formerly associated with the local headquarters of the Knights of St John of Jerusalem. Now its tumbling walls and derelict squat church tower are sadly

St David's Cathedral, one of the most beautiful religious buildings in Wales.

surrounded by thick undergrowth. It is not certain when the church was built, but it may date from the fourteenth century.

The most imposing of the early medieval churches were built in the main towns, where there were rich patrons, large congregations and skilled stone-masons and carpenters. We have already referred to the fine churches of Haverfordwest, and it is worth noting here that St Mary's Church at the top of High Street is thought by some to be the finest parish church in Wales. It is austere and spacious, and has a fine thirteenth-century arcade of pointed arches made by skilled craftsmen. In its style and size it gives some indication of the importance of the medieval town. St Mary's Church (Pembroke) is another fine Norman church dating from the thirteenth century; and St Mary's (Tenby), with its fine tower and spire, is said to be the largest of the medieval parish churches in Wales. There is yet another large parish church dedicated to St Mary in Cardigan.

Of all the ancient churches of Pembrokeshire, the crowning glory is of course St David's Cathedral. It is at least the third to stand on this site, for the Viking raiders seemed to enjoy the occasionally sally into Dewi Sant's "Vale of the Roses". The present structure was begun about 1180, but several centuries of work under a succession of bishops were needed before the building assumed anything like its present form. The plan of the cathedral is a simple one, and is not much different from that designed for Bishop Peter de Leia in 1180. Some of the internal ornament was the work of Bishop Gower, and the exterior has been much modified because of structural defects. The first tower collapsed in 1220, and an earthquake demolished part of the structure in 1248. The present tower is a low one, but it was even lower in the fifteenth century and lower still in the fourteenth century. It did not acquire its pinnacles until the cathedral was safe from raiders. The exterior is plain to the point of austerity. The west front was rebuilt in 1789 by John Nash, when it was about to collapse from the outward pressure of the Norman arches, and there was further rebuilding under the guidance of St Gilbert Scott in 1863. The result is somewhat drab, but at least these remedial works rescued the cathedral from ruin, for parts of it had been in a sad state of decay in the seventeenth and eighteenth centuries.

While the exterior may be uninspiring, the interior is exquisite. The slope of the floor gives the building a strange feel, but the eye is attracted by other things. There is the magnificence of the late Norman arcades, the superb nave ceiling of black Irish oak, dating from about 1500; the fourteenth-century stone screen built by Bishop Gower; the fine fifteenth-century choir stalls; and the delicate fan-vaulted ceiling of the Holy Trinity Chapel. Then there is the shrine of St David, the altars, and the tombs of assorted notables. And one can see delicate carving in stone and wood, reaching perfection in the rich pendants of the nave roof.

Like most cathedrals, St David's is not exactly consistent in style either without or within, and a troubled history has left its mark. But it is still very much the symbol of the power of the church in this remote and saintly corner of the western world, even if it came to be the symbol of Normal ascendancy and Welsh decline. It is still a worthy place of pilgrimage, set serenely in its hidden valley together with the Bishop's Palace, St Mary's College and the houses and cottages of the close.

Lamphey Palace, used by the Bishops of St David's as their country retreat.

The Monastic Houses

The monastic communities of the Age of the Saints were succeeded by a number of Norman foundations,and the buildings from these later foundations still survive in a number of localities. Religious houses were St Dogmael's Abbey, Pill Priory near Milford, Haverfordwest Priory and Friary, Monkton Priory and Caldey Priory. There were medieval hospices at Llawhaden and at Whitewell, St David's. Then there was the Commandery of the Knights of St John at Slebech, mentioned earlier in this chapter. All of these establishments were of immense importance in the confused world of Anglo-Norman Pembrokeshire; as Major Francis Jones has said, "together with the parish priests, the good monks were the main, indeed the only, civilizing agents of that barbarous age..."

The best known of the monastic ruins is at St Dogmael's, where the abbey was founded with rich endowments in 1115 on the site of an older Celtic monastery. Most of the building took place after 1200, but the greatest construction work was during the fourteenth century. Building was still going on right up to the Dissolution of the Monasteries in 1536; after that time the abbey fell into ruin, but the abbey church became the parish church and continued in use for a while. The north and west walls of the church stand almost to their full height, and the many other remnants of buildings around the cloister are today carefully preserved by the Department of the Environment.

St Mary's College, adjacent to St David's Cathedral, must have been a fine building. It was founded in 1377 and later built in the perpendicular style with a single tower at the south-west corner of the chapel. However, by the 1700's it was derelict. John Nash was allowed to use it as a stone quarry during his restoration of the west front of the cathedral, and this did it no good at all. The College chapel still remains, gaunt but impressive with its high walls and large windows. It has now been substantially restored, and is used for exhibitions and other events.

No other monastic ruins in the county are so well preserved. Haverfordwest Priory stands in ivy-covered ruin on the banks of the River Cleddau just below the town, but it is unlikely to deteriorate further since a comprehensive archaeological "dig" now in progress is proving the site to be immensely valuable. Pill Priory near Milford is nowadays simply a twelfth-century chancel arch in the midst of much later dwellings. Parts of Monkton Priory are incorporated in Priory Farm, and the choir and sanctuary became the chancel of the parish church. This was restored in 1887, and its lofty spaciousness gives a clue to its origins. There are few traces of the hospices at Llawhaden and Whitewell, or of the once-famous Whitland Abbey.

At St Non's, near St David's, there is a modern monastery which is used for retreats; but of greater interest is the little Chapel of Our Lady and St Non, built in 1934 and closely modelled on the old Celtic style. There is an ancient holy well. Nearby, in a field, is a ruined chapel which probably dates from the early Middle Ages and which may have been part of a monastery. There are certain well-informed people who say that this is the loveliest spot in Pembrokeshire, and they may well be right.

At Caldey the old Norman priory has been subject to alterations and repairs over the years, but many of its medieval rooms remain in use to this day. Here, as at St Non's, the monastic tradition of the Celtic saints and their Norman successors has been revived; the Cistercian community of Caldey is very much part of Pembrokeshire life today.

Chapter Seventeen

Buildings: Homes for Rich and Poor

Most of the buildings in Pembrokeshire are the homes of its inhabitants - town and suburban houses for rich and poor, farmhouses, country cottages, and country mansions. The majority date from the past 100 years or so, but there are many interesting domestic buildings of much greater age in both Englishry and Welshry.

On the whole this was not a county of vast, rich estates, so there is little to compare with the magnificent country houses and parks so lovingly created in the counties of England between 1550 and 1800. The Pembrokeshire country houses were smaller and less imposing, but they have many interesting architectural features, and like the medieval churches and fortified residences they provide a link with the castle-building techniques of the Anglo-Norman community. The smaller farmhouses and country cottages have many features of interest, and in the towns there are fine buildings ranging from the well-known Tudor Merchant's House in Tenby to the town houses of the eighteenth-century gentry in Haverfordwest.

Near the old ports of the county there are commercial buildings such as the warehouses of Haverfordwest, St David's and Fishguard; and in Chapter 11 mention has already been made of the wide range of buildings connected with various industrial activities. There are also bridges, harbour works and jetties, lighthouses and monuments, stations, embankments and

viaducts dating from the railway era, and military buildings like the Milford Haven forts, many of them still in a good state of repair. In this short chapter there is space only to look at a few of these buildings, but the following paragraphs may give some idea of the architectural heritage of domestic buildings in Pembrokeshire.

Country Cottages

Most of the cottages scattered around the Pembrokeshire countryside used to be the dwellings of farm labourers and small craftsmen. Probably they were similar in style in both parts of the county, although there were of course local differences according to the raw materials available and the wealth and skill of the builder.

Many of the simplest and most primitive cottages have of course disappeared or have been altered and enlarged over the years. The most primitive cottages of all, which were still being built after 1840, were the "one-night" shacks put up on waste or common ground by the landless peasants. We have already referred to such cottages on page 72. The squatters would seek the help of neighbours, relatives and friends in the provision of raw materials and especially labour for the nocturnal building operation; but the **ty unnos** was not meant to last. It was built of turf and rough wooden beams, perhaps with a roof of grass or rushes, and it was usually built in May or June so

One of the most attractive of the remaining old cottages of Pembrokeshire. This one is at Treleddyd Fawr, near St David's.

that it could be replaced during the summer months by a second, more permanent, dwelling. Once this second dwelling was habitable, the original turf building became the cowshed or pigsty. Not surprisingly, most of the squatters' homes have vanished long since, for they did not have the quality of permanence about them. But several of the little hamlets which arose out of the squatters' settlements do remain, particularly in the north of the county on the fringes of Mynydd Presely.

Many of the Pembrokeshire country cottages of the 1700s and 1800s were built with mud walls and a rough-thatched roof. If help was forthcoming in the construction of the cottage, the total cost even at the end of the eighteenth century might be no more than £10. Most cottages were built to a simple rectangular plan, with mud or clay walls up to 2 m high and up to 1.5 m thick. These were referred to as "clom" walls, and they were strongest where clay could be employed in their construction, strengthened with chopped straw, rushes or twigs. Generally there was a low, thatched roof. The quality of the thatching was generally poor, and the bundles of hay or straw were kept on with long poles or cord running along the length of the roof. There was a fireplace at one end, and a rough wattle and daub chimney, more often than not leaning out from the gable end of the cottage at a crazy angle. There was generally a low front door, centrally placed in one of the longer walls, with a small window on each side. The windows were simply openings in the walls for glass panes did not come into common use until much later. The floors were of compacted earth. The simplest cottages had only one room, although articles of furniture were often used as partitions to create separate rooms. They

A photograph of the Old Post Office in St David's, taken around 1870. Such thatched cottages were common at the time.

had only a single storey and no lofts. Nowadays it is difficult to imagine the poverty and squalor of life in cottages such as these.

Not all of the cottages of this type were in the country districts, for they were common in the towns and villages also. Some of the most wretched cottages were built at the time of Pembrokeshire's "industrial revolution", when many farm labourers were forced to leave the land and seek employment in the coal-mining districts. Many cottages for colliery workers were hastily erected around Begelly (where many of them seem to have been built by squatters) and at Kilgetty and Saundersfoot. In the middle of the nineteenth century the squalor of the buildings and of their inhabitants attracted much comment. Each cottage was made of a mixture of mud, road scrapings and

stones, and its roof was thatched with straw. Sometimes a low wall of earth and wooden boards served to divide the cottage in two. A fire was kept burning continuously in the hearth, filling the interior with fumes and smoke but helping to keep the walls and floor dry. Not surprisingly, when the collieries and the Stepaside Iron Works closed, the cottages were abandoned and soon crumbled away. Within living memory there were over forty clom cottages in and around Stepaside. Now they are all gone.

In some parts of the county, especially where clom walls could be strengthened with shale fragments, cottages of this type are still in use, although not as dwellings. Generally they have been preserved because the old thatched roofs have long since been replaced by slate or corrugated iron. Thatch was never a very

Typical Pembrokeshire cottage shapes. Above, one-roomed cottage with thatch. Below, five-roomed cottage with shale or slate roof. (After Martin Davies)

The building materials varied according to the nature of the local bedrock; hence the cottages are made of limestone blocks in parts of south Pembrokeshire, slate slabs at Abereiddi and Trefin, Old Red Sandstone slabs on some of the shores of Milford Haven, and purple Cambrian sandstone near St David's. Mudstone or "rab" fragments were often used around Haverfordwest, and where flagstones were available in Ordovician and Silurian shales, these were occasionally used for roofing purposes also. Very often the exteriors of cottages were colour-washed in pink, white, grey or yellow, and it was not at all uncommon for each of the four walls to be given a different colour. This custom probably arose from the need to seal the outer walls of clom buildings with a lime wash, and it was later extended to stone-built walls also.

good roofing material in the wet and windy climate of Pembrokeshire, and hardly any thatched buildings remain. The best preserved is at Penrhos, near Maenclochog, where it is kept as a miniature museum.

The majority of eighteenth-century cottages still standing in the county have stone walls and slate roofs. Generally they conform to the traditional design; but the later cottages (dating particularly from the decades following the arrival of the railway in West Wales) are more elaborate. They have higher walls, larger windows with glass panes, back doors, internal walls, paved floors, and sometimes fireplaces and chimneys inside both gable ends. Some cottages were given interior ceilings and second floors or lofts, and porches and out-houses were often added. But still the design of these cottages was basically rectangular and symmetrical.

Slate roofs have been used since the medieval period in some of the areas of Anglo-Norman settlement, but slate only became widely available for use on the cottages of poor people within the last 150 years or so. Naturally this coincided with the growth of slate-quarrying operations at Abereiddi, Rosebush, Sealyham and elsewhere. The original method of roofing with slate was to drill a hole through each slate, and then to fasten it to a thin, split batten by means of a wooden peg. All the battens were nailed onto the rafters, but no nails were used on the rows of slates themselves. The finished roof was rendered underneath with lime mortar, which had the effect of cementing slate, peg and batten together and keeping out the wind. As the decades passed and the wooden pegs began to rot, a thin coat of mortar would be applied to the outside of the roof in an effort to keep the slates in place. Over the years more and more mortar, or a sand and cement wash, would be applied, making the roof heavier and more liable to rot. Sometimes wires would be passed from one eave to the other, over the ridge, and again heavily grouted. Eventually the whole roof would slide off or collapse, or else be repaired with a patchwork of corrugated iron sheets.

Farmhouses

There are several different types of farmhouse in Pembrokeshire, showing the influence of both Welsh and Anglo-Norman building traditions. From the Middle Ages onwards, the homes of the yeomen were much more substantial structures than the cottages of the agricultural labourers, and they were generally built of stone. Many were completely rebuilt in the later sixteenth and seventeenth centuries, and many more were enlarged. At this time new farmhouses also appeared in many areas as agriculture became more prosperous, more efficient, and free of the conflict and destruction of the preceding centuries. But most of the new farmhouses were built to a fairly consistent local style.

Many of the Pembrokeshire farmhouses are based upon the medieval tradition of the open hall. The early medieval buildings were built with massive stone walls and they probably had no chimneys. But then gigantic fireplaces and chimneys were added, sometimes in awkward positions attached to the outside of an end wall or a side wall. Sometimes later renovations and alterations to farmhouses involved the demolition and rebuilding of nearly all the walls, so that the rebuilt structure was in effect added to the old fireplace and chimney! It follows that Pembrokeshire fireplace and chimney units were built to last, like that which stands in glorious isolation today in the middle of a cottage garden in Carew. From medieval times they were a part of the local building tradition, and there is no doubt that they are among the most remarkable architectural features of the region.

The chimneys come in three types. The tall round chimneys which occur in

"Stepped longhouse" on a steep slope in the village of Trefin.

Pembrokeshire are well known, and they are locally referred to as "Flemish chimneys". However, there is no evidence that they had anything to do with the Flemings, for their distribution does not at all coincide with that part of the Englishry settled by the Flemish immigrants. They are, however, found on the halls and large farmhouses of the medieval gentry, and there are at least twenty-three of them. All occur in the Englishry, and the greatest concentration is found in a belt between Monkton, Pembroke and the Tenby area where limestone was

An old farmhouse on the flanks of the Presely upland ridge. Sadly, many of the oldest farms are now in ruins.

commonly available as a building material. The slightly lower and less elegant conical chimneys are found mostly on the St David's peninsula, although there are at least two to the south of Milford Haven and another at Garn, near Fishguard. These generally belong to very old farmhouses which may have been the homes of the lesser gentry or the more prosperous yeomen. The most unusual are the square chimneys which are often built above fireplaces of extraordinary

size, sometimes out of all proportion to the building which they serve. Occasionally there are exceptionally capacious ovens, too, fitted on to fireplace and chimney in unusual forms. These units are often situated to one side of the ridge. There are some splendid examples in the Englishry, as at Dover (Bosherston), Bangeston (Stackpole Elidor), Palmer's Lake (Penally) and Thornton (Bosherston).

There are various types of farmhouse plan, and these can be classified according to the number of rooms, their arrangement, and their relationship with the fireplace and chimney unit. The simplest subdivision seems to be between houses with gable-end chimneys (located either inside or outside the house wall) and houses with partly projecting fireplaces. The farmhouses at Rhosson, Clegyrfwya, Croftufty and Llaethdy, all near St David's are, or were, typical examples. Generally, there is a central passage running across the house from front door to back door. There are large rooms on either side of this passage, and sometimes smaller rooms as well under the main roof. There may be a loft to increase the living area beneath part of the roof, as in the magnificent fifteenth-century farmhouse at Garn. Small side-aisles or "pent-houses" built on to the side wall are used as storerooms, dairies or extra bedrooms, and they effectively increase the size of the living-room without increasing the span of the roof. In centuries past the main roofs of farmhouses such as these would have been thatched, with stone slabs or slates used on the roofs of the side-aisles.

An old type of farmhouse which is particularly common in the Welsh parts of Pembrokeshire is the so-called long-house. This is even more common in adjacent Cardiganshire and Carmarthenshire, where several splendid examples have been studied. The typical long-house consisted, as its name implies, of a long, rectangular

An example of exotic domestic architecture, on the arcades of the Bishop's Palace in St David's.

building, which was divided into three main segments. At the upper end was the dwelling-house, and at the lower end the cow-byre; between these was a connecting section used as a cattle-feeding walk. This central section usually had the main door and the main hearth. Some of the long-houses had lofts providing a second storey to the dwelling-house, and indeed haylofts were necessary for the cattle-shed also. Sometimes the lowest section of the building was a stable, entered through a separate door. Some of the long-houses had cruck-construction roofs, and they were originally thatched with straw or reeds. Turf was sometimes used to protect the ridge of the building, and often the dwelling-house was whitewashed. There were many local variations on the long-house theme, and in the last century or so some of the more successful farmers, have ejected the cattle

from their homes into separate cow-sheds, thus allowing the whole of the long-house to be used for domestic accommodation. There is a fine example of a long-house in the village of Trefin, where the building is in four connected segments running straight down a steep slope.

Many of the old Pembrokeshire farms are hybrid buildings showing some characteristics of the long-house tradition and some of the Anglo-Norman tradition. The Welsh tradition is seen in the highly elongated rectangular form, the small windows and the central passage running between opposite doors; and the style of the Anglo-Norman castle-builders is seen in the massive, thick stone walls, the arched doorways, the peculiar fireplaces, chimneys and ovens, and the stone staircases, recesses and benches.

Country Mansions

While the farmers were farming and the poor cottagers were trying to survive, the landed gentry of Pembrokeshire flourished. During the sixteenth century the manors of the Middle Ages were consolidated, and the landed gentry on their fine estates still wielded almost feudal power over their tenants. In addition to the old-established families there were many squires and lesser gentry. Some of these kept their place in the ranks of the gentry through their ancient pedigrees, but others rose through successful trading in the towns to join the ranks of the socially acceptable. From about 1570 onwards, there was a burst of house-building in Pembrokeshire as affluent families renewed or rebuilt their family seats to reflect their living style and (especially) their status. Many of the fine mansions of Pembrokeshire date from the period 1570-1800.

Among the great families were the Philippses of Picton Castle, the Owens of Orielton, the Barlows of Lawrenny, and the Campbells of Stackpole; and there were other well-known families at Slebech, Boulston, Llwyngwair, Sealyham and Manorowen, to mention but a few. Some of these families prospered, and as they did so their fine stately homes were rebuilt and enlarged. Other families (particularly the smaller gentry) built their homes and found their small fortunes dissipated. Between 1670 and 1750 many of the lesser Pembrokeshire gentry mortgaged or sold off their estates, and in 1810 Richard Fenton wrote that "...in several parts of this county mansions frequently occur in ruins, some abandoned for others more suited to the taste or views of the different owners, many by falling to heiresses, who have conferred their hands and properties on strangers, but the far greater number owing to the vicissitudes of human affairs and the precariousness of human possessions...".

Some fine mansions remain to remind us of past glories. The house at Orielton was originally a fortified medieval manor, but the powerful Owen family rebuilt it with a plain, classical east front in 1743. The south front was more elaborate, and there was a landscaped vista across lake and woodland. During the eighteenth century the estate and the house were great centres of the county's social life, and as the family prospered the house was extended even further in 1810. Now the complex of buildings houses the Orielton Field Centre, run by the Field Studies Council. At Picton Castle, as we saw in the last chapter, a large, new, castellated block was added in 1800, and the old west tower of the castle was demolished to make way for it. In 1768 Sir William Hamilton incurred great expense in making improvements to Colby Hall, and the cost of rebuilding Slebech Hall in 1776 was so crippling that the owner was forced to sell the estate soon afterwards. The great house at Landshipping was improved in 1789. Completely new mansions were built in this period at Ffynhone (1790, designed by John

Orielton, one of the finest country houses in South Pembrokeshire. It is now used as a Field Study Centre. (Robert Evans)

Nash) and at Boulston (about 1800). The former, although remodelled in 1904, is still the finest country house in the whole of the Welshry. Close to the idyllic harbour of Lower Fishguard, Richard Fenton built the fine house called Glynamel. There are other interesting stately homes still in a good state of preservation at St Brides (Kensington Castle), Saundersfoot (Hean Castle), Lydstep, Llwyngwair near Nevern, Manorowen, and elsewhere.

Sadly, or perhaps inevitably, some of the great houses are now demolished or have been reduced to ruins. The stately mansion at Stackpole Court, home of Baron Cawdor, which was embellished within by works of art and beautified without by extensive renovations in 1715, has now been demolished. Close to Haverfordwest are the ruins of Haroldston mansion, the home of the picturesque Elizabethan Sir John Perrott. We can still gain some impression of its former grandeur even though it has been in ruins for over 200 years. In the south of the county there are the last remnants of Scotsborough in the little valley of the Ritec. Henllys, the home of our old friend George Owen, is lost without trace. The same can be said of the mansions of Rickeston and Llanrheithan in Dewisland, and many other fine houses. Unlike the castles and the churches, the mansions of Pembrokeshire were, sadly, not built to last.

Town Houses

By way of conclusion to this chapter it is worth mentioning some of the fine domestic architecture of the main towns. Most of the interesting buildings date from the period when the Pembrokeshire gentry were at their most affluent and when the merchants of Haverfordwest, Pembroke and Tenby could still afford to live in reasonable style. All of the best-known local families showed off their wealth through their town houses.

The most interesting of all the old buildings is the Tudor Merchant's House in Tenby It dates from the fifteenth century, and it has a gabled front and a corbelled chimney. It is still carefully preserved, and is a popular tourist attraction. Next door is Plantagenet House, of similar age; this has a fine round chimney. There are few other traces of medieval buildings in the town, for the greatest part of its fabric dates from late Georgian to early Victorian times. Nevertheless, the regiments of hotels and boarding-houses along the cliff-tops above both North Beach and South Beach are quite magnificent monuments to the early efforts of Sir William Paxton, the creator of the modern holiday resort.

Haverfordwest has a number of fine town houses, some of them dating from the affluent years of the eighteenth century when many of the gentry built and maintained winter residences there. While the local gentry congregated in Tenby during the summer, Haverfordwest was the centre of the winter social scene. A number of the houses of High Street and Hill Street were the residences of the elite, and parties and balls were held virtually every night during "the season". The best-known of the town houses is Foley House in Goat Street, built by John Nash in 1794 for Mr Richard Foley. It has been preserved (somewhat garishly) and is now used as a local government office.

Elsewhere in the town there are other interesting buildings, but local people apparently failed to notice them until many of them were recently scheduled for preservation. Hermon Hill House has a Regency bow front, and may also have been designed by Nash. In Barn Street, Gloucester Terrace and elsewhere there are most attractive rows of town housing in a variety of different styles. The splendid wrought iron work of the terrace at the bottom of Barn Street is particularly fascinating.

Along the main street of Pembroke there is a wide variety of domestic architecture, from houses at the castle end with projecting Tudor corbels to the more familiar styles of the modern shop fronts. The irregular roof-line of the street has a medieval look about it, and this is of course enhanced when one is looking towards the castle. Here again is a reminder that in Pembrokeshire the medieval world is not very far away even when we are within sight and smell of Pembroke power-station.

The "new wing" at Roch Castle, built to change the old castle into a desirable modern residence around 1900,

Chapter Eighteen

The Rediscovery of Milford Haven

The most recent chapter in the life story of the Milford Haven waterway is part of the story of the British oil industry. During the early 1950s the oil companies were thinking in terms of vastly increased tonnages for their oil tankers, to enable them to keep pace with the enormous rise in the demand for petroleum products and to reduce their own transporting costs. Both the BP and Esso petroleum companies began planning for oil tankers of 100,000 tonnes or more, and the immense advantages of Milford Haven as a potential oil port became apparent. It had a wide and sheltered waterway, and could accommodate vessels of 16.5 m draught at all states of the tide. Tidal scour was efficient, and there was no silting problem and thus no need for continuous dredging. Land was cheap on both sides of the Haven, and was available for large-scale construction projects. Moreover, the government favoured the development of the Haven. Consequently the decision was taken in 1957 to embark upon the creation of a major oil port, and in 1958 government legislation was passed setting up the Milford Haven Conservancy Board (now called the Milford Haven Port Authority). By 1959 the Esso and BP companies were hard at work with building projects on the shores of the Haven, and the modern oil port was born. Since then there have been a number of other major developments.

The Oil Industry

The Esso oil refinery, near the village of Herbrandston, was the first refinery to be built on the shores of Milford Haven, and in 1983 it was the first one to close. It began working in the autumn of 1960 and became the second largest refinery in the British Isles. At its peak, 375 staff were employed at the refinery. At first it was able to refine only about 4.5 million tons of crude oil each year; but in the 1970s, after a large expansion project costing £26 million to complete, its refining capacity increased to 15 million tons per year. The refinery site covered 515 ha, and the refinery plant itself was more or less surrounded by almost a hundred oil tanks. The largest tanks, on the clifftops around the western edge of the refinery, stored the crude oil. The smaller tanks held various products such as petrol, diesel oil and jet fuels. Most of the crude oil was imported in the Esso supertankers which were a common sight on the waters of Milford Haven. The Esso jetty, stretching over 900 m out from the shore, has a long pier head with five berths for shipping. These were used by tankers of all sizes up to 285,000 tons and in the refinery's heyday more than 2,000 vessels used the jetty each year. Most of these were small tankers which carried about 80% of the refined products to other British ports. About 18% of the products were pumped along a pipeline (called the "3Ms Pipeline") owned by Esso, Gulf and Texaco which links the Haven refineries with the Midlands and Manchester.

In 1983, only a few years after a major expansion programme, the refinery was suddenly closed following a management decision to concentrate all production at Fawley near Southampton. At that time

A 215,000 ton BP supertanker berthed at the Popton Point jetty in 1970. The jetty is now owned by Texaco. (Photo: BP)

there was great oil refining over-capacity all over Europe. Within a few years the refining plant was dismantled, sold and shipped abroad. The huge storage tanks were taken to pieces, and the hundreds of miles of on-site pipelines were also removed, leaving at last a barren wasteland which included much land which was heavily polluted. Later the railway line to the refinery site was lifted, and the 132 kV electricity sub-station was dismantled.

The deep-water terminal at Popton Point, near Angle, was built by the BP company in the years 1958-60 and was officially opened in 1961. Its cost was approximately £7 million. There was no BP refinery on the site. Instead, the terminal was built to import crude oil for the existing BP refinery at Llandarcy, near Swansea, which had no facilities suitable for

handling supertankers. The terminal and the refinery were connected by a buried pipeline over 95 km long. Its construction was an impressive civil engineering project. It involved the crossing of twelve major roads and thirty-seven rivers. The greatest obstacle of all was the River Tywi below Carmarthen, crossed at a point where it was about 450 m wide at high tide. When it was brought into use the pipeline was the longest crude oil pipeline in the British Isles, able to carry 5 million tons of oil per year. Between 1960 and 1975 the Llandarcy refinery was expanded to refine over 8 million tons of crude oil per year, and the capacity of the pipeline was also increased (by the building of a "booster station" with three pumps at St Clears) to 9.2 million tons per year.

The jetty at Popton Point stretches 300 m from the shore, and the "jetty head" is

722 m long, providing three berths for supertankers. In 1965 the first 100,000 ton ship to enter the Haven berthed at the BP terminal amid great publicity. Nowadays even this vessel seems small in comparison with tankers of 250,000 tons which are frequent visitors to the Haven.

In the early days of the Milford Haven oil industry BP held 155 ha of land on the south shore of Milford Haven, of which less than 100 were used. The offices and control centre for the terminal were inside the old Popton Fort where there were also storage tanks for bunker oil and water supplies. The main tank-farm was about a mile away at Kilpaison, on the shore of Angle Bay. The tanks held a total of half a million tons of crude oil, and four of them (each holding 75,000 tons of oil) were among the largest in Europe. In the 1970's two 50,000 ton tanks were built on Popton Point to store heavy fuel oil for the Pembroke power-station.

In 1985 the BP operations at Angle Bay and Popton Point were closed down as a result of a decision to concentrate all BP activity at Llandarcy. It was predicted that with the rise of oil production in the North Sea the need for supertanker crude oil imports from the Middle East would reduce, and BP management recognized that the Queen's Dock terminal, not far from Llandarcy, could handle the smaller vessels carrying oil from the North Sea production platforms. The Kilpaison tank farm was quickly dismantled. The Popton Fort administrative centre was leased by the Field Studies Council's Oil Pollution Research Unit, and the jetty was sold to Texaco. Finally the Llandarcy pipeline was "plugged" or filled, making it impossible to use again.

In 1962 Texaco chose Milford Haven as the site for its first UK refinery. It was opened in October 1964. It is the only refinery on the south shore of the Haven. The tank-farm and refinery are built in the middle of a 500 ha site, near the small village of Rhoscrowther. Since it was built the refinery has been enlarged so that it can now refine about 10 million tons of crude oil per year. The actual refining complex and tank farm occupies 223 ha of the site. The most important of the capital investments in the last 20 years involved an expenditure of £400 in the period 1977 - 1982 on a new cat cracker, financed jointly with Gulf Oil and now operated by the Pembroke Cracking Co. The crude oil is imported in supertankers and smaller vessels, although only two of the five berths on the jetty can accommodate tankers of more than 100,000 tons. The largest berth can now handle vessels up to 280,000 dwt, and the acquisition of the BP jetty allows the company to load or unload up to five vessels per day. The refinery produces petrol, jet fuels, kerosene, diesel oils, fuel oils and liquefied petroleum gases. About 72% of these products are shipped out, with another 26% moved by pipeline, for road access to the refinery is poor and there is no rail link. The refinery employs about 320 persons, and Texaco estimates that it contributes about £29 million annually to the local economy in the way of rates, salaries and local purchases.

In 1966 the Gulf Oil Refining Company started to build its refinery, petrochemical plant and deep-water marine terminal in the inner reaches of Milford Haven near the village of Waterston. The installations, which cost £39 million, were formally opened by the Queen in August 1968. The refinery and its tank-farm are built on an exposed flat site near the coast. The three berths of the jetty are quite close to the shore and they are not nearly so noticeable as the Esso, Amoco, Texaco and BP jetties further down the Haven.

Because the Gulf refinery is 9 km from the mouth of Milford Haven it does not have access to the deepest channel. The largest vessels which can be handled at the jetty at present are 139,000 tonners. However, this presents no great difficulty to the company for it has an importing strategy based almost entirely upon North Sea crude oil. The refinery can process c 5.5 million tons of crude oil per year, and although there is a rail link most of the products are sent out by sea. Prior to 1982 some of the refinery products were used in a petrochemical plant, which was the only one in the Milford Haven area. Following the closure of this plant in response to market changes in the oil industry, the company has embarked upon a number of major capital projects. As mentioned above, between 1977 and 1982 Gulf Oil was a 35% partner in the "Pembroke Cracking Company" project on the Texaco Refinery site, and this involved the installation of five new product pipelines under the Haven. In 1990 - 1991 the company invested heavily in an up-grade of the cracking unit and also in a Co-Gen unit, which now uses refinery wastes to generate all the electricity needed on site and even to export surplus power to the grid. In 1991-1993 a £45 million isomerisation unit was installed on the site of the old petrochemical plant, in order to enhance the production of unleaded petrol. And a recent modernisation project has given the company the ability to produce diesel fuel which will conform to new anti-pollution standards.

Twenty years ago there were several Gulf installations in Europe, including the Bantry Bay supertanker terminal in Ireland, which was used for Middle East crude oil trans-shipment. However, following the rationalisation of the industry the Waterston refinery is the only one left. The Gulf Oil company is now a wholly-owned subsidiary of the Chevron Corporation. Currently it is preparing to protect its long-term interests by making plans for a new terminal extending into the deep-water channel from the old Newton Noyes RN Armaments Depot, which the company has recently purchased.

The £30 million Elf - Murco refinery was the last of the oil installations to be built on Milford Haven. Building started in 1971 and it came "on stream" in October 1973, with a refining capacity of 4 million tons per year. Originally it was owned by Amoco Ltd, but in 1990 it was taken over on a 70:30 basis by Elf and Murco. There are currently about 300 employees. Unlike the other Milford Haven refineries the Elf site lies well away from the coast, about two miles inland near Robeston Cross. It does, however, have its own jetty a short distance east of the Esso terminal. The jetty runs 715 m from the shore near Gelliswick Bay out to the deep-water channel. The main berth can handle tankers of 275,000 tons, and the second and third berths are designed for loading smaller tankers with refined products. Thirteen underground pipelines connect the jetty to the refinery. Since it was built the refinery has been up-graded through the addition of a cat cracker in 1981 and an isomerisation unit in 1992. Capacity has now been increased to about 5 million tons per year. All of the processing operations, and the tank-farm, are contained within a more or less rectangular perimeter. Closest to the sea are the large crude-oil storage tanks. To the east of them, and around the "process area" itself, are the smaller tanks which hold the refined products. The refinery and administrative buildings are in the north of the site, and on the eastern edge are the railway sidings. Like the branches serving the Esso and Gulf refineries, these were specially built to link up with the main railway line between Milford and Johnston.

Pembroke power-station, which is located in the Pennar Gut on the south shore of the Haven, is one of the largest in Europe. It was planned in 1964 and completed in 1973, having cost £105 million to build. It currently burns heavy fuel oil which is

The 2,000 MW Pembroke Power Station, located on the south shore of the Haven. (Studio Jon)

carried from the local oil refineries by buried pipelines. It is cooled by sea water pumped from the Haven at a rate of up to 55 million gallons per hour. In its early days the power-station burned about 2 million tons of oil per year, but it was designed to burn up to 4 million tons per year. At full capacity, using all four 500 MW generator sets, the power station can feed 2,000 MW into the overhead power-lines of the national "supergrid" which run towards the industrial areas of South Wales, the Midlands and the Bristol region. These power-lines, which carry 400kV, are supported between the huge metal pylons which are now a spectacular and not very beautiful part of the south Pembrokeshire landscape.

The power station has always been something of a white elephant, for following the oil crisis of the 1970's its fuel costs have been very high in comparison to those of competing coal-fired power stations. As a result, for much of the last decade only one or two of the four gigantic generator sets have actually been in use. Following the privatisation of the industry, National Power (which took over the station from the old CEGB) has had to compete in the electricity "pool" against even cheaper power stations burning North Sea gas. The power-station originally provided employment for 495 people, but this figure has since dropped to c 150, partly as a result of the under-utilisation of the plant and partly because of the drastic staffing cuts made by National Power in the name of efficiency. Currently the company is seeking consent to burn Orimulsion fuel at Pembroke, involving the large-scale import of this bitumen-based emulsion from Venezuela, the import of bulk cargoes of limestone for use in a new flue-gas desulphurisation unit, and the export of waste gypsum. If the plan goes ahead, National Power will boost production at the station up to the design level of 2,000 MW. This will involve a range of large-scale environmental impacts, including the construction of a new jetty in the waterway, followed by thousands of additional shipping movements each year and a great increase in atmospheric pollution. Environmentalists are very concerned, not least because Orimulsion has been called "the dirtiest fuel on the international market" and because it has never before been burned on such a scale in the UK.

Of the vast network of pipelines which are essential to the workings of the Milford Haven oil refining complex, the most important is the "3Ms" pipeline mentioned above. It was built at a cost of £15 million in 1972-3. with the Esso company taking the lead in the ownership consortium. Now it carries a variety of refined products (mainly petrol, kerosene and diesel fuel) in a pipeline which runs from Waterston to Seisdon in Staffordshire. From Seisdon there are smaller pipelines to terminals in Birmingham, Nottingham and Manchester. The pipeline now has the capacity to carry about 9 million tons of high-value products each year. It is now operated by Mainline Ltd, and all the local oil companies book space and time on the pipeline as required.

While the developments of the oil-refining industry have been proceeding apace, the Haven has failed to attract any other type of major industry. Many industrial schemes have been proposed, amid great local interest, but none of them has come to anything. Even the petrochemical industry has failed to materialize, except for a short-lived appearance on the Gulf refinery site, although it was widely thought at one time that companies like Fisons would be attracted to the Haven. Many other schemes for industrial developments have fallen through, and although some of them have encouraged great local hopes of increased industrial employment, others have raised great local opposition on environmental grounds. Above all, however, it is still true that the factor which militates most strongly against a more diverse industrial base around Milford Haven is remoteness from the major British markets.

The Modern Port

The trappings of the oil industry in and around Milford Haven are considerable. The most important of the "ancillaries" is the Port Authority, the body mainly responsible for controlling shipping operations in the waterway. It was set up as a unique civil port authority by Act of Parliament in 1958, since Milford Haven is the only new port in the UK to be established in the twentieth century. The Port Authority was charged with maintaining and improving the navigation of the whole tidal area of Milford Haven and the Daugleddau, regulating seaborne traffic, and providing lights, buoys and communications. Also, in 1960 it was given the right to levy dues on all vessels entering the Haven, in order to finance its operations.

The Port Authority has its offices, signal station and small boat harbour at Hubberston Point, which gives easy access to all the refinery jetties and to the harbour entrance. The authority has much greater powers than its predecessor, the Milford Haven Conservancy Board, and it now owns Marine and Port Services Ltd and DV Howells Ltd, as well as providing pilotage services to ships entering and leaving the Haven. The pilot launches are on duty round the clock. In effect, the Port Authority now operates as a private limited company.

The biggest project undertaken by the Port Authority prior to 1975 was the £7 million rock-dredging scheme of 1967-70, designed to improve the deep-water channel so that it could be safely used by 285,000 ton tankers at all states of the tide. New day

and night transit lights were put up at West Blockhouse and Watwick Point, to supplement the existing navigational lights. The Watwick Point lighthouse is forty-eight metres high, making it the third tallest lighthouse in Europe. Subsequent capital investments have included the £8 million Pembroke Dock Ro-Ro Terminal used by the B & I Irish ferries, and a £10 million development programme within Milford Docks. In addition to operating the VHF radio port information service, the Port Authority signal station is the hub of telephone communications for Milford Haven. It controls the round-the-clock information and emergency services and co-ordinates the movements of the fleet of powerful tugs owned by Cory Ship Towage Ltd. It is also the operations centre for the sophisticated radar navigation system for vessels entering and leaving the waterway.

The Milford Haven oil industry has grown as a spectacular rate. From the small beginnings of the oil trade the Haven had risen by 1968 to become Britain's leading oil port, handling 30 million tons out of a UK total of 180 million tons. In 1992 almost 39 million tons of shipping (3,861 vessels) used the port, and the cargo handled was mostly crude oil and petroleum products. Since 1992 annual shipping and cargo tonnages have fallen in response to the global recession and the reduction in the use of oil products in the United Kingdom.

The impact of the oil developments on Pembrokeshire has been enormous, and this can be measured in a variety of different ways. In terms of capital investment, something like £1500 million has been spent on the oil installations, and capital expenditure is still going on, partly in response to the need for cleaner and cleaner fuels. Each phase of refinery construction has provided jobs for over 2,000 temporary workers, some from the ranks of the project "travellers" but many of them locally

The Port Authority jetty and headquarters building at Hubberston. The ruins of Hubberston Fort can be seen on the left.

recruited; and the completion of each refinery has been followed by severe unemployment. The number of people directly employed in the oil installations is now around 1,350, and this is substantially lower than the figure for 1975. However, the industry is also responsible for the creation of at least another 1,500 jobs in local firms. It is difficult to calculate the contribution of the industry to the local economy in cash terms; but including rates and local expenditure by the oil companies and National Power, one calculation puts the figure at about £60 million each year. As noted in Chapter 12, the need to provide services for the oil industry has resulted in better local roads, the reopening of Haverfordwest aerodrome to light aircraft, and the construction of the Cleddau Bridge. In addition, electricity supplies were improved and the county acquired a new reservoir at Llysyfran, which not only improved water supply but also now provides a welcome amenity for local people and tourists.

Most of the direct impact of industrialization is of course felt around the waterway itself - in its farms and villages and in the three Milford Haven towns. Around the Haven, more than 2,000 ha of farm land has been lost to industry, and in the 1960's the appeal (and high wages) of refinery construction work attracted many farm workers away from agriculture. Most of them have never returned to the land. But over the years the farmers have obtained good prices for the land lost, and they have been forced to rationalize their farming activities to cater for their problems in finding farm labour. This may be no bad thing. The towns have experienced greatly increased trade, and many small firms have expanded to provide services for the oil industry. The oil companies have provided social and recreational facilities which have benefited all three of the town communities, and the arrival of many newcomers in the area has given a boost to social life and land values.

Very few people have complained about the economic or social impact of the oil industry, although there has been much disquiet about the small number of permanent local jobs provided by the industry. Something like seventy per cent of jobs in the oil installations are held by local people, but the dreams of 10,000 local jobs were never realistic. Since the oil companies came to Milford Haven technological developments in the industry have been so rapid that it has become one of the most capital-intensive of all. And the oil companies have come to Milford Haven to refine petroleum products as cheaply as possible - not to provide local employment.

Milford Haven and the Celtic Sea Oil Search

Studies of the Celtic Sea and St George's Channel have shown geologists that there are probably large reserves of crude oil and natural gas. These may not be as large as those of the North Sea and the offshore waters of northern Scotland, but there is still a powerful incentive for both the government and the oil companies to discover and exploit all possible offshore oilfields. Drilling for oil and natural gas commenced in the Celtic Sea in 1973, and by mid-1974 natural gas had already been discovered in the Irish sector. Since then there have been

several rounds of oil and gas exploration, with some licenses issued for sea-floor blocks within a few miles of the Pembrokeshire coast. Most of the results of the drilling work are shrouded in secrecy, but it is rumoured that substantial reserves have been located. Following the issue of the 14th round of exploration licenses, four drilling consortia are at work in Cardigan Bay and St George's Channel, and there is considerable expectation in the industry that large discoveries are imminent.

Milford Haven is extremely well placed for taking part in the Celtic Sea oil search. It has its own oil industry and there are sites which can be used as shore bases; the best of these are the Port of Pembroke and Milford Docks. Before 1973 the old Pembrokeshire County Council encouraged the use of shore bases in the county, and between 1973 and 1995 Dyfed County Council maintained this policy. Some local companies were initially involved in providing ship-building and repair and storage facilities. A company called Celtic Sea Supply Base Ltd built up its work-force and expanded the range of its industrial and service work; Govan Davies Estates and Marine and Port Services developed their bases in the Pembroke Dockyard; and the Milford Docks Company experienced a new lease of life. And the vast number of services required for drilling operations in the difficult waters off the Pembrokeshire coast encouraged many smaller firms to commit themselves to the Celtic Sea oil search as well. Near Haverfordwest the runways of Withybush aerodrome were resurfaced, and were then used frequently by air taxi and helicopter services. Other helicopter bases were in use closer to Pembroke Dock.

By the beginning of 1975 the oil search had not really begun in earnest, partly because the oil exploration companies were fully occupied in the North Sea and partly because of a world shortage of deep-sea drilling equipment. This rather slow build-up caused some local frustration, but it at least allowed local commercial interests to prepare themselves carefully. In the summer of 1973 Shell drilled the first unsuccessful "wildcat" in the British section of the Celtic Sea, using the drilling rig **Transworld 61**. By August 1977 only nine wells (all dry) had been sunk, and the local bases had seen very little servicing activity. For the most part, the drilling rigs and drill ships remained well offshore. Things became very quiet during the 1980's as the oil companies moved their activities from the North Sea to the north coasts of Scotland and even to the deep waters of the Atlantic.

Under the latest phase of exploration work, planned to conclude in 1996, the main drilling consortia including Arco, Chevron, Marathon and BP are making remarkably little impact on the local economy. Their drilling rigs have no need to come into port, and many of them are moved from one exploration site to another in a fully loaded state. Even those which are partly unloaded stay well out to sea, and only their small service vessels come into the Haven for chandlery, loading and discharge of fuels and drilling liquids, and some storage and support services. The Celtic sea drilling "bonanza" has not happened and will not happen, largely because the industry has now become adept, after many years of working around the Scottish coast, at minimising the need for shore-based support.

Local naturalists are worried that if oil (or gas) is found close to the Pembrokeshire coast the resulting pipelines will come ashore in the National Park, requiring coastal terminals and pumping stations. Increased flying over the bird islands of Skokholm, Skomer and Grassholm by oil company helicopters could do great damage to local wildlife. There has been grave concern in the mid-1990s about seismic exploration and spillages of drilling lubricants, not to mention oil and gas leaks from the sea bed or from drilling rigs, because of fears for the resident Cardigan Bay populations of porpoises and dolphins. Naturalists are only too aware of the potential damage to the seabird populations, especially in the case of a major oil spill during the breeding season.

Again, some people fear that now that oil has been found further out in the Celtic Sea the oil companies will soon want to establish offshore terminals in St Bride's Bay to handle ships of 500,000 tons and more. The effect of oil spills from such terminals could be disastrous for the local holiday trade, for the oil would come ashore on the sandy beaches of Broad Haven, Newgale and Whitesands Bay.

These fears are probably exaggerated, and most analysts agree that even if there is a major oil find close inshore it will probably not be exploited for at least a decade. However, the exploration consortia have sought to calm local fears by commissioning a detailed Environmental Appraisal of their activities; and at the time of writing there are signs that the local government authorities are taking local protests seriously enough to evolve new strategies for controlling future offshore and onshore oil industry developments. This is just as well, for the central government seems thus far only to have been concerned with maximum development of St George's Channel and Cardigan Bay "in the national interest", regardless of the cost to the environment or the local community.

Chapter Nineteen

Environment in Focus

Twenty years ago very few people in Pembrokeshire took environmental issues seriously. Those who sought to draw attention to the local ecological impact of pesticides or herbicides, or the scale of air pollution from the Milford Haven oil installations, were looked on as "eco freaks" or even political subversives. Not any longer. Environmental issues are now high on the political agenda, and demand constant attention from local councillors and council officials as environmental organizations publicise them through the use of increasingly sophisticated public relations techniques.

Pembrokeshire people have a long and honourable tradition of public protest and political campaigning where there is a widely-perceived and large-scale threat to the environment. In the 1970s there was an effective campaign, with the Dyfed Wildlife Trust playing a vociferous role, to eliminate the use of herbicide chemicals on roadside verges and hedgerows. The County Council adopted a new strategy of cutting after the spring and early summer flowers had set seed, and the result is that verges and hedgerows are now more colourful, and support a wider variety of flowers, than for many decades past. Another example of a perceived threat came a few years ago when the MoD proposed to build a huge "over the horizon" radar installation on the old St David's Airfield, just 4 km from the cathedral. Coming as it did after the end of the Cold War, local people (and many defence experts) considered it to be a classic piece of strategic planning which was twenty years behind the times, and the proposal was killed off by a storm of protest and by a professional and highly effective lobbying and publicity campaign organized by local people. In 1992 there was another vociferous (and ultimately successful) campaign when National Power sought to burn Orimulsion fuel at Pembroke Power Station without the fitting of flue-gas desulphurisation (FGD) equipment.

Just as new threats to the environment are now tackled head-on by environmental campaigners in Pembrokeshire, so old-established and environmentally-damaging practices are increasingly coming under the spotlight. Twenty years ago, it was acceptable to dump raw untreated sewage into the sea all around the Pembrokeshire coast. Now the practice is not acceptable anywhere, and groups of local citizens in Tenby, Fishguard, Newport and other coastal towns are prepared to take on Welsh Water (Dwr Cymru), the National Rivers Authority, and the local councils in order to obtain full sewage treatment facilities where none exist. One reason is that beach pollution by sewage is now highly publicised by Friends of the Earth, the Marine Conservation Society and other bodies, and in an increasingly competitive tourist market no seaside community wants its beach to fail the EC "bathing water" test or to risk a single case of viral infection among swimmers or water sports enthusiasts.

Similarly, the old somewhat laid-back attitude of farmers to farmyard slurry spills into water courses is no longer tolerated. members of the public are now quite watchful of pollution incidents in streams or rivers, and the NRA has strong powers to prosecute offending farmers who have allowed their slurry tanks or pits to overflow. A few years ago there was widespread local outrage when Nevern Dairy (now closed) allowed surplus whey from the cheese-making process to wash into the Caman Brook which flows past Nevern Church.

In this brief chapter there is no space to survey the whole environmental scene. However, it is worth highlighting some of the current issues of concern in the fields of urban and rural land-use, planning, and the Milford Haven oil industry.

Urban Problems

In previous chapters we have already examined some of the characteristics of urban life in Pembrokeshire However, it is worth drawing attention to the main types of environmental damage associated with urban lifestyles. Even quite small towns such as Fishguard and Narberth suffer at times from air pollution. Some of it is related to the burning of central heating oil and solid fuel, although in recent years there has been a sharp decline in the use of patent fuels, coal and coke. Vehicle fumes certainly make a contribution to town centre pollution, and Milford Haven, Neyland, Pembroke and Pembroke Dock all suffer on occasions from pollution from the Milford Haven oil installations. Most often this is simply manifested as a heavy smell of oil in the air, but sometimes there is a fallout of soot and other corrosive substances which causes great local distress. More to the point is the rising frequency of asthma in children in Pembrokeshire; partly this is related to the complexity of the chemical substances with which children nowadays come in contact, but there appears little doubt that man-

made pollution by the oil industry is the major culprit.

The heavy level of car usage in towns is partly a matter of lifestyle preference, but it must be said that planners and politicians must share the blame for a number of factors which have driven people into their cars. The fashion for out-of-town and edge-of-town supermarkets and hypermarkets has been encouraged by local planners, with the consequence that town centre traders have found it increasingly difficult to compete with the "big names" in retailing. High business rates in town centres have also helped to force small family concerns out of business, with the result that some of the Pembrokeshire town centres seem to be dominated nowadays by banks, building societies, estate agents and charity shops, none of whom provide the daily necessities of life for the average shopper. Another factor driving people into their cars is the scarcity (and the high cost) of public transport. Very few people now travel in to the town centres from the rural parts of Pembrokeshire by rail to do their shopping, and relatively few even travel by bus. Bus deregulation in recent years has made it possible for small companies to offer bus services within the built-up areas of towns, but very few of the new breed of bus entrepreneurs are prepared to take on the rural services which are generally loss-making. To its credit, Dyfed CC has sought for some years to subsidise rural bus services, but many rural people still find the services too expensive and too infrequent to be useful.

Urban sewage disposal is another problem which challenges some communities. Welsh Water has unfortunately made a name for itself in recent years as a privatised monopoly more concerned with profits than sewage provision and more concerned with "image" than service. It has shot itself in the foot several times on public relations matters, and the inhabitants of Fishguard,

Town centre decay in High Street, Haverfordwest, in the 1970's, caused partly by inappropriate planning policies.

Goodwick, Newport and Tenby (for example) have been particularly incensed that the practice of dumping raw macerated sewage into the sea appears not be be of undue concern to Welsh Water bosses. Naturally enough, now that beaches are carefully monitored, no community is satisfied with the thought of a sewage system in the year 2010 when it is needed immediately! Public pressure is building up inexorably for instant action on the sewage front, particularly in coastal towns which experience very large population increases over the summer holiday months.

Housing policy is another matter which has a strong environmental dimension. The cut-back in council house building under the Tory government of the 1980's caused a severe housing problem in some towns. To a degree this was relieved by private house building and by the building projects of housing associations, and it is good to report

that various derelict or semi-derelict sites in Haverfordwest, for example, have now had good-quality houses, flats or maisonettes built on them. However, private or speculative builders almost always prefer houses with gardens on the fringes of towns, preferably on "green field" sites. This means that over the years the main towns like Haverfordwest, Pembroke and Pembroke Dock have seen their edges pushed out inexorably into the open countryside, especially along the main roads.

Ribbon development is all too apparent, although the planners seek to control it. Again, the planners seek to release land for housing provision at a controlled rate, and through the Local Plan process they seek to establish town and village limits within which building is permissible and outside which building is resisted. But consensus is very difficult to achieve, and as people move out inexorably from the town centres into designated housing areas the increased use of cars is an inevitable consequence. The community becomes less "energy efficient" -- and socially less coherent -- than a community living in and around the historic town centre, and the environment is the loser.

Rural Land Use

In Chapter 12 we have already looked at some of the characteristics of the farming industry in Pembrokeshire today. However, environmental damage in the countryside is not by any means the sole responsibility of the farmer, for there are many other users of the rural environment. For example, tourism is now a major industry in the countryside, especially within the National Park. In south Pembrokeshire in particular, the impact of holiday developments on the landscape of the area around Tenby, New Hedges and Saundersfoot has been dramatic; caravan parks, holiday clubs, bungalow estates, shops, filling stations, and "tourist enterprises" have in places converted green and pleasant countryside to a sort of "rural suburbia" which some people love and others hate. It would be arrogant to deny the rights of local people to capitalise on tourism as best they can, and since tourism is now vital to the Pembrokeshire economy we cannot wish it away. The planners have a difficult task in controlling such development, and they have wisely decided to restrict it to a small number of areas where pressure is greatest. Even those who live and work on "the south-east holiday coast" would probably agree that the style of development which has evolved there would not be appropriate in Dale, Newgale or Newport.

A related problem is the spread of large-scale "theme park" developments outside the National Park in the Tenby -- Saundersfoot area. As mentioned in Chapter 15, the clustering of developments such as the Manor House Wildlife Park, the Great Wedlock Dinosaur Experience and the Heatherton Country Sports Park near St Florence, and then Oakwood Park, the Canaston Centre, Folly Farm and Heron's Brook Country Park only a few kilometres to the north, may be sensible from a planning point of view, but the environmental impact of such concentrated development must be questioned. All the developments have come to the area in order to capitalise on a nearby holiday population which adds up to about half a million people over the course of the summer, and in order to enjoy the benefits of easy access now provided by the M4 and its dual carriageway extension on the A40 route west of Carmarthen. All of these developments work hard to attract local holiday business, but in the future they will also embark upon marketing campaigns designed to pull in day trippers from other parts of South Wales and even further afield. Most of the visitors to these attractions travel by car, and the long-term environmental impact of traffic congestion and air pollution may be considerably more severe than anticipated by the planners. Exhaust fumes in particular are invisible, and are all too easily forgotten about.

Another "problem location" is the newly-designated City of St David's. Although it has been a place of pilgrimage for at least a thousand years, many Pembrokeshire folk now think that it is becoming too popular for its own good. Local people have (and who can blame them?) set up a number of imaginative tourist enterprises in the city over the last decade or so, specifically in order to entertain visitors and to convince them to part with a few pounds of their holiday spending money. The community, after all, has to make a living. But how much development is appropriate in such a small and sensitive community? Retired people (of whom there are many in St David's) often resent local entrepreneurial activity on the grounds that it changes the place they love, and creates noise and bustle when all they want is peace and quiet. Local councillors, on the other hand, argue that the community has to find other sources of income to compensate for the long-term decline in farming fortunes in the surrounding countryside. The dilemma is a real one, and planners are already aware that the city's image as an old and precious centre of Celtic Christianity is dangerously close to disappearance. Will it be replaced by the image of a typical tourist honeypot, with gift shops, purveyors of plastic buckets and spades, cafes, ice cream shops and galleries lining every street? The most virtuous of organizations have been dragged into the world of tourist souvenirs, and the National Trust, Cadw, the NPA and even the Dean and Chapter of the Cathedral now have retail outlets (in the best possible taste) designed to make as much money as possible during the short summer season!

Out in the open countryside farmers and landowners have their own environmental problems to cope with. The over-use of agri-chemicals (fertilisers, pesticides, and herbicides) still causes concern, and some farmers are responding to the growing demand for organic produce by returning to the older and more benign methods of land management that their grandfathers used. The trend towards specialisation on farms has led to near-monoculture in places, and farmers who are totally dependent upon dairying or sheep husbandry are particularly vulnerable to the effects of political decisions concerning, for example, milk quotas or headage payments. Of equal concern are the ecological characteristics of specialised farm units, for they lack the habitat diversity of the old mixed farms.

However, there are some glimmers of light in the expansion of set-aside land (which can, if adequately planned, be used for the creation of wildlife refuges in the midst of intensively cultivated areas) and in the range of grants now administered by the Countryside Council for Wales (CCW) for the creation of new ponds, woodland areas and water meadows. The designation of the Preseli Environmentally Sensitive Area (ESA) in 1994 is a major step forward, and has been described by a local farming leader as a "change away from production support to environmental support" for the agricultural community. Under the ESA scheme administered by the Welsh Office Agriculture Department, volunteer participants can receive payments for reductions in stocking levels, the creation of wetlands and hay meadows, and the use of "conservation headlands" around arable fields. On these headlands, the use of herbicides and pesticides is not allowed; and the result should be a widespread increase in hedgerow wildlife.

From the viewpoint of an environmentalist, it is somewhat ironic that whereas grant aid was paid to farmers twenty years ago for **destroying** wildlife habitats through boulder clearance, stream channel straightening, land drainage and hedgerow removal, grant aid is now available to farmers who want to take land out of food production and allow it to revert to nature! Similarly, the coniferous plantations established in the 1950s and 1960s are now extremely unpopular, partly because of the role they play in soil acidification and because they support very little wildlife; the latest trend is towards deciduous tree planting using native species, not for any particular long-term financial gain on the part of landowners, but because of the long-term environmental benefits that an increased woodland cover will bring to the county. We live in a strange old world.

Finally, a rural issue with a very powerful environmental content is the potential use of renewable energy resources in the countryside. As recently as fifty years ago energy was produced and consumed on a decentralised and local basis. Coal was produced and used, if possible, close to its source. Electricity was generated in small hydro plants or in local power stations such as that which I remember as a child in Cartlett, Haverfordwest. Gas for domestic use was even produced in places like Porthclais. Many rural dwellings used their own timber for fuel and their own tallow for lighting purposes. Then, with mass-production, nationalisation, centralisation and the development of the national electricity grid, the means of energy production were taken out of local hands. Coal and liquid fuels began to be produced on a vast scale and were shipped around the country in bulk. Electricity production became more and more centralised into larger

Supergrid electricity pylon in south Pembrokeshire, not far from Begelly.

and larger power stations, and the population as a whole has subsequently been "educated" into the strange belief that power production should be gigantic in scale and preferably somewhere else. This is a

historical aberration, and should be seen as such, for the environmental costs associated with installations such as the Pembroke Power Station and the Milford Haven oil refineries are only now being properly calculated, and are ultimately too high to be carried by the nation or the world. In the future renewable energy will have to be developed, even in rural areas like Pembrokeshire, if we are to have any hope at all of holding the "greenhouse effect" in check. One of the ironies of the situation is that the most beautiful areas close to the western coasts of Britain are precisely those areas where the most abundant wind, tidal and hydro resources are to be found.

In 1992 the government committed itself, at the Rio Earth Summit, to a reduction in national emissions of carbon dioxide and other pollutants. It is therefore inevitable that renewable energy resources will be used on an-increasing scale in the UK; the developments using wind power, water power or tidal power will be relatively small in scale, and they will be for the most part in rural locations. In recent years the government has chosen to create a support mechanism to allow renewable energy technologies to establish themselves in the energy market-place, and as a result there have been several development proposals in Pembrokeshire for windfarms, wood fuel generating plants and hydro schemes.

For example, a proposal from a local wind energy company for a small project involving four wind turbines near Square and Compass and Croesgoch was greeted with something akin to mass hysteria in the local area, fed by certain national organizations which specialize in the provision of disinformation concerning wind turbines. A planning application from National Power for a large windfarm of 45 turbines on Mynydd Cilciffeth was greeted with great hostility in 1995, not only from the residents of Puncheston but also from many individuals who are pleased to call themselves environmentalists. The NIMBY syndrome was much in evidence, and it became clear that most of the objectors were preoccupied with the fact that the proposed wind turbines would be visible over a large distance and that they would produce "remarkably little electricity". Many local and national organisations joined the furore. Only the West Wales Energy Group, based in Newport, was prepared to go on the record and register its support in principle for the proposed development near Puncheston, and was prepared to point out that wind turbines are more cost-effective and "energy efficient" than fossil-fuelled or nuclear power stations, use less land per installed kilowatt, and are free of air-pollution effects.

The environmental dilemma is very difficult to resolve. It is certainly true that some people feel threatened by a new and unfamiliar technology, especially if it is likely to be located in their own home area. It is their privilege in a free society to sign petitions and to submit objections to planning applications. Some feel that no matter how clean and benign wind turbines may be, they must not be located on hilltops in a beautiful and sensitive area like Pembrokeshire.

No developers have suggested that windfarms should be located in the National Park, but does the NPA have any right to object to proposals for sites which are near, or visible from, the Park boundary? And do we, the ultimately selfish users of electricity, have any right to expect that the power stations which keep us supplied should always be out of sight and out of mind? More to the point, are we prepared arrogantly to slam the door on a clean and sustainable energy technology in Pembrokeshire in the full knowledge that it will work less efficiently elsewhere, and that the alternatives (fossil fuel burning and nuclear power) are infinitely more damaging to the global environment?

Oil and the Environment

It is inevitable that there should have been environmental problems in developing Britain's largest oil-refining complex in the county which contains Britain's only coastal National Park. The oil installations are built around the middle reaches of Milford Haven, mainly between the coastal and inland sections of the park. But there has been much building inside the Park also; the old BP terminal is entirely within the Park and the Elf and Texaco refineries straddle the boundary. The Esso refinery (now closed) was also partly within the Park. The Gulf refinery, further up the Haven, is built very prominently on a flat site, and although the Power Station buildings are well shielded in the depression of Pennar Gut the 230 m chimney stack is now Pembrokeshire's most prominent landmark. In the south of the county, as we have seen from Chapter 18, there are now two rows of gigantic pylons transporting electricity solidly and inexorably towards the eastern horizon.

Nobody expected that the oil industry would be invisible, but it could have been made very much less visible than it is. During Milford Haven's first decade of development the oil companies, conscious of the fact that they were building on the fringes of a relatively new National Park, attempted to minimize the visual impact of their installations. The Esso company embarked upon an elaborate landscaping scheme and an even more elaborate public relations exercise during the building of its refinery, and used earth embankments and sunken storage tanks on the slopes of a small valley in its attempt to blend massive structures into the landscape. The Texaco refinery was made considerably less obtrusive from the town of Milford because of a careful siting and landscaping scheme. The large BP tank-farm was built close to sea-level on the south shore of Angle Bay, and was well landscaped and coloured. And it was a happy idea on the part of BP to use the old Popton Fort as the administrative centre for the Angle Bay ocean terminal. On the other hand some aspects of the original construction works undertaken by the oil companies before 1970 were rather less pleasing to the eye. It was a planning aberration, for example, to allow the construction of five storage tanks for bunker oil and water on the rocky tip of Popton Point. It was a mistake to allow Texaco to build a group of storage tanks on another prominent clifftop site. And many local people now feel, in retrospect, that it was a planning disaster to have allowed the building of the Gulf refinery at all, on its prominent site adjacent to the village of Waterston where effective landscaping was impossible.

In the waterway itself the rocky headlands (such as Popton Point, Wear Point and Hubberston Point), which are the focal points of coastal landscapes, sprouted their inevitable jetties. The first three were built with long piers projecting to the edge of the central deep-water channel of the Haven. Having reached it, they spread their tentacles laterally towards east and west. In addition, navigational aids of various shapes and sizes appeared in and around the waterway, particularly during the major project undertaken by the Milford Haven Conservancy Board in 1967-70 to improve port facilities. These aids are prominent in the Haven entrance and on the cliffs to the west and north.

In the years following the building of the oil installations, visual pollution around the waterway has steadily increased. The Elf refinery, subject to stringent landscaping controls on the site itself, nevertheless makes a strong visual impact on many parts of the Park which previously had no views of modern industrial buildings. The Esso company was given the blessing of the Alkali Inspector (who had the final word in

such cases) to construct a 152 m smoke stack as part of its expansion programme. Extensions to the refinery tank-farms also made an impact. In order to store and supply fuel oil to the Pembroke power-station, the BP company constructed two 50,000 ton capacity tanks on a clifftop site immediately behind Popton Fort. These tanks were deeply sunk into bedrock in an attempt to reduce their effect upon the skyline. On the other hand, as part of its expansion programme Esso built equally large tanks on clifftop sites on the seaward margins of its original tank-farm. The visual impact of these was much more violent, for three of them occupied the hill summit adjacent to South Hook Battery, in an area which was strictly excluded from the first phase of refinery construction. Both the Esso and BP companies used strong civil engineering arguments to show that their new tanks could not have been sited elsewhere, and the planning authorities believed the civil engineers. Some of these environmental problems were ameliorated with the closure of the Esso refinery in 1983 and the BP installation in 1985, followed quite quickly by the removal of all above-ground structures. But it emerged afterwards that there were other environmental problems that had not previously come to light; for example, the Esso company proved to be very reluctant to dispose of its site for any other type of development, partly because its land was heavily polluted with herbicides including the particularly unpleasant poison called 245-T.

The Port Authority prides itself that Milford Haven is the cleanest oil port in the world, but there are still occasional oil spills at the refinery jetties. These spills are always heavily fined, but this is no real deterrent since most spills are due to human error in piping crude oil or petroleum products between ship and shore. As commercial pressures increase so does the risk of spillage and small spills are quite frequently reported in the press. A big collision or berthing accident could cause fearsome pollution, and would provide a stern test for the emergency services. The Haven tugs are equipped for salvage operations, and they all carry fire-fighting apparatus including foam jets mounted 20 m above the water-line. In case of oil spills the anti-pollution vessels **Seamop** and **Seasweep** are always on call with stocks of emulsifiers. In addition there are frequent patrols in search of floating oil, and the oil companies have paid for research into the best ways of fighting oil spills.

But accidents will happen even in the best regulated of situations within the confines of the waterway. A disaster was narrowly averted in 1960 when explosions and a severe fire crippled the tanker **Esso Portsmouth** while it was berthed at the Esso refinery jetty. There was almost another disaster one August evening in 1973 when the product tanker **Dona Marika**, loaded with high octane spirit, went aground during a gale at Lindsway Bay, close to the village of St Ishmael's. So great was the danger of explosion that most of the villagers were evacuated from their homes for the night. In the event there was no loss of life, but a substantial spillage of aviation fuel from the vessel caused a major headache for the emergency services.

Outside the Haven, in the Celtic Sea and St George's Channel, there is still far too much pollution arising from small "accidental" spillages of bilge oil or from tank-cleaning operations on tankers in ballast. And every now and again a major oil tanker wreck occurs to remind us just how vulnerable our coastal environment really is. Pembrokeshire's most serious accident occurred in October 1978 when the 58,000 ton tanker **Christos Bitas** went aground on a reef not far from the Smalls Light. She refloated, but then headed off towards Belfast trailing a huge oil slick from her damaged tanks. In all, she spilled about 2,000 tons of crude oil into the sea. Luckily,

Condemned to death. An oiled guillemot found after the "Christos Bitas" incident.

she did not sink, and the rest of her cargo was transferred under hazardous conditions to other tankers; but when it was all over a great deal of oil came ashore on the Pembrokeshire coast, killing at least 9,000 seabirds and many seals. Local naturalists were left wondering what might have happened if the accident had occurred at the height of the nesting season.

Great concern has been expressed locally about noise and atmospheric pollution, particularly with respect to the Gulf refinery and the Pembroke power-station. The Gulf refinery plant is far too close to the village of Waterston, and in the 1970's the villagers were involved in a long campaign against the company in their attempts to lessen the impact of noise, smell and dirt fall-out. The campaign was at times quite bitter; the company offered to buy the whole village and evacuate the population, and the villagers resorted to various legal devices to obtain compensation and even to close the refinery down. But Gulf is no more and no less guilty of pollution than the other companies operating around Milford Haven, and something similar happened at Rhoscrowther, very close to the Texaco refinery. The village is dwarfed by the huge bulk of the refinery, and after a long history of complaints about noise and smell, matters came to a head in 1992 when a refinery "flashback" occurred during a plant shut-down. Nobody was hurt, but the emergency services turned out in force and the villagers were very frightened. An Action Committee was formed by the villagers, and some members of the community asked Texaco to buy the whole village and re-locate the residents. In the event a relocation package was worked out between the company, the residents and the local authority, and a majority of Rhoscrowther families chose to move out in favour of a more peaceful life elsewhere.

Few people seem to have grasped the sheer scale of local atmospheric pollution associated with the oil industry. Working at full capacity in the late 1970's, each refinery ejected more than 20,000 tons of sulphur dioxide in its flue gases each year. At a conservative estimate this meant that about 300 tons of sulphur dioxide was added by the refineries to the atmosphere above Milford Haven each day. In 1989 the government introduced much stricter pollution controls, and to their credit the refinery operators worked hard to minimise SO2 emissions. Nowadays actual refinery stack emissions are down to about 75 tons per day. Much of this falls to earth again a few kilometres downwind, but some is carried hundreds or even thousands of kilometres to the east and north-east to fall in the form of acid rain.

The power-station is in a different league, for at full production, under its original "pollution consent", it ejected 650 tons of sulphur dioxide daily. It still burns heavy (ie cheap and filthy) fuel oil, and at present has no "scrubbing" devices in its chimney flues to remove sulphur dioxide and other poisonous substances. Government regulations have not in the past insisted on their installation, and the simplest and cheapest method of disposal is (as in Victorian times) to eject the waste gases at high velocity to an altitude of over 600 m in the hope that the wind will carry them away towards the Midlands, the North Sea and Scandinavia. The greatest fall-out of sulphur dioxide occurs about 10 km away from the power-station, and above certain critical levels (already attained in parts of Mynydd Presely and the Cambrian mountains) plants are killed. All in all, the Milford Haven oil installations are still capable of ejecting perhaps 500 tons of poison into the Pembrokeshire atmosphere each day, and nobody seems to have noticed.

Not surprisingly, with this background, more and more Pembrokeshire people are expressing grave concern about the National Power proposals for Orimulsion burning at Pembroke Power Station. As indicated in Chapter 18, the plan to reduce sulphur dioxide emissions through the use of FGD technology deals with one problem but also creates a whole set of other problems, including a much enlarged condensation cloud above the power station stack, an increase in emissions of fine dust, toxic metals and nitrogen oxides, and a huge increase in CO2 emissions to a level of about 9 million tonnes per year. During the planning process the "jobs card" has been effectively played by the company and its work-force, to the extent that none of the local authorities has seen fit to object to the Orimulsion planning application. Environmental organizations -- which are after all made up of local people --are dismayed by the apparent unwillingness of their elected council representatives to force a Public Inquiry at which all of the environmental and economic implications of Orimulsion burning can be properly examined.

Chapter Twenty

Conclusion: Pembrokeshire Past and Present

In the foregoing chapters we have traced a number of threads which run through the landscape and the way of life of Pembrokeshire. Woven together these threads make up a rich tapestry - a tapestry which has more beauty and more variety than one has any right to expect in an area so small. And the tapestry is unique. It has a combination of colours and textures quite unlike those of adjacent parts of Wales. And yet these adjacent parts, the old counties of Cardiganshire and Carmarthenshire, were forced in 1973 to join Pembrokeshire in the new county of Dyfed. In a period of turmoil the seat of local government was removed to Carmarthen, and the UK government assumed that Pembrokeshire was dead and buried. In this book we have seen that the spirit of Pembrokeshire has continued to inspire the minds and hearts of local people, even though their home territory may have lost its official name for twenty years or so.

When the plans for local government reorganization began to take shape in 1970, Pembrokeshire was slow to react. However, when it became clear that the county was to lose its identity and lose much of its control over its own destiny, a ground-swell of public disapproval started. During 1971 this swell gained momentum, with the enthusiastic support of the local press, and a "Save Pembrokeshire" committee was formed to lead the fight for independence. Soon there was a thriving campaign in full swing, and the culmination of its activities was a

delegation to the Welsh Office in London bearing a petition of 55,560 signatures. This represented the corporate voice of seventy-nine per cent of the Pembrokeshire electorate, requesting the abandonment of the amalgamation scheme. However, unlike some other parts of England and Wales, Pembrokeshire was short of a strong establishment lobby, and the campaign failed. When the Local Government Act was passed it signalled the end of Pembrokeshire as a local government unit.

This was bad enough, but the crimes of officialdom were compounded by the demarcation of the two district councils that replaced the old Pembrokeshire County Council. As we have seen in Chapter 13, Preseli Pembrokeshire DC (which should have become the "Welsh" district and which should have included all land north and east of the Landsker) was designated so as to include Haverfordwest, Neyland, Milford and the Dale peninsula. South Pembrokeshire DC (which should quite simply have included the whole of the Englishry) was given the area south of the Milford Haven waterway and also a sizeable part of eastern and north-eastern Pembrokeshire which was Welsh-speaking. Clearly the officials who were responsible for drawing the boundaries of the new districts were seeking to achieve some sort of balance in population numbers and economic strength; but the apparent total disregard for culture, tradition and language in the whole

*People like this made the modern
Pembrokeshire. Mr John (pictured here with
his wife around 1845) was a landscape
gardener at Castle Hall, Milford.*

process cannot have been entirely accidental. At the time, it was "politically correct" to make gestures towards an increasingly aggressive Welsh-language movement. One must conclude that in the eyes of the Welsh Office ministers (and their advisers from the old counties of Carmarthen and Cardigan) the idea of an economically powerful English speaking South Pembrokeshire coinciding with the ancient Englishry was simply not politically acceptable. Such a district would certainly have become something of an "enfant terrible" and would have caused untold trouble in the council chamber and offices of the new and predominantly Welsh-speaking Dyfed authority!

An interesting feature of the "Save Pembrokeshire" campaign was that it revealed a strong unity of purpose in both Englishry and Welshry. The people of both halves of the county showed that, in spite of their traditional bickering in local council meetings and their petty animosities towards each other, they were united in their affection for the idea of Pembrokeshire. People from both north and south showed that they felt themselves to be, above all else, Pembrokeshire people. This was to be expected in the Englishry; but it was perhaps surprising that Welsh-speaking people showed themselves more inclined to face the future alongside Little Englanders than alongside their Welsh-speaking neighbours of Cardiganshire and Carmarthenshire.

Once Pembrokeshire belonged to Dyfed, it was forced reluctantly to adapt itself to the new situation. To many the most interesting feature of the new county council was its aggressive pride in its own quality of Welshness. This was a consequence of the increasing self-respect of Welsh people throughout Wales, and of the upsurge in the popularity of the Welsh language after 1965. The campaigns of the Welsh Language Society and other groups were remarkably

successful, and came just in time to save the Welsh language and culture from an irreversible decline. The language suddenly became respectable, and it has become acceptable in many spheres where previously it was not tolerated. By 1975 Welsh lessons were in full swing in Cardiff, Swansea, Carmarthen, and even in Haverfordwest.

The implications of the new situation were fascinating, especially when looked at with respect to Little England. After centuries of numerical superiority over the Welsh-speaking people of Pembrokeshire, the people of Little England now found themselves very much in the minority in an aggressively Welsh new county. This did not do them any harm, and indeed they had always considered themselves Welsh, deep down, in any case. Eisteddfodau, welsh-cakes, Welsh costumes and cawl (leek broth) have always been as much a part of life in the Englishry as the Welshry; and in 1972 Haverfordwest, below the Landsker, acted as host, for the first time ever, to that most Welsh of all Welsh institutions, the Royal National Eisteddfod of Wales.

Sadly, the great occasion proved somewhat traumatic for many local people. The extremes of Welsh nationalism were demonstrated a little too openly for some tastes, and there seemed to be some disrespect for local traditions and for the use of English, which happens to be the native language of the Englishry. Perhaps the Eisteddfod officials were insensitive towards local feelings, and perhaps local people were hypersensitive about quite small incidents which were not at all calculated to cause offence. But offence was certainly caused by the lunatic fringe of the Welsh language movement, which defaced and smashed road signs all over Pembrokeshire. In all, damage costing £2,000 was caused, almost entirely to road

Are two names better than one? A typical bilingual road sign not far from the Landsker.

signs which had English place-names such as Haverfordwest, Fishguard, Rudbaxton, and Milford Haven. This vandalism caused much local resentment, and although it was condemned instantly by the Eisteddfod organizers, it caused a quick backlash of vandalism against road signs bearing Welsh village names.

Peace was restored, and the Welsh language lobby won a major victory in forcing the government to adopt bilingual road-signs for the whole of Wales. This involved the resurrection of Welsh place-names for south Pembrokeshire localities which had been English for about 900 years. Many of the medieval settlements of the Englishry needed to have Welsh place-names specially manufactured or dredged up out of ancient Welsh chronicles. South Pembrokeshire people were not quite sure how to react. Some were furious. Others accused Dyfed CC of a lack of respect for the unique heritage of Little England, and of attempting to destroy Pembrokeshire's cultural identity. Most were amused by the farcical nature of the whole bilingual road-

sign exercise. After all, they thought, when the new road-signs were all erected, the lunatic fringe of the Englishry would have some convenient road signs right on their own doorsteps to daub with red, white and blue paint.

While much changed in Pembrokeshire after 1973, local people actually had no need to fear for the identity or for the state of health of the old county. It had problems to face, certainly, particularly in its attempts to control the operations of Britain's greatest concentration of oil installations on the fringe of its smallest and most vulnerable National Park. But the old county was economically quite healthy, and it was involved in national economic affairs to a greater extent than ever before. The tourist industry was expanding, agriculture was relatively efficient, and manufacturing activities were gradually becoming more important. Pembrokeshire people were now better off than they had ever been, and they knew that their home area was a vital part of the new county of Dyfed. Most enticing of all was the prospect, or the hope, of industrial wealth and abundant side-benefits from the discovery and the piping ashore of oil from the sea bed. As in the Age of the Saints, the people of Pembrokeshire were looking with faith towards St George's Channel and the Celtic Sea.

By the mid-1980s, after a decade of belonging to the new county of Dyfed, Pembrokeshire's optimistic self-esteem was undiminished. By that time most of the road signs in Pembrokeshire (even in the south) bore both English and Welsh versions of place-names, causing some confusion among visitors and some concern about costs among the locals. The seemingly inexorable process of local government centralisation had led to the closing down or contraction of small-town council offices and the steady growth of Carmarthen as the new commercial and administrative centre of affairs. Anti-Dyfed

*St Brynach's Cross in Nevern Churchyard --
an enduring symbol of Pembrokeshire's Celtic
past and present.   (Robert Evans)*

feeling was as strong as ever, and the old "Save Pembrokeshire" campaign was transmuted into a vigorous "Bring Back Pembrokeshire" campaign which had much support particularly in the south. Many local people consistently refused to use the word "Dyfed" in their postal addresses, and the Post Office had to reluctantly accept this as a fact of life.

Shemi Wad (James Wade), one of the great characters of Goodwick, pictured in 1887.

By the time Dyfed was twenty years old the campaign (which by then had changed its name yet again to "The Campaign for Pembrokeshire") had already won some small victories, for example in the naming of the Pembrokeshire Health Authority and the new Pembrokeshire College. The Ordnance Survey had agreed to keep the name "Pembrokeshire" on some of its maps. And the local tourist industry --

with the support of the Wales Tourist Board -- was also determined not to let the Pembrokeshire label disappear, following research which indicated that the great British public still recognized the old county as a desirable holiday destination with a strong "brand image" whereas it knew hardly anything about Dyfed. Many of those questioned had not even heard of Dyfed, and a significant proportion of those who had were blissfully unaware of where it was in the British Isles.

Among the other important changes of the Eighties was the gradual decline of the oil industry. Falling demand for petroleum products led to the closure of the Esso refinery on Milford Haven, and the high price of heavy fuel oil resulted in a great reduction in the electricity output of the Pembroke Power Station. The eternal but unfulfilled promise of oil riches in the Celtic Sea continued to be a topic of conversation, but the prospects of an oil exploration boom in Milford Haven receded further and further into the future. In the end, the farming industry appeared to be reestablishing itself as the real pillar of the Pembrokeshire economy, with tourism adding invaluable support during the all-too-short summer season.

Now, in 1995, Pembrokeshire can confront its own identity again. Agriculture has taken a severe battering over the last few years, and the effects of milk quotas, reduced headage payments on livestock, and set-aside arrangements have shaken the confidence of many farmers and forced some out of business. The Whitland dairy has closed, as have the MoD establishments at Trecwn and Newton Noyes. The future of the old RAF base at Brawdy is still far from certain. The oil industry has contracted, and "black gold" from the Celtic Sea has still not been piped ashore. The deep economic recession of the early 1990s has destroyed or damaged hundreds of small businesses. The

View from the New Bridge, Haverfordwest, around 1910. On the left is the site for the new Pembrokeshire CC Offices.

decline of town centres has been accelerated by the expansion of out-of-town or edge-of-town superstore developments in which the local authorities have connived; in most cases they have been tempted by infrastructure developments paid for by the developers and euphemistically referred to as "planning gains". The tourist industry has declined, and is having to adapt to changing patterns of holidaymaking and to a tourist challenge mounted by virtually every other part of the UK. The powers of local government have inexorably been whittled away during fifteen years of Tory rule, and at the same time local people have seen a greater and greater centralisation of political and economic power in Westminster and Cardiff and in the hands of a host of unelected quangos. As a consequence Pembrokeshire, like most of Wales and Scotland, has moved politically towards the left, and there is a degree of scepticism and even cynicism about the democratic process. Closer to home, the new Pembrokeshire

County Council will have to take over some of the functions of Dyfed CC and will have to translate the policies and the services of two district councils into the policies and services of a new unitary authority. This will prove very difficult, even after transitional arrangements have been made and after the deliberations of the new "shadow" authority elected in 1995.

The language issue is likely to become particularly contentious. The new authority will be dominated by "Little Englanders" from the more densely-populated south of the county, and they will have to face up to the financial implications of bilingual road-signs, bilingual forms and leaflets, and a bilingual teaching policy. Will Council and Committee meetings be bilingual, and if so what will be the cost of translation facilities? More to the point, is there any merit in continuing some of the Dyfed CC policies regarding Welsh-language teaching in south Pembrokeshire,

Some of those who have fought to keep craft traditions alive over the past 15 years.

and in appointing bilingual teaching staff to primary schools in places like Marloes, Cosheston or Manorbier?

For the last twenty years there has been an evolving conspiracy to assimilate the Englishry into a new bilingual Wales; Dyfed officials and councillors, backed up by legislation, have apparently believed that their "super-county" should be given a sort of cultural uniformity stretching from Castlemartin to Tregaron and Aberystwyth to Llanelli. In the minds of Pembrokeshire folk this constitutes an insensitive and even wicked denial of a unique cultural identity which is a thousand years old. In the event there may well be support for an extension of Welsh language policies north of the Landsker, but the trade-off will be a demand from South Pembrokeshire councillors for a recognition of the fact that Welsh is a **foreign language** in the deep south. They will say, and I will agree with them, that

there is really no official place for the Welsh language south of the Landsker

So the new county faces a series of difficult problems. But Pembrokeshire has proved itself in the past to be nothing if not resilient. Those of us who were born and bred in the county, and those of us who have made it our adoptive home, have a powerful vested interest in its future prosperity. We love its clean air and its wide windswept skies, its landscapes of brambled lanes and tumbled rocks and blazing gorse, its pretentious blustering castles and its unprepossessing towns and villages, and its strange split personality. It is not quite Welsh and not quite English, and because of this its people look on themselves first and foremost as **Pembrokeshire folk**. They are the inheritors and the upholders of a thousand years of cultural tradition, and as far as they are concerned Dyfed never was a good idea.

Page 236

Acknowledgements

I am very much aware that the text of this book contains a great deal on topics which are difficult if not obscure. I have taken advice and received information from a multitude of kind people during my research, and I thank all of them for their generosity. Where appropriate I have acknowledged my main sources of written information, and it will have been obvious to the reader how much I have depended upon earlier published works. However, in a book of this type it is not possible to cite chapter and verse as often as I would have liked. There are many Pembrokeshire writers who will recognise parts of the text as based upon information provided by them; I am happy to acknowledge my debt to them, and I hope I have succeeded in reporting their ideas honestly. Some of their key publications are listed in the bibliography which follows. Needless to say, the opinions and the factual shortcomings in this book are my own, and I take the blame for them.

Most of the maps and other illustrations are my own. Others have come from my book called "Pembrokeshire" first published in 1976. I gratefully acknowledge the kindness of many photographers for allowing the use of their material. In particular I should like to thank Robert Evans, Studio Jon, John Havard, and Squibbs Studios. Where possible I have given credits in the photo captions, but I have been unable to trace the copyright holders of certain photos, and I will appreciate any information which will enable me to make due acknowledgement in future editions of this book.

Finally I thank Tony Case for his patience and his sound advice on all matters to do with computers and image scanning; Sally Rudman for her help with typesetting; Jonathan Lewis and his colleagues at Lewis Printers for many practical suggestions and for their professional expertise; and my wife Inger for sustaining me while I have been obsessed with this book, for helping with the index and the choice of illustrations, and for her careful proofreading.

Ruined Castle
at Angle

A Select Bibliography

Chapter 1
The Region and its Character

Curtis, T. (ed) The Poetry of Pembrokeshire (Bridgend, 1989)

Evans, R.O. and John, B.S.   The Pembrokeshire Landscape (Tenby, 1973)

Fenton, R.   A Historical Tour through Pembrokeshire   (Brecon, 1803, reprinted by Dyfed CC, 1994)

Giardelli, A. and others,   Pembrokeshire Painters   (Newport, 1991)

John, B.S.   Pembrokeshire Coast Path (National Trail Guide, London, 1990)

Jones, L.   Schoolin's Log (London, 1980)

Lockley, R.M.   Pembrokeshire (1957)

Miles, D.   A Pembrokeshire Anthology (Llandybie, 1983)

Miles, D.   Portrait of Pembrokeshire (Hale, 1984)

Morgan, P. (ed)   Writers of the West (Carmarthen, 1974)

Reeves, Bob,   My Blood, My Earth (Pembroke Dock, 1989)

Seymour, J.   About Pembrokeshire (Haverfordwest 1971)

Chapter 2
The Natural Landscape

Bassett, D.A and Bassett, M.G.   Geological Excursions in South Wales and the Forest of Dean (Cardiff, 1971)

Campbell, S. and Bowen, D.Q. Quaternary of Wales (Geological Conservation Review, NCC, 1989)

Ellis-Gruffyd, I.D.   Rocks and Landforms of the Pembrokeshire Coast National Park (Newport, 1977)

John, B.S.   Coastal Scenery of the Pembrokeshire Coast National Park (Newport, 1977)

George, T.N.   South Wales Regional Geology (HMSO, 1970)

John, B.S.   The Rocks: Geology of Pembrokeshire, Pembrokeshire Handbooks (Llanychaer, 1973)

John, B.S.   Scenery of Dyfed,   The Face of Wales Series, No 3   (Lanchester, 1976)

Lewis, C.A. (ed) The Glaciations of Wales and Adjoining Regions (1970)

Owen, T.R.   Geology Explained in South Wales   (Newton Abbot, 1973)

Saunders, D. (ed)   The Nature of West Wales   (Buckingham, 1986)

Whalley, T. (ed)   The Secret Waterway (Milford Haven, 1988)

Wright, C.J.   A Guide to the Pembrokeshire Coast Path   (London, 1986)

Chapter 3
Myths, Monuments and Mysteries

Burl, A.   The Stonehenge People (London, 1987)

Burl, A.   Prehistoric Henges : Shire Archaeol (Princes Risborough, 1991)

Dyfed Archaeological Trust,   Archaeology in Dyfed   (Carmarthen, 1986)

Dyfed Archaeological Trust,   The Landsker Borderlands   (Narberth, 1992)

Gregory, D.   Wales Before 1066. (Llanrwst, 1992)

John, T.   Sacred Stones. (Llandysul, 1994)

Laing, L.   Celtic Britain (London, 1979)

Lewis, T.P.   The Story of Wales, Pembs Edition (Llandybie, 1959)

Lewis, E.T.   Mynachlog-ddu: a guide to its antiquities (Cardigan, 1972)

Rees, S.   Dyfed: Cadw Guide to Ancient and Historic Wales (London, 1992)

Chapter 4
The Welsh, their Saints and their Stories

Bowen, E.G. Saints, Seaways and Settlements in the Celtic Lands (Cardiff, 1969)

Bowen, E.G.   Britain and the Western Seaways (1972)

Charles, B.G. Old Norse Relations with Wales (Cardiff, 1934)

Howells, R. Total Community (Tenby, 1975)

James, D.W. St David's and Dewisland (Cardiff, 1981)

Jones, G. and Jones T. (eds) The Mabinogion (1973)

Lofmark, C. Bards and Heroes (Llanerch, 1989)

Rees, N. St David of Dewisland (Llandysul, 1992)

Sharkey, J. (ed) Ogam Monuments in Wales, Llanerch (1992)

Chapter 5
The Creation of "Little England"

Davis, P.R.   Castles of the Welsh Princes (Swansea, 1988)

Fraser, D. The Defenders (Cardiff, 1967)

Giraldus Cambrensis, The Itinerary through Wales and The Description of Wales (ed. W. Llewelyn Williams, 1908)

Gregory, D. Wales Before 1066 (Llanrwst, 1989)

Gregory, D. Wales Before 1536 (Llanrwst, 1993)

Laws, E. The History of Little England Beyond Wales (1888)

Miles, D.   The Castles of Pembrokeshire (NPA, 1983)

Miles, D. The Ancient Borough of Newport in Pembrokeshire (Carmarthen, 1995)

Miles, J. Princes and People (Llandysul, 1969)

Morris, W. Castles (Dyfed CC, 1991)

Rees, S. Dyfed -- A Guide to Ancient and Historic Wales (London, 1992)

Rees, W. An Historical Atlas of Wales (London, 1972)

Reeves, A.C.   The Marcher Lords : A New History of Wales (Llandybie, 1983)

Vaughan-Thomas, W. The Splendour Falls (Cardiff, 1973)

Chapter 6
George Owen's Pembrokeshire

Charles, B.G. George Owen of Henllys (Aberystwyth, 1973)

Howells, B.E. (ed) Elizabethan Pembrokeshire: the evidence of George Owen (Haverfordwest, 1973)

Howells, B. Early Modern Pembrokeshire : Pembrokeshire County History, Volume 3 (Haverfordwest, 1987)

John, B.S. The Ancient Game of Cnapan (Newport, 1986)

Jones, G.E. Tudor Wales (Llandysul, 1986)

Lloyd, H.A. The Gentry of South-West Wales 1540-1640 (Cardiff, 1968)

Owen, George, The Description of Pembrokeshire (1603), ed D. Miles (Llandysul, 1994)

Owen, G.D.   Elizabethan Wales (Cardiff, 1964)

Thomas, H.A.   A History of Wales 1485-1660 (Cardiff, 1972)

Chapter 7
War and Peace

Carradice, P. The Last Invasion (Pontypool, 1992)

Dodd, A.H. Life in Wales (1972)

Horn, P. The Last Invasion of Britain (Fishguard, 1980)

Jenkins, G. Nets and Coracles (Newton Abbot, 1974)

Jones, E.H.S. The Last Invasion of Britain (Cardiff, 1950)

Kinross, J.S. Fishguard Fiasco (Tenby, 1974)

Leach, A.L. The History of the Civil War in Pembrokeshire and its Borders (1937)

Lockley, R.M. Orielton (London, 1977)

Toulson, S. The Drovers (Shire, 1980)

Toulson, S. and Forbes, C. The Drovers Roads of Wales, Vol 2, Pembrokeshire and the South (London, 1992)

Williams, G. The Land Remembers: A View of Wales (1977)

Chapter 8
Religious and Social Awakening

Brinton, P. and Worsley, R. Open Secrets (Llandysul, 1987)

Dyfed CC, Haverfordwest in Old Photographs (Carmarthen, 1992)

Evans, G. Land of My Fathers (Swansea, 1974)

Fenton, R. A Historical Tour Through Pembrokeshire (1810, republished by Dyfed CC, 1994)

Horn, P. The Tithe War in Pembrokeshire (Fishguard, 1982).

Howells, B. (ed) Pembrokeshire County History, Vol 3 (Haverfordwest, 1987)

John, B.S. Honey Harfat (Newport, 1979)

Lewis, W.J. The Gateway to Wales (Dyfed CC, 1990)

Molloy, P. And they blessed Rebecca (Llandysul, 1983)

Morris, J. The Railways of Pembrokeshire (Tenby, 1981)

Morris, R.M. The Rebecca Riots (OUP, 1989)

Padfield, R. and Burgess, B. The Teifi Valley Railway (Haverfordwest, 1974)

Rees, V. South -West Wales (Shell Guide, 1976)

Williams, D. The Rebecca Riots (Cardiff, 1971)

Chapter 9
Seafaring and Life by the Sea

Bennett, T. Welsh Shipwrecks (Vols. 1, 2, 3) (Haverfordwest, 1981)

Bennett, T. Shipwrecks Around Wales (Newport, 1992)

Bennett, T. Shipwrecks around St David's (Newport, 1994)

Davies, P. Deadly Perils (St David's, 1992)

George, B. Pembrokeshire Sea Trading Before 1900 (London, 1964)

Goddard, T. Pembrokeshire Shipwrecks (Llandybie, 1983)

Hampson, D. G. and Middleton, G.W. The Story of the St Davids Lifeboats (St David's, 1989)

Howell, F. Stories at the Mill (Haverfordwest, 1969)

Howells, R. The Sounds Between (Llandysul, 1968)

Howells, R. Across the Sounds to the Pembrokeshire Islands (Llandysul, 1972)

Jenkins, G. The Coracle (Carmarthen 1988)

John, B.S. Ports and Harbours of Pembrokeshire, Pembrokeshire Handbooks (Llanychaer, 1974)

Raggett, P. Solva (Solva, 1990)

Warburton, F. W. The History of Solva (1944)

Chapter 10
Milford Haven and its "New Towns"

Carradice, P. The Book of Pembroke Dock (Buckingham, 1990)

Dyfed CC, Along the Cleddau in Old Photographs (Carmarthen, 1990)

Evans, J. Flying Boat Haven (Pembroke Dock, 1985)

Griffith, S. A History of Quakers in Pembrokeshire (Milford, 1990)

McKay, K. The Story of Milford Haven (MH Museum, 1993)

McKay, K. A Vision of Greatness (Chevron, 1989)

Morris, J.P. The Pembroke and Tenby Railway (Haverfordwest, 1976)

Peters, E.E. The History of Pembroke Dock (1905)

Price, M.R.C. The Pembroke and Tenby Railway (Oxford, 1986)

Rees, J.F. The Story of Milford (Cardiff, 1954)

Richards, W.L. Pembrokeshire under Fire (Haverfordwest, 1965)

Scott, V. An Experience Shared (Pembroke Dock, 1992)

Scott, V. Inferno 1940 (Haverfordwest, 1980)

Chapter 11
Coal, Stone, Slate and Iron

Davies, P. Dewisland Limekilns (St David's, 1989)

Davies, P. Forgotten Mines (St David's, 1990)

Edwards, G. The Coal Industry in Pembrokeshire (London, 1963)

Gale, J. The Maenclochog Railway (Milford, 1992)

Hall, G.W. Metal Mines of Southern Wales (Gloucester, 1971)

Howells, R. Old Saundersfoot from Monkstone to Marros (Llandysul, 1977)

Jermy, R.C. The Railways of Porthgain and Abereiddi (Oxford, 1986)

Price, M.R.C. Industrial Saundersfoot (Llandysul, 1982)

Price, M.R.C. The Saundersfoot Railway (Oxford, 1969)

Rees, D.M. Industrial Archaeology of Wales (Newton Abbot, 1975)

Richards, A.J. A Gazetteer of the Welsh Slate Industry (Llanrwst, 1991)

Stickings, T.G. The Story of Saundersfoot (Tenby, 1970)

Williams, M. The Slate Industry (Shire, 1991)

Chapter 12
Town and Country Today

Carter, H. The Towns of Wales: A Study in Urban Geography (Cardiff, 1965)

Davies, R.W. Old Pembrokeshire (Llandysul, 1988)

James, D.G. The Town and County of Haverfordwest and its Story (Haverfordwest, 1957)

Morris, J. The Railways of Pembrokeshire (Tenby, 1981)

Morris, J.P. The North Pembroke and Fishguard Railway (Lingfield, 1969)

John, B.S. Rural Crafts of Wales (Newport, Dyfed, 1976)

John, B.S. and Evans, R.O. The Pembrokeshire Landscape (Tenby, 1973)

Morgan, W.R. A Pembrokeshire Countryman looks back (Tenby, 1988)

Price, M.R.C. The Saundersfoot Railway (Lingfield, 1964)

Richards, W. L. Changing Face of Haverfordwest, 1992)

Western Telegraph, Pembrokeshire Then and Now, Vols 1 and 2 (Haverfordwest, 1988 and 1989)

Chapter 13
The English, the Welsh and the Landsker

Aitchison, J. and Carter, H. A Geography of the Welsh Language 1961 - 1991 (Cardiff 1994)

Awbery, G.M. Pembrokeshire Welsh (Cardiff, 1986)

Dyfed Archaeological Trust, The Landsker Borderlands (Narberth, 1992)

Jones, L. Schoolin's Log (London, 1980)

Charles, B.G. The English Dialect of South Pembrokeshire (Haverfordwest, 1982)

Charles, B.G. The Place Names of Pembrokeshire, 2 vols (Aberystwyth, 1992)

Gallie, M. Little England's Other Half, Pembrokeshire Handbooks (Llanychaer, 1974)

Harris, P.V. Pembrokeshire Place-Names and Dialect (Tenby, 1974)

James, D.W. St David's and Dewisland -- a Social History (Cardiff, 1981)

John, B.S. Fireside Tales from Pembrokeshire (Newport, 1993)

Jones, J. Welsh Place Names (Cardiff, 1979)

Jones, T.G. Welsh Folklore and Folk Custom (Cambridge, 1979)

Lewis, E.T. Llanfyrnach Parish Lore (Haverfordwest, 1969)

Lewis, E.T. North of the Hills (Haverfordwest, 1972)

Morgan, P. (ed) Writers of the West (Carmarthen, 1974)

Owen, T.M. Welsh Folk Customs (Cardiff, 1968)

Parry-Jones, D. My Own Folk (Llandysul, 1972)

Peate, I.C. Tradition and Folk Life: a Welsh View (1972)

Thomas, W.G. Llangwm Essays and Sketches (Haverfordwest, 1992)

Chapter 14
Natural History

Barrett, J. and Nimmo, M. Identifying Flowers common along the Coast Path (NPA, 1988)

Davies, B. Provisional Distribution Maps of the Mammals, Reptiles and Amphibians of Pembrokeshire (Haverfordwest, 1990)

Donovan, J. and Rees, G. Birds of Pembrokeshire (Haverfordwest, 1994)

Kruys, I. Butterflies of Pembrokeshire (Newport, 1981)

Davis, T.A.W. Plants of Pembrokeshire (Haverfordwest, 1970)

John, B.S. (ed) Wildlife in Dyfed (Haverfordwest, 1979)

Howells, R. Cliffs of Freedom (Llandysul, 1961)

Condry, W.M. The Natural History of Wales (London, 1981)

Lockley, R.M. Grey Seal, Common Seal (1966)

Perry, A.R. Welsh Wild Flowers (1973)

Saunders, D.A. A Brief Guide to the Birds of Pembrokeshire (Tenby, 1976)

Saunders, D. (ed) The Nature of West Wales (Buckingham, 1986)

Saunders, D. A Waterway for Wildlife (Haverfordwest, 1991)

Sutcliffe, A. A Tourists Guide to the Pembrokeshire Islands (Haverfordwest, 1990)

Chapter 15
The National Park: for Better or for Worse?

Barrett, J. The Pembrokeshire Coast Path (HMSO, 1974)

John, B.S. Presely Hills (Newport, 1981)

John, B.S. The Pembrokeshire Guide (Newport, 1992)

John, B.S. Pembrokeshire Coast Path : National Trail Guide (London, 1990)

John, B.S. (ed) The Carningli Walks (Newport, 1995)

McEwan, A. & M. National Parks: Conservation or Cosmetics? (London, 1982)

Miles, D. (ed) Pembrokeshire Coast National Park, National Park Guide No 10 (HMSO, 1973)

Pembs Coast National Park Authority Handbook (Haverfordwest, 1993)

Pembs Coast National Park Authority, Local Plan, Part 1, General Policies (Haverfordwest, 1994)

Shepherd, A. A Visitor's Guide to Pembrokeshire (Tenby, 1995)

Williams, H. The Pembrokeshire Coast National Park (London, 1987)

Wright, C. J. A Guide to the Pembrokeshire Coast Path (London, 1986)

Chapter 16
Buildings: Castles, Palaces and Churches

Ball, P. Every Single One (Pembroke Dock, 1990)

Davies, M. The Story of Tenby (Tenby, 1979)

Fitzgerald, M. Pembrokeshire Churches (Newport, 1989)

Miles, D. Castles of Pembrokeshire (Haverfordwest, 1983)

Rees, V. South-West Wales, Shell Guide (1963)

Salter, M. The Old Parish Churches of South-West Wales (Upton-upon-Severn, 1994)

Savory, H.N. et al. Ancient Monuments of Wales (HMSO, 1973)

Stickings, T.G. Castles and Strongholds of Pembrokeshire (Tenby, 1973)

Vaughan-Thomas, W. The Splendour Falls (Cardiff, 1973)

Wales Tourist Board, Castles and Historic Places in Wales (Cardiff, 1974)

Chapter 17
Buildings: Homes for Rich and Poor

Barnes, T. and Yates, N. (eds) Carmarthenshire Studies (Carmarthenshire CC, 1974)

Colyer, R. The Teifi: Scenery and Antiquities of a Welsh River (Llandysul, 1987)

Davies, M. Save the Last of the Magic (Pentrecwrt, 1991)

Davies, R.W. Old Pembrokeshire (Llandysul, 1988)

Fitzgerald, M. Pembrokeshire Castles and Strongholds (Newport, 1991)

Fitzgerald, M. Pembrokeshire Architecture (Newport, 1993)

Howells, R. Tenby Old and New (Llandysul, 1981)

Peate, I.C. The Welsh House (Liverpool, 1946)

Rees, S. Dyfed -- A Guide to Ancient and Historic Wales (London, 1992)

Rees, V. South-West Wales (Shell Guide, 1976)

Smith, P. Houses of the Welsh Countryside: Royal Commission (London, 1988)

Timmins, H.T. Nooks and Corners of Pembrokeshire (1895)

Worsley, R. The Pembrokeshire Explorer (Abercastle, 1988)

Chapter 18
The Rediscovery of Milford Haven

Celtic Sea Advisory Committee, The Celtic Sea: Land Use Implications in South West Wales (Cardiff, 1975)

John, B.S. Milford Haven Waterway (Newport, 1981)

McKay, K. The Story of Milford Haven (MH Museum, 1993)

McKay, K. A Vision of Greatness (Chevron, 1989)

Wright, C.J. A Guide to the Pembrokeshire Coast Path (London, 1986)

Chapter 19
Environment in Focus

Bunyard, P. and Morgan-Grenville, F. The Green Alternative (London, 1987)

Smith, J. and Yonow, N. The Coast of Dyfed and South-West Glamorgan: an Environmental Appraisal (Field Studies Council, 1995)

Dyfed CC, County Structure Plan Review, Proposals for Alteration (Carmarthen, 1987)

Lyons. G. and Sweet, J. Orimulsion - Trials and Tribulations (World Wildlife Fund, 1991)

Maynard, R. Off the Treadmill (FoE London, 1991)

Saunders, D. A Waterway for Wildlife (Haverfordwest, 1991)

Swedish NGO Secretariat on Acid Rain,
Critical Loads for Air Pollutants
(Goteborg, 1992)
Texaco Ltd.   Pembroke Plant and the
Environment (Pembroke, 1994)
Welsh Affairs Committee, Wind Energy
(HMSO, 1994)
Whalley, T. (ed) The Secret Waterway
(Milford, 1988)

Chapter 20
Pembrokeshire, Past and Present

Dept of Environment, Sustainable
Development: the UK Strategy
(HMSO, 1994)
Office of Population Censuses and Surveys.
Censuses 1971, 1981 and 1991 (HMSO)
Pembs Coast National Park Department,
National Park Plan, Second Review
(Haverfordwest, 1995)
Preseli Pembrokeshire DC, Preseli
Pembrokeshire Local Plan : Draft
(Haverfordwest, 1993)
Richards, W.L. Changing Face of
Haverfordwest (Haverfordwest,
1992)
Western Telegraph, Haverfordwest, press
cuttings 1993-95

Pentre Ifan (John Havard)

Index

A

B

C

CND 151
Caldey 25, 105, 133, 194
Caldey Abbey 42
Caledonian mountain chain 19
Cambrian rocks 17
Camps 43
Cantref y Gwaelod 27, 42
Cantrefi 45
Caravans 177
Carboniferous Limestone 18, 21, 24
Cardigan 45, 94
Cardigan Bay 20, 27, 169, 217-218
Carew 53
Carew Castle 53, 54, 189
Carew Mill 54, 83
Car ferry 122, 144, 215
Carmarthen 161, 229
Carn Alw 30, 34
Carningli 34, 65, 148
Carn Meini (or Menyn) 17, 24, 30
Carns 17
Carreg Wastad 78
Carter, H. 162
Castell Henllys 34, 176
Castell Malgwyn 134
Casting out 88
Castlemartin peninsula 71, 76
Castlemartin tank range 24, 152, 183
Castle Mills 82
Castle mounds 45-47, 192-194
Castles 44, 49, 187-194
Cat cracker 211, 212
Cattle 28, 36, 57, 71, 76, 148
Cattle pound 56
Caves 25
Cawdor, Lord 71, 78, 106, 206
Ceibwr 24
Cells, monastic 40
Celtic Sea 38, 73, 217, 234
Celtic Sea oil search 122
Celtic settlers 37
Celtic tribes 33-36, 42
Cemais (Cemaes) 47, 55, 65
Cenarth 76, 138
Census data 162
Cerrig Marchogion 44
Chapels 40, 85, 87
Chapel Bay Fort 80

Charles, B.G. 55, 155
Chartists 91
Cheese 59, 140, 180
Chevaux de frise 34
Chimneys 203-204
Church, "Celtic" style 87, 157
Church, "Norman" style 48, 51, 53, 195
Church types 48, 153, 156
Cilgerran 75
Cilgerran Castle 189
Circulating schools 85-87
Civil War 67-70, 187
Clay Marl 60
Cleddau Bridge 144, 145
Cleddau Coracle 75
Clegyrfwya (Clegyr Boia) 28, 41
Clergy 98
Cliffs 19-20, 171-174, 183
Climate 94, 146, 166
Clom 200
Cnapan 62-66
Coal industry 112, 123-128, 201
Coal Measures 17, 18, 126, 128
Coastal scenery 19-20, 165
Coastal trading 99, 112
Coast path 166, 183-184
Cosheston 101, 122
Coedmore Forge 134
Colby Moor Rout 68
Common land 43, 49, 71, 91
Compass nets 74
Conservation 166, 171, 175, 182
Copper Mines 133
Coracle 75, 158
Cordell, A. 76
Corn 58, 148
Corn mills 53, 82, 180
Cottages 139, 199-203
Country life 76, 91-95, 146-150, 199-207
Countryside Council for Wales 184
Countryside Unit 181
Crafts 36, 82, 180
Cromlechau 28-30, 44
Cromwell, Oliver 69-70
Crop rotation 71-72
Cropper, Edward 96
Crops 92, 142, 148
Crymych 29, 33, 76, 93, 97
Culm 107, 124
Cymydau 43

W